Francis of Assisi

A Prophet for Our Time

Francis of Assisi
A Prophet for Our Time

by
Fr. N. G. van Doornik

translated by
Barbara Potter Fasting

Francis of Assisi: A Prophet for Our Time by Fr. N. G. van Doornik, translated by Barbara Potter Fasting from the Dutch *St. Franciscus van Assisi,* Gooi en Sticht B.V., Holland, Copyright © 1979 by Franciscan Herald Press. All rights reserved.

Library of Congress Cataloging in Publication Data

Doornik, Nicolaas Gerardus Maria van.
  Francis of Assisi: a prophet for our time.

  Translation of Franciscus van Assisi.
  Bibliography: p. 239
  1. Francesco d'Assisi, Saint, 1182-1126. 2. Christian saints—Italy—Assisi—Biography. 3. Assisi—Biography.
BX4700.F6D413   271'.302'4 (B)   78-671
ISBN 0-8199-0695-6

IMPRIMATUR:
  Msgr. Robert Schlund
  Vicar General, Freiburg im Breisgau

February 14, 1977

MADE IN THE UNITED STATES OF AMERICA

Contents

Chronology

1182 Birth of Giovanni Francesco Bernardone
1198 The deacon Count di Segni is elected pope (Innocent III)
1199 Destruction of the Rocca by the citizens of Assisi
1202 Francis joins the army on its way to Perugia
1203 He is taken prisoner and ransomed by his father
1205 Return to Assisi, after he joined Walter of Brienne. Pilgrimage to Rome
1206 Francis visits the annual market at Foligno (Jan. 24). Incident in the church of San Damiano. Encounter with his father before Bishop Guido (March)
1208 Francis receives the first followers
1209 Journey to Innocent III, to whom he presents his First Rule
1211 Unsuccessful journey to Syria
1212 Clare flees to Francis
1213 Count Orlando offers Francis the use of Alverna
1214 Unsuccessful journey to Morocco
1215 Fourth Lateran Council. Probable meeting between Dominic and Francis
1216 Death of Innocent III. Successor Honorius III
1217 General chapter (strong influence of the missionary ideal)
1218 First papal decree on the Franciscan Order (the brothers are to be received as fellow Catholics).

Introduction

Assisi in the sun is a celebration. I've often wondered what it is about this town that I find so fascinating. And now I think I've found at least part of the answer: the walls. The outer walls of the city, walls of buildings, walls that wander randomly over the rolling hills, walls built over a period of almost 3,000 years. They shade from tawny beige into rust, and no two stones are exactly the same color or shape. The town is the child of the mountain on which it is built. From its sides great blocks of stone were hewn for the houses, churches, and *palazzi* which adorn the four or five different levels of the town. Carved into the face of Monte Subasio, they are embellished with towers, balconies hung with greenery, and magnificent wrought iron dragons. Through the maze of shops on the sloping streets the ruins of the Rocca, "the Fortress," are ever visible on the verdant mountaintop. And every side street offers a glimpse of the plains of Spoleto, one of the most charming panoramas of all Italy.

In the sidewalk cafes of the Piazza del Comune tourists bask in a glorious sun, that Umbrian miracle which per-

ambulates across the sky only to evaporate in a veil of
indescribable color at the end of the day. My faithful
Giovanni brings my *espresso* and my eyes wander around
the square. I contemplate the walls, the Minerva Temple,
which sent Goethe into ecstacy, the Palazzo of the Capi-
tano del Popolo, the Palazzo dei Priori, now the city hall,
the old fountain and the archway leading to the Chiesa
Nuova. It has never occurred to the city fathers to sand-
blast the walls or turn the square into a tourist attraction.
Traffic is a good-natured muddle, under the baton of a
policeman-conductor. I watch as he jovially slaps an of-
fender on the shoulder, causing a brown-habited figure on
a motorcycle (his order does not approve of horseback
riding!) to swerve sharply.

The hands of the Minerva clock point to XII and out of
nowhere the pigeons appear to devour the food which has
been scattered for them. Small boys with enchanting little
caps on their heads and *spumante* in their blood frolic
about, darting low to catch the pigeons, who do not allow
themselves to be caught. This summer day the square is
a delight which no *platz* or *plaza* in the world can equal.

Everything in Assisi is picturesque. I've never had a high
regard for travel folders, but they speak the truth when they
say that Assisi is one of the most charming cities in Italy.
Through the ages man has built up, torn down, and blended
colors, unwittingly conforming to some unwritten law which
decrees that the artistic whims of sculptors and bricklayers
shall not touch the soul of the city.

Wandering down a side street, I come upon a dilapidated
structure. It is a poor excuse for a house, but it is beautiful. In Assisi houses sag aesthetically. The town, like its
most illustrious citizen, emanates the beauty of the un-
prententious and the humble. Francis of Assisi has made
it the Assisi of Francis.

A study of the archives of Assisi and other Umbrian
towns has recently brought to light new information about
Francis. So I am on my way to the Via Portica, to the

office of Signore Fortini, lawyer and former mayor of Assisi, a man who knows her history as no one else. In fact, Professor Fortini[1] knows everything there is to know about Assisi. For half a century he has combed archives and libraries for details which will help him to situate an authentic Francis against the background of an authentic Assisi of the thirteenth century. The fruits of his study are neatly arranged in chronological order; books, lectures, and brochures take up more than a yard of shelf space. Among them is his greatest work, *Vita Nova di San Francesco,* in five volumes, published in 1963.

He welcomes me with typical Italian charm and we enter into animated discussion. For readers who look for the nearest door at the mere mention of footnotes, let me hasten to assure you that I have used as few notes as possible and have placed them at the end of each chapter; but there is one source which I feel I must mention here: the archives. Dry as dust, totally lacking in imagination, municipal records are nevertheless the most reliable of historical documents. The medieval scribe with his quill pen, laboriously entering names, dates, donations, and bills of sale, must have taken on something of the stiff, unyielding quality of the parchment on which he wrote. But his ideal was accuracy. Perhaps it would have cheered him to know that hundreds of years later his documents would be taken from the vaults so that we might study Francis, so to speak, in his natural habitat.

This, then, is the work of a specialist, to which the specialist Fortini has devoted his whole life. He is an Italian, and nothing Italian is foreign to him. In moments of excitement his voice is that of an orator. But when he quotes from the archives of Assisi or the Cathedral of San Rufino, the very matter-of-factness of these long-forgotten names and dates is dramatic, compelling. What they have to say to us has an undeniable appeal for modern readers. It is true, genuine, actual fact. No one is trying to sell us a legendary Francis. Here they stand—old, dull, trustworthy witnesses, who rise to proclaim the truth and nothing but the truth.

Fortini has his critics and they have their Fortini. They need one another. By their meticulous checks and counter-checks, Franciscologists all over the world are shaping the image of a medieval Francis, an image which is not unrecognizably gilded by pious fantasy, but which attempts to answer the fundamental question: Who was Francis of Assisi?

But still we have not penetrated the deepest essence of his character. Francis will always remain shrouded in mystery and entombed in time. But we can perhaps uncover enough of the truth—and here we touch on the aim of my book—to ascertain whether Francis is inextricably bound up with the past or whether this unusual personality has indeed some significance for us today.

Fortini is not the only historian I visited, nor is his the only work I consulted; but the above is intended to show that there is more to St. Francis than a myth. We still rely on the interpretation of the biographer—or rather the biographers, for "the character and life of Francis were too rich and complex for a single interpretation."[2]

We can go even further: the very plenitude of publications about Francis proves that there is some quality that continues to elude us. Even now his true personality has not been discovered. He shares the fate of Napoleon, of whom the Russian historian Mereschkowsky once said, "Under 40,000 books, like so many tombstones, lies the unknown soldier Napoleon." I take my leave of Professor Fortini.

In the Corso Mazzini I pass a small gate above which hangs a Gothic inscription. "Descend these stairs and discover the place where 'poor Francis' was born." I obey and find myself in *lo stalletto,* the "little stable" of St. Francis, one room with an altar, commonplace and unexciting. "When Francis' mother Pica felt that her time had come," the guide tells me, "a pilgrim knocked at her door and prophesied that the child would be born as soon as she exchanged her elegant quarters for a poor stable."

He goes on talking but I am no longer listening. What interests me is not the story but the storyteller. He is an old man who believes what he is saying. When he cries out "It's a miracle, a great miracle!" it is not the spiel of a paid guide but a profession of faith. His smile is friendly and he pats me on the shoulder. I feel that the old man is deeply affected by Francis. He grew up in the shadow of this great citizen of Assisi, and it is almost as if he has absorbed something of his spirituality. His mission in life is to proclaim the wonders of Francis, and something of their supernatural light enhances his old age. Hesitantly, I offer him a few coins. He shakes his head and drops them into the poor box. The *Santo* would not have done otherwise.

I do not believe his story. No pilgrim ever knocked on Pica's door, nor was there ever a manger here. Cruel research has destroyed what pious imagination constructed. I don't even believe that Francis was born in this house. Even Fr. Abate's extensive study has not been able to convince me. Historians recognize three possible birthplaces, and if the manner of his birth was not in itself a miracle, then only one of them is the real thing. I believe—and I am not alone—that a house about a hundred meters from the *"stalletto"* is St. Francis' birthplace.[3] Next to the Franciscan church, Chiesa Nuova, part of the house is still standing, the stone steps leading to the front door and the servants' entrance to the left. These remains not only remind us that Francis was born into a well-to-do family but also bring us closer to him, to the life he lived here, on this very spot.

The records of city hall tell us simply that Giovanni (Francesco) Bernardone was born in 1182 and was baptized in the church of Maria Maggiore. But as one walks through the church or sees the remains of the house where that child lived and played, the rooms through which he was carried in his mother's arm, this simple fact takes on a new dimension. And one experiences that strange ambiance which through the years comes to permeate the birthplaces of famous men.

At the end of my tour I cross the city to visit the tomb of St. Francis in the dark crypt under the basilica. I ask myself if there is any sense in resurrecting this man and compelling him to embark anew upon the pathways of his life. If Francis were to appear today in the Piazza de Comune to speak to the people of Assisi and the tourists assembled there, how many of them would follow him to the caves of the Rieti Valley or Alverna? Anyone who has ever seen these caves will realize that the age of hermits is long past. In late autumn it would be rash to spend more than an afternoon there. More important, few modern Christians would be willing to desert a world where they stand in the midst of life itself and where they believe they have a mission to fulfill.

And yet lamps are still burning round this tomb. Less than a century ago, Renan, Sabatier, Jörgensen, and many others initiated a new study, a new cult which rivals that of recently deceased philosophers and poets. And few visitors to Umbria are so rushed that they cannot spare the time to visit Assisi and this tomb.

We live in a period in which Christianity is developing at such a staggering pace that many people wonder whether a Christian from the past has anything at all to say to us. Do bare poverty and bitter loneliness mean anything to a world where charity is organized on a national scale, where people express brotherly love (or think they do) in terms of aid to developing countries? And what can he possibly mean to us—this man who reads the gospel as it was written, who is convinced that the earth and stars were created in seven days, and that on the last day angels will appear with their trumpets to summon mankind, to call us out of the grave and carry us off to the Valley of Jehoshaphat? Has the time not come to let the dead bury the dead and to let the living free themselves from the past to build a better

world for the future?
I asked myself these questions. This book is my answer.

Footnotes

1. Fortini died in 1970.

2. E. Gilson, "S. François et la culture medieval," lecture at the Sorbonne, quoted in *L' influence de S. François sur la civilisation italienne* (paris, 1926), p. 98.

3. G. Abate, "La casa natale di S. Francesco e la topografia di Assisi nella prima meta del secolo XIII,". *Miscellanea Francescana* (Rome, 1966). In any case, all historians agree that Francis' birthplace was near the present Piazza del Comune. Since the discovery of a parchment in the city archives (B. 424-P.C9) which clearly describes the Bernardone house, there is little room for doubt; Francis was born in the house near the Chiesa Nuova.

1

Son of a Merchant

Two years after the death of Francis his first biographer writes: "In the town of Assisi lived a man called Francis, who from earliest childhood was brought up by his parents to a life of senseless luxury."[1]

The man who wrote these words was the poet and pulpit orator Thomas of Celano,[2] who was received into the order by Francis himself. What he goes on to tell us of the man who is to go down in history as the *Poverello* is unexpected, to say the least. "Until his twenty-fifth year he surpassed all his companions in wild and irresponsible frivolity. He dressed elegantly, was very rich but not in the least avaricious. On the contrary, he was a spendthrift. Shrewd in business matters, he thought nothing of squandering large sums of money on meaningless pleasures."[3]

Here Celano unknowingly puts in a good word for the early Francis he is describing. A high-spirited young man, frivolous and fashionably dressed, is less likely to frighten off twentieth-century readers than a pious child prodigy. Especially when he knows how to spend money—and not only on himself. He is a product of his day, which stood

1

on the brink of a new age of prosperity. He is also a product of the social class in which both he and his father grew up: the world of commerce. He emerges as the prototype of the medieval man of business.[4] Quite probably there was nobility on his mother's side, for we see in Francis the adventurous spirit of the medieval merchant, combined with the elegant charm of the knight.

The merchant class remained outside agrarian society as the former developed under the Carolingians. The first merchants did not live in the fortresses of the knights, but neither did they belong to the class of feudal serfs. They had escaped that life and made their way as adventurers and rovers, crisscrossing Europe. Their fortune was in their courage, their initiative, and their cunning sense of business. The Crusades brought back costly goods which, owing to the introduction of coinage, could be turned into solid cash. They coursed the rivers, pirated the coasts, imported and exported, lost every penny, or made a fortune —in which case they were a welcome resource for destitute knights and prelates in need of additional finances.

They are also the first to counter the feudal system. When, later, they settle in the cities, they come to consider themselves above the nobility. The archives of Assisi (1207) tell us that merchants enjoyed the same status as military men and took part in the administration of the city.

It is of historic importance that these merchants also employed people, and long before the era of great industrial development one can see the early beginnings of capitalism. Celano's reference to excessively elegant dress is a reflection of this culture. One has only to stroll through any museum in Italy to see the richness of color and style which characterized the period. Satin, silk, brocade, and golden sashes embellished men, women, and horses. The extravagance of ladies' attire reached such proportions that in Assisi the authorities felt called upon to introduce certain restrictive measures, "with the exception of the neckline and the back."![5]

The cloth shop of Pietro Bernardone, Francis' father, was one of the fashion centers of Umbria. Pietro emerges from the archives as a man who is conscious of his wealth and influence and accustomed to being obeyed. And he must have had something of the adventurer. He traveled with the caravans—necessary in those days for protection against marauding raiders—over the Alps to France and Flanders, where he saw new ways of life and where he met Pica, whom he later married. He returned from one of his journeys to find his firstborn, Giovanni.[6] The name did not appeal to him and, full of all he had seen abroad, he renamed his son Francesco.

The child grew up in luxurious surroundings and there is nothing to indicate that he voiced any objections.[7] It will be some time before he shows signs of the phenomenon of "conservative parents begetting revolutionary children," or of the twentieth-century dropout with unkempt hair and jeans, who lounges in his father's impeccable living room. For the time being, he is more like the wealthy son of an industrialist at the turn of our century, who views the social abuses around him as a normal part of life. Later, after a long and painful process of soul-searching, he will expose the injustices of his day, and he will do so in his own inimitable fashion.

Those who knew Francis did not consider him particularly handsome,[8] but he was an entertaining talker and a good friend. The latter trait seems to have annoyed Celano, for he says, "This unfortunately only made his folly worse. He attracted a whole band of young people who indulged in all kinds of vice and wickedness." Then, in an allusion to St. Augustine's *Confessions,* he says, "Francis was seen at the head of this worthless bunch, dressed in beautiful clothes, head held high, striding through the streets of Babylon."[9] The tones of a fire and brimstone sermon seem to echo around us.

Celano is probably referring to Assisi's Piazza del Comune, where festivals were customarily held. The city records shed more light on these practices. Mention is made of the *societas trepudantium,* an organization which performed dances in the public squares of Assisi. The solo dance, performed by a young woman, was meant to convey certain romantic emotions connected with martyrology, the heroic deeds of knighthood, and sometimes of erotic love. Most striking of all was Salome's dance with the head of John the Baptist, meant to arouse shock and horror among the spectators.

As leader or *podestà,* Francis played an important role in these mysterious rites, in which individual consciousness was lost in that of the group. Religious-erotic sensations kept dancers and spectators enthralled throughout whole nights of revelry. Although for various reasons it was not customary to allow citizens to wander about the city streets at night, the authorities sometimes gave permission for this sort of "recreation." The records of the neighboring city of Perugia show that such wild celebrations often led to fist-fights, adultery, and crime. It was up to the leader to avoid these excesses.

The affluent society was not the only dominant theme in the early life of St. Francis. Like many of his contemporaries, he was fascinated by the ideals of knighthood. In those days Assisi was a good deal smaller than it is now, and within its walls lived a powerful semimilitary nobility alongside the wealthy merchant class. In addition to these *maggiori* were the *minori,* the craftsmen with their guilds of butchers, shoemakers, weavers, etc. One wonders how all this could be contained within those city walls. Life in the streets and squares, devoid of crosswalks and traffic controls, must have been sheer chaos. People lived close to one another; everyone knew everyone else, shared both sorrow and joy. A single spark tossed into the inflammable masses could set off a wild celebration or a riot. Usually a riot.

In the thirteenth century, Italian society was not yet aware of such things as the rights of man. When two cities signed a treaty, they were motivated not by ideals of equality and humanitarian treatment for the oppressed, but by a thirst for commerical gain, power, and territory.[10] When a primitive economic situation made way for a money market and urbanization began to make itself felt, the gap between *maggiori* and *minori* became steadily wider, until a rebellion of the latter was inevitable. Moreover, the rivalry between merchants and nobility, citizens and soldiers, was a constant source of legal suits, feuds, and small-scale revolutions. The distorted idea of honor which was common among the chivalrous classes did not help matters much. Person and possessions were considered inviolate, so that a single offensive word could be avenged only by the shedding of blood. It takes no great imagination to picture the situation in a small town, where hot-headed groups lived side by side, while currents of greed and ambition flowed all around them.

There was only one point on which all agreed. High up on the mountain stood the Rocca. Built in 1174 by order of Frederick Barbarossa, it put an end to Assisi's freedom. Such fortresses had a precarious existence. In 1199 the imperial duke, Conrad of Lutzen, who lived in the fortress, was summoned by Pope Innocent, who wished to bestow Assisi upon him officially. In his absence, the entire population set about breaking up the Rocca until no stone was left upon another.[11]

Innocent III issued a formal protest against this destruction and even threatened to forbid the celebration of Mass.[12] The citizens of Assisi calmly went on with the work of repairing the outer walls of the city. Experience had taught them that as soon as one enemy disappeared over the horizon, another helmeted head rose up to threaten their existence. This time it was Perugia less than 15 miles away. Perugia was on the crest of a wave of victories and its influence and power reached nearly to Citta di Castello on Lake Trasimeno. Now it saw an opportunity to rise up as the "protector" of Assisi. From the heights of their city the Perugians watched the *castelli* of the nobility being razed and saw how the power of the citizenry was reaching dangerous proportions. When certain members of the nobility of Assisi appeared in Perugia to complain about this injustice, the Perugians were only too glad to come to their assistance.

For several years (1202-1209) the two cities remained enemies, a prime example of the terrible city wars which were the scourge of the Middle Ages. Officially, the hostilities involved the supporters of the pope, the Guelfs, and those of the emperor, the Ghibellines, but none of these worthy gentlemen played any great role in the day-to-day life of the Italian cities. They were far too busy fighting among themselves. Seaport cities, merchant cities, small cities, bitterly jealous of one another, all sent their armies marching to the accompaniment of pealing church bells. They fought battles, signed treaties, broke them, and marched off to war again. Never has war been waged with such ferocity as during the small-scale altercations of the thirteenth century. Florence and Siena, Bologna and Modena, Venice, Genoa, and Pisa jostled each other in their headlong rush toward the future, ready to elbow the others into oblivion if necessary. Anyone who wanted to impress his fellow citizens or his lady would don helmet and armor and march over the fields, prepared to kill or be killed.

Francis too strode over the plains of Spoleto to Perugia, to do battle and win fame, fortune, and fair lady. But he was soon captured, and his father paid a ransom to free him. Ambitious as he was, Francis continued to yearn for fame on the battlefield, where the burning questions of the day—the city wars, the recapture of the Holy Land, and the colossal clash between pope and emperor—were being fought out. His hero was Walter de Brienne, who rode at the head of the papal troops, acclaimed by the troubadours and idolized by the anti-German youth. At one point Francis had hoped to join his idol, but on the way to Apulia he suddenly turned back to Assisi, according to his biographers, after a warning dream. He put away for good his costly armor and took his place behind the counter, dispensing lengths of cloth from great rolls. Rather an anticlimax for a young man with knightly ambitions! But whatever one may think of his ideals, Francis had no inbred dislike of violence.

The childhood of St. Francis is presented to us by the hagiographers as a kind of gallery of Giottos, like those of the upper church of Assisi. They are not in the least concerned with Francis' psychological development; they are trying to establish the saintliness of the saint. Instead of the wealth of precious detail which one might expect to find, we see only a series of pious scenes unrelated to one another. The moment we think we've discovered a psychologically explicable reason, the biographer hastens to explain it away as divine intervention. Thus Francis' youth is drawn into the exalted spheres of sin and grace.

Nevertheless, it is possible to arrange the "Giottos" so that something of Francis' psychological development emerges. Thus these two themes, wealth and chivalry, are forerunners of the central theme of Francis' life, which is now beginning to emerge: God.

This is first apparent in the following. Francis was probably about 23 when, during one of the pilgrimages to Rome which were the order of the day, he climbed to the top of Vatican Hill. On the spot on which now stands the magnificent edifice conceived by Bramante and Michelangelo rose the old basilica with its five naves, which Constantine had ordered to be built over the tomb of St. Peter. On entering St. Peter's, Francis noticed that visitors were extremely frugal in their offerings. Like an indignant *grand seigneur,* he pulled out his purse and threw all its contents through the grating of the poorbox. He then exchanged clothes with a beggar and took his place on the steps to beg for alms. Feeling very noble, he played the part of the beggar.

Besides a decidedly whimsical bent, this incident reveals a character trait which was deeply ingrained in the ancestral

makeup: extravagance. Francis spends his money spontaneously, charmingly, with a modest little smile, as Celano
grudgingly recounts. Money is the key to happiness, for
himself and for others.

A beggar once came into the crowded shop in Assisi to
beg for alms, but was turned away. Francis called him back
and, to the man's amazement, presented him with a roll
of cloth.

Once, when he still entertained hopes of a military career,
Francis exchanged his costly armor for the trappings of an
impoverished knight.

He was fond of appearing at dances elegantly attired,
according to the latest fashion.

It was as if he had some uncontrollable urge to set the
whole world dancing, singing, and merrymaking—to pile up
everyone's troubles and worries in the middle of the *piazza*
and set them all alight in one huge bonfire.

Another "Giotto scene" has been immortalized by Celano.
During this period Francis fell prey to a serious illness,
which completely transformed him. Each of us reacts to
sickness in his own way, and Francis, that spoiled con-
noisseur of the *joie de vivre,* who once dreamed of military
glory and deeds of chivalry, experiences the undeniable
shock of incapacity. Helpless, bound to a few square feet,
he is suddenly confronted with the tragedy of human existence. He is shut off from the vibrant life of the city outside the walls of his room. While his friends tramp the highways of Apulia, he is doomed to the emptiness, boredom,
and aimlessness of the sickbed.

When, finally, he is able to leave the house, leaning on a
cane, and looks upon the sunny plains, he is seized by a
deep melancholy. Those who know those plains can picture
the sight that met his eyes that day. Umbria, with its hills
and olive groves, streams and fields, is not an imposing
sight, but it has a sweet charm about it, a touching quality.
Such beauty produces not the epic but the lyric poet. The
Roman Propertius is one; Francis is another. Whoever makes

his way upward, over the green Subasio hills, through the fields of grain and the meadows of grazing sheep, and sees the plains below fade from view, knows how depressed this young man must have been to sink into melancholy in the presence of such beauty. One of the loveliest sights of all Italy has no power to comfort him! It is like the loneliness of a lost love that will not die. Everything has changed, everything speaks a language he no longer understands. "From this day onward," Celano tells us rather abruptly, "he began to despise himself and everything which up to then he had loved and admired."[13]

During this period something has indeed changed, but it is not in the plains below. Months of sickness and solitary contemplation have stirred something deep inside Francis, opening untouched depths. And when one's inner world alters completely, one's view of the outside world cannot but change with it.

The spontaneous abandonment to pleasure is gone. But that does not mean that he has been transformed overnight into an ascetic or a hermit. Celano tells us that he "returned to the company of the sons of Babylon."[14] They drew him in a direction which led away from his calling. With his wealth and charm, he was still their darling. The nocturnal feasts resumed, and the rambles through the streets and the Piazza Grande, up Subasio and back over the green hills, until the dawn showed.

Inner tensions lead inevitably to a crisis, and in Francis' case this came one evening at the very height of the merry-making. (I am following the description given by the Three Companions, who probably heard the story from Francis himself.) He had been elected "king" by his friends and was requested to organize and finance a magnificent celebration, as he had so often done in the past. When all the guests were more than sated, everyone went outside. His comrades strode ahead of him through the city streets, singing. Francis, their king, staff in hand, brought up the rear of the procession. He was not singing, but listening carefully. "And suddenly," the writer tells us, "he was visited by our Lord. His heart was filled with such a glorious sensation that he could neither speak nor move. He could hear nothing, feel nothing but a joy so intense that it seemed to raise him off the face of the earth. As he was fond of saying later, if anyone had threatened to tear him to pieces he would not have been capable of moving from that spot."[15] This man had come to the point of no return. What follows is a farewell.

Footnotes

1. *I Celano* 1, in *English Omnibus of the Sources for the Life of St. Francis*, ed. Marion A. Habig O.F.M. (Chicago: Franciscan Herald Press, 1973), p. 229 (hereafter referred to as *Omnibus*).

2. For details on Thomas of Celano, see *Omnibus*, pp. 179–200.

3. The description of Francis' youth in *I Celano* is difficult to reconcile with the account which appeared twenty years later in *II Celano*. We will probably never know for sure if Francis really led the life of a charming and hotblooded young man sowing his wild oats. Ugolino, later Pope Gregory IX, who knew Francis well, praised him "because he had embraced chastity, after having succumbed to the temptations of the world." See the work of Sbaralea, *Bullarium Franciscanum*, I, 242.

In all probability, Pica, Francis' mother, was French and belonged to the nobility. For supporting evidence see D. Vorreaux, "Thomas de Celano," in *Vie de S. Francois d'Assise* (Paris, 1957), pp. 113–114 and footnotes. Francis was baptized in the church of S. Maria del Vescovado (St. Mary Major) in Assisi. The baptismal font was later transferred to the cathedral of San Rufino, where it stands today. St. Clare and Frederick II were baptized at the same font.

4. H. Pirenne, *History of Europe*, 4th ed. (Amsterdam), pp. 151ff.

5. A. Fortini, *Nova Vita de San Francesco* (Assisi, 1957), III, 619.

6. Francis was born during a period in which every country, some-

times every city, had its own chronology. It was not until the fifteenth century that it became customary to begin the year on January 1. Although Assisi adhered to the chronology of Florence, Celano departs from this system on several occasions. This (among other things) makes it extremely difficult to establish the exact chronology of the events of Francis' life. In this book we have taken 1182 to be the year of Francis' birth. Thereafter we have adhered to the work of A. Terzi O.F.M., *Cronologia della vita di S. Francesco d'Assisi* (Rome, 1963).

7. Bernardone was a wealthy man who enjoyed his wealth and had a strong desire to be respected by his fellow citizens. The last will and testament of Francis' brother, Angelo, which Fortini unearthed from the archives (Francis had been disinherited), shows that Bernardone owned extensive property, country homes, olive groves, and grazing lands, in addition to his house and warehouse in the city. See *Archives S. Convento*, 1.27; Fortini, op. cit., I, 103–113.

8. *I Celano* 2; *Omnibus*, p. 230.

9. Celano, who knew Francis personally, describes him as follows: "Francis was of average height, on the thin side. His head was round and of normal proportions, the face slightly pointed, the forehead small and straight, the eyes dark and clear. He had dark hair and a thin, straight nose. His ears were small and always appeared to be listening. His beard was dark and thin. He had a vibrant voice, clear and pleasant, and his words had a calming influence on people" (*I Celano* 83; *Omnibus*, p. 298).

10. In this century, city wars were inevitable. "For the people of the cities, war was a natural part of life, springing from nowhere and synonymous with freedom itself. To put an end to such wars one would have had to renounce every aspiration, every hope for the future" (G. Ferrari, *Histoire et révolution d'Italie* (Paris, 1856), I, 545).

11. Through the treaty with Lombardy (1183), Frederick Barbarossa lost most of his privileges with respect to the Italian cities. But his successor, Henry IV (1183–1198), won back almost all these rights, and Conrad, who lived in the Rocca, atop Assisi, was his nephew. Innocent III, the guardian of Henry's son, Frederick II, regained Assisi. In all probability, Francis, as a boy of 17, helped to demolish the Rocca.

12. A local ban forbade the faithful of the town, with few exceptions, to hold or to attend religious services. See Innocent III, *Regestorum,* lib. I, 88 (*Mirari cogimur*), *Register Innocenz' 3rd Uber Die Reichsfrage, 1189–1209,* ed. Georgine Tangl (Johnson Reproductions, 1923).

13. *I Celano* 4; *Omnibus,* p. 232.
14. *II Celano* 7; *Omnibus,* p. 366.
15. *Leg. 3 Comp.* 7; *Omnibus,* p. 896.

2

Metanoia

Metanoia is an impressive term. It signifies that process of inner change by which one's past life disintegrates, as it were, and is reassembled on a higher level to form a harmonious unit. We can compare the mind to the nocturnal half of the earth's sphere, turning slowly from dark toward light. Metanoia is often mentioned in the Bible—a process accompanied by contrition, penance, and that old-fashioned term "the breaking of hearts."

Anyone who has gone through such an experience, in which a definite break with the past takes place, knows how excruciating this process can be. There is a schizophrenic period, a time of disjointment. The past keeps calling out but the new ideal is equally enticing, and one cannot manage to balance the two. Wrenched from the security of the old way of life, one falls prey to anxiety, loneliness, and wanderlust.

For Francis, this process is about to begin with frightening intensity. Tortured by constant inner turmoil, he looks back on his life with a mixture of horror and longing. He sees the past exposed in all its futility. His consciousness

13

narrows, concentrating on the very fundamentals of his existence, in which he discovers the God of the Apocalypse. Not philosophically, but in a highly existentialist way, he sees—to his amazement—the absolute triumph over the relative. And everything is drawn to that absolute center, as metal filings are drawn to a magnet. Plagued by restlessness and tortured by doubt, he searches, prays, and hesitates; he sees a ray of hope and this obsession drives him onward, closer and closer to God, whom he is now to meet, personally, for the first time.

It is clearer to him now than ever before that God is a secret God. And it is this quality of mystery which makes him realize that only God can reveal God to us. No one on earth can help Francis through this process. An original, intuitive personality such as Francis would be bound to experience any human intervention as an obstacle, an interference.

His whole view of life is changing. The scarlet-blooming walls and the sun over the plains of Spoleto cause no melancholy pain now, but neither has he regained the vibrant, carefree love of life which characterized him as leader of the local *jeunesse dorée.* One of Francis' most striking characteristics is slowly developing, though the germ of it must have always been present: that strange oneness with the cosmos, which emanates the presence of God to him. He knows that he is approaching a break, one which will alienate him from his family and friends. He knows that there has been some kind of short circuit between him and his environment. Past interests have no meaning for him; what repelled him now fascinates him.

The following is a striking example of his new attitude, a story destined to be told and retold by countless generations. On one of his rides through the valley he suddenly saw before him a leper. Having been expelled from the city, this living corpse was wandering along the roads. In the Middle Ages, a leper who found himself a place in the leper colony could consider himself one of the chosen few. Outside such a colony he was branded an outcast.

Francis felt revulsion rising in him. He could toss the man a few coins and ride away . But then a new vision dawned. In the person of this leper, God was holding out his hand to him. He sprang from his horse, pressed some money into the man's hand; then he grasped that hand and brought it to his lips. He kissed the hand, which received as if it had given. It was the hand of God which gave him strength to turn deep revulsion into deep love.

This gesture is characteristic of Francis. He will never be the type to serve on a committee for aid to victims of leprosy. His kind of charity does not go about "doing good works." What he sees before him is not a "life work" but a human being. What he gives is not a handful of money, but himself. Organization will never be his strong point. What moves him, what will always move him, is the suffering of the man standing before him at that moment. He improvises, gives help where it is needed, even if only to an animal.

One cannot dispute the importance of the organization. But hundreds of well-meaning organizations have long been forgotten, while the act of this rich merchant's son still speaks to us. He did no more and no less than raise this disfigured leper from the depths of his humiliation to the level of a fellow man. Kissing his hand was a mark of respect which gave the leper status in the eyes of others and in his own eyes. It was a foolish gesture, as he might have been infected himself, but he pays no heed. His earlier fear and horror of leprosy have been conquered and he has penetrated the world of the leper. From this moment on, he is the friend of these outcasts and a frequent visitor to their hospital.

We will realize how deeply this incident remained imbedded in Francis' memory when we read the Testament he dictated on his deathbed. It begins: "Thus God has ordained that I, Brother Francis, should begin life in penance. For when I led a life of sin I could not bear to look upon a leper. And the Lord himself sent me to them and I showed them mercy."[1]

Francis begins to realize how tortuously divided his life is becoming. He slides lengths of elegant cloth over the counter, extolling its merits to knights and prelates, studies the many complexities of textile bindings, and travels from one trade market to the other. And all the while, especially on the long road back at night, his thoughts are occupied by that inner world which is slowly overwhelming, devouring him. Until he has had enough and, radical as ever, decides to force a decision.

One market day in 1206[2] Francis fits out his horse, loads the costly rolls of cloth, and sets out for Foligno, a well-known marketing area in the thirteenth-century. There he sells both cloth and horse, and with this money in his pocket he returns to Assisi on foot, along the route which Goethe later described in his travel journal as one of the loveliest in Italy.

Near Rivo Torto he turns right, along the Umbrian and Roman mausoleums, and arrives at the tiny tumbledown chapel dedicated to San Damian. Entering the dark recesses of the building, he is fascinated by the almost seven-foot-high painted crucifix.[3] It is at this moment that he is overcome by the mystical ecstasy which many see as the decisive moment in his metanoia. The visible world fades from his consciousness and a voice, which seems to come from the crucifix, says to him: "Francis, do you not see how my house is falling to ruin? Go and repair it for me."[4]

It is difficult to say whether Francis' biographers intended that these words be taken in a wider, symbolic sense, or as pertaining only to the chapel. In any case, Francis seems to have taken them literally. When the trance had left him, he stood up and turned from the dim interior into the bright sunlight. The path upward lay before him. But he knew that it was not the road for him. He would not be going back to Assisi, to his father's house. A new phase of his inner existence had begun: flight. This flight from the world is vital to him in this initial period. He must devote himself, calmly and quietly, to his own reform and the task he had vowed to fulfill: the restoration of San Damian's. It is a seemingly profitless task, a useless absurdity. Throughout his life we will see again and again the paradox of a folly which defies the ages. What earthly good was it to undertake the repair of this chapel, which any bricklayer could have done better? And yet the tiny church of San Damiano is today one of the most impressive relics of all Italy, an enduring Franciscan sermon on poverty and simplicity.

Francis goes to the old priest who lives near the church, asks for shelter, and offers him all the money he has to pay for the restoration. Celano notes the utter stupefaction of the old man. A well-known young man from Assisi, until recently leader of the gilded youth, offers him all the money he possesses and wants to restore the dilapidated chapel with his own hands! Medieval man was rather cynical about sudden conversions, and the whims of Francis were sufficiently well known for the old man to view this offer with a certain reserve. He agrees to allow Francis to stay with him but, fearing the reaction of Francis' father, refuses to accept the money. Then the young man's fiery temperament rises to the surface. He throws the money onto a window ledge in the church, and never again will he possess a cent.

The period which follows, in which Francis wanders through city streets and along country roads, culminates in a father-son conflict which even today we find perplexing. Pietro Bernardone learned that his son, who had been gone for a month, had been seen in town. Disheveled, gaunt from fasting, he was hooted and jeered at. Beside himself with rage, Pietro raced into the street, not to protect his son from his persecutors but to attack him. The biographer may be exaggerating when he tells how Pietro can no longer control himself, seizes Francis, and—under a storm of blows, threats, and recriminations—drags him home and locks him in a dark closet. But this strange episode is not as strange as it sounds. The legal records of Assisi shows that, as in old Roman law, the head of the family had the power to imprison a son at home for squandering his father's money. He was not required to show proof of the son's misdeeds, and was even allowed to put him in chains, as long as he gave him enough to eat.

We must not forget that a hagiographer always tends to shower every opponent of his hero with criticism. But Celano is rather superficial in his treatment of the conflict, and the background goes much deeper. A leading figure in the world of commerce, though himself without lineage, associates freely with the nobility and envisions a future in which he may even surpass them in wealth and power. And then he is forced to look on while his eldest son, upon whom he has placed all his hopes and who seemed destined for a successful career, throws away the popularity and influence of the family and allows himself to be laughed at like a village idiot. His anger and disappointment are not entirely unreasonable. There had for some time been a conflict between father and son, for the simple reason that Francis unconsciously saw in his father the symbol of a world which he was beginning to despise.

This conflict is ageless, but in each period it takes on a characteristic form. In chaotic times such as our own, many will sympathize with the young man who hammers away at the establishment in which his father has become comfortably, inextricably settled. But as long as a society considers itself strong and healthy and feels in its bones the coming of spring, as in the initial surge toward the Renaissance, any protest against the existing order is absurd. It takes unbelievable courage to turn one's back on that world and the luxury and comfort it offers.

To Francis, his father was the exponent of that society, with its ideals of prosperity, success, influence, and prestige. Nothing could be more diametrically opposed to Francis' calling than obedience to his father. And Pietro sincerely believed that he would be betraying honor and conscience if he were to give in to his son.

The two Bernardones opposed each other and the outcome of their conflict was to be as radical as the character of both men. Everything surged toward a climax. With Francis locked up at home, the stage was set for the familiar story of a mother who listens only to the dictates of her heart. Pica opened the doors and set her son free, and Francis sped back to San Damiano. But Pietro would not leave it at that. He appealed to the consuls of the town, who sent officials to force Francis to come back and answer for his deeds.[5] It is a remarkable story from here on. According to the chronicler Salimbene, the road was almost impassable due to a heavy snowfall. The men waded through, found Francis, and exhorted him according to the formula of the day, "Francis, son of Pietro Bernardone, let it be known to all that by order of the consuls you are charged and summoned." The young man refused to yield. His motive was unlikely to impress a judge today: "By the grace of God I have become a free man and the servant of the Most High. I am no longer obliged to obey the consuls."[6]

One may view the validity of this argument with some skepticism, but it was sound in those feudal times. The consuls were not prepared to take a stand. They sent Pietro Bernardone away with the message: "He has entered the service of God and is out of our reach."[7]

But one does not dispose of a Bernardone so easily. Pietro leaves the consuls and goes straight to the palace of Bishop Guido, where he repeats his indictment. This man, who is to play such an important role in the life of Francis, is worthy of close consideration. We see in him a prelate in whom greed and love of poverty exist side by side. Some sources record that Guido Secundus, bishop of Assisi from 1204 to 1228, took Francis' side from the beginning. But there are also records which show Guido to be an irascible potentate, who did not care how many court cases he had to fight or how many sentences he had to pass to obtain what he considered his due. He could squabble over a barrel of wine, though he possessed huge estates, vineyards, and castles. One might well wonder why a man like Pope Innocent III, who later became an admirer of Francis' poverty ideal, does not point out to this bishop the true meaning of the gospel. Instead he issues a decree by which it is forbidden, under pain of interdiction, to interfere in the affairs of Bishop Guido.[8] It was not until he decided to forgo the funeral oration at a burial service, in favor of a tirade on the high cost of the services, that the pope finally reprimanded him for his miserliness. The *Regesta* of Honorius III reveals that Guido once struck a monk across the face and that monks and canons alike trembled before him. And he was not even classed among the more unworthy officials!

It was against this background that the famous case of Bernardone vs. Bernardone was to take place—to be exact, on the spot where the bishop exercised his legal authority: the church square. If today you were to stroll the length of the Via Bernardone di Quintavalle, where the Middle Ages seem to have stood still, you would arrive in the Piazza del Vescovado, with its lion fountains. Among the staid houses rises the facade of the Maria Maggiore, designed by Giovanni da Gubbio in 1163.[9] It was here, in March of 1206, that Bishop Guido stood as he announced his verdict. Around the Mediterranean Sea, time is a gift of God, like water and air, and without doubt, the entire population of Assisi crowded around the square in front of the houses, even then staid and stately. From every window and *loggia* heads appeared, voices were raised, and with typical Italian outspokenness everyone made clear whose side he was on and why. They were treated to a spectacle which would be talked of for many years.

It is indeed strange to think that a bishop who is capable of bickering over a few olive trees is now about to pass a mild judgment on a young man who "defrauded" his father of hundreds of ducats. He spoke from experience when he said, "Your father is worried and upset. If you really want to serve God, give back the money you still have, and which you most likely came by unlawfully. It is not God's will that you should spend money on that chapel."

Many a pious young man of medieval times might have returned the money without a word and drifted back into the obscurity of his former existence. But not Francis. He displays a talent for imagery, and his personality finds expression not only in words but in actions, full of grace and wit. He "plays" the situation unself-consciously and with deep conviction. Words are inadequate and he resorts to pantomime.

Celano recounts: "Led before the bishop, Francis does not hesitate. Without a word and before a single order has been given, he removes all his clothes and throws them into his father's arms. He stands there before the assembled crowd, completely naked." Celano then describes how the bishop, moved by the young man's courage, rises, goes straight to Francis, and throws his arm around him. He then places his cloak over Francis shoulders. "He was convinced that the scene which he had just witnessed had some secret significance, and from this moment on he was Francis' patron."[10]

But this is not all that happened. Francis' pantomime requires more than a superficial explanation. In front of all his fellow citizens he breaks his silence and calls out, "From now on I can say freely: Our Father, who art in heaven. Pietro Bernardone is no longer my father and I return to him not only my money but also my clothes. Naked I will stand before my Lord."[11]

Cruel words. Incredibly cruel in light of the Francis we will come to know. But the emotional process he was undergoing had thrust him brutally from one phase into the next. When the moment of truth comes, Francis knows only one solution—a complete break. By word and gesture he takes leave of his father forever. Two worlds have separated—and never the twain shall meet.[12]

It is no simple matter to try to follow another's process of metanoia. It is deeply personal, unique, irreproducible. Often there is one theme which plays a leading role throughout. This is no accident; it is embedded in the whole structure of the process. In Francis' case this theme is wealth. He has grown up during a period in which, after centuries, a certain prosperity has begun to emerge. He has experienced what it is to be wealthy, how the possession of wealth can influence relationships between men, how it can widen the gulf between the haves and the have-nots. Everywhere, not least in his own circles, he has seen how a life of luxury draws one away from a more spiritual world. Now he has forever banned money from his life. This alone shows him to be a prophetic figure, a progressive far ahead of his day, far ahead of his cautious bishop, and indeed far ahead of his pope and cardinals, who try to curb him, though later he is proved right. He takes and keeps the initiative. Not one to dream over the past, he already lives in the future.

Footnotes

1. *Omnibus,* p. 67.

2. Probably Jan. 24, 1206, since the markets were usually held on the nameday of the patron saint of the city, in this case St. Feliciano, the patron of Foligno.

3. The early history of the little church of San Damiano is unknown. It is first mentioned in an *instrumento* dated 1030, which speaks of the "holy altar dedicated to San Damiano" (see L. Bracaloni, *Storia di San Damiano in Assisi* (Todi, 1926)). The crucifix of San Damiano is approximately 8 feet by 5 feet; it is painted on linen-covered wood, and dates from about 1100. Such crucifixes appear shortly after the year 1100. They are Italian products but show a strong Byzantine influence, and are found only in Italy.

During the building of the basilica of St. Clare, where the saint was buried in 1253, the old church of San Giorgio (where Francis had attended school as a child) was left standing and transformed into a choir for the nuns. This choir has disappeared, but the crucifix of San Damiano still hangs in front of the altar, a relic which attracts many visitors. See L. Bracaloni, *Il crocifisso che parlo a S. Francesco.*

4. *Leg. 3 Comp.* 13; *Omnibus*, p. 903. See also *II Celano* 10, *Omnibus*, p. 370, and *Leg. Major* II, 1, *Omnibus*, p. 640.

5. From the year 1198 onward the citizens selected two consuls each year; they enjoyed executive and judicial power and headed the army. Their power was not dictatorial for they were obliged to consult the representatives of the people on important matters. Their seat was the Casa dei Consoli, next to the cathedral of San Rufino. After 1212 the consuls were replaced by a *podesta,* who in Francis' day was elected for only a short period as a kind of dictator. See Fortini, op. cit., II, 231.

6. *Leg. 3 Comp.* 19; *Omnibus*, p. 908.

7. *Leg. 3 Comp.* 19; *Omnibus*, p. 908.

8. See Fortini, op. cit., III, 543–550.

9. This church took the place of an earlier one, which probably dated from the fourth century and underneath which a Roman fountain, inlaid with mosaics, was discovered. In the apse of the church a document was unearthed which has proved to be of considerable importance in the dating: "1216, *indictione quarta,* and the tenth year in the time of Bishop Guido and Brother Francis." The term *indictio* can mean a period of fifteen years. *Indictione quarta* would mean the 81st *indictio* A.D., that is, 1216. It is generally assumed that this commemorates the 10th anniversary of Francis' "performance" before Bishop Guido. This coincides with *I Celano* 88 (*Omnibus*, p. 303), which maintains that Francis lived for twenty years after his conversion. Thus we arrive at the dates 1206 and 1226.

10. *I Celano* 15; *Omnibus*, p. 241.

11. *II Celano* 12; *Omnibus*, p. 372. See also *Leg. 3 Comp.* 19, *Omnibus*, p. 909, and *Leg. Major* II, 4, *Omnibus*, p. 643.

12. We once referred to this as "the corresponding moment" (see N. G. van Doornik, *Pelgrims naar de Una Sancta,* 4th ed. (Utrecht, 1949), pp. 412ff.). In Francis' case these were luxury and prosperity, on the one hand, and evangelical poverty on the other.

3

The Desert Years

After the confrontation with his father, Francis leaves the city and retreats into the hills. The tension has gone. Feeling gloriously liberated, he climbs snowy Subasio with a song on his lips. Having renounced all, he has nothing more to lose. He wanders over the quiet paths he used to roam with his cronies, but now he is alone and his songs are heard only by a few startled birds. Before him lies his mission: the restoration of San Damiano.[1]

How strange is the symbolism of his act: the reformer of the medieval Church began as a bricklayer, repairing tumbledown chapels. But this work of restoration was essentially a symbol of what all Church reformers have done from that day to this: tear down old walls, erase forgotten images, and bring light and air into old, stuffy spaces.

The repairs to San Damiano were of no great consequence, probably no more than a layer of plaster and a new coat of paint. The church was still in use and the elderly priest lived nearby. According to a document which Cristofani discovered in Sacro Convento (the present convent next to the basilica) and which was later lost again,

actual restoration was not made until 1233—after Francis'
death, and under the auspices of the city.

After completion of his task, Francis withdrew into the
countryside around Assisi, into a calm and quiet now unknown. On one of his walks he came upon a tiny church,
several kilometers from the city, which was in an extreme
state of deterioration. It stood like a relic from the past,
surrounded by trees and visited only by birds. In a bill of
sale dated 1045, the place is mentioned under the name
il cosidetto Porziuncola (the forest of the holm oak, known
as Porziuncola). It belonged to the Benedictines of Subasio.[2]
The church, which is also called Maria Degl' Angeli, has
been preserved in its original form and is one of the most
striking souvenirs of Francis. In this small space he knelt
in prayer for many days and nights, and today it is strange
to think that some of the bricks in the old wall were laid
by Francis himself. The woods are gone now and a baroque
basilica has been built around the chapel, like a rich Rubens
encircling a modest Giotto. The "Giotto" alone would have
been more impressive.

With this church as his headquarters, Francis roamed
through Umbria, walking the lonely paths of one who is
misunderstood by the world and has taken his stand outside society. Though he had broken with the past, memories
could not be brushed aside. The hagiographers say nothing
of the inner conflict which tormented him here. But without
advice from any man, he sought, and found, the way to
a spirituality that was uniquely and completely his own.

There is a striking similarity between this spirituality and
the countryside of Umbria. Both are of touching simplicity
and mysterious depth. The Umbrian woods have a quality of
grace and charm. They lack the overpowering beauty of the
northern woods, but they give one a feeling of peace. These
hills are not even vaguely menacing, as are the high Apennines. The grays and greens of the slopes flow into one
another in an endless succession of folds and furrows. Walking over these modest heights, gazing down at the rolling

hills and valleys stretched out in circular form, one thinks of nothing—or of God.

Francis thought of God. In these woods and valleys he was in loving communion with his Lord, in prayer.

Because the hagiographers have chosen to portray Francis as one who at a stroke achieved full and complete spiritual maturity, it is impossible for us to trace his spiritual development. But to this man, who could not look at a flower or hear a brook without feeling his heart reach out to God, life was prayer, in the sense of breathing in the divine milieu. When he began his prayers with an *Oremus,* his biographers tell us, he seemed to be snatched away from this world of three dimensions and five senses. Suddenly, behind these words of prayer, the reality of God appeared. If we were able to penetrate Francis' consciousness and, with his sense of God's overwhelming presence, pronounce the words of the Our Father, we might understand what Jesus meant when he said, "Thus should you pray."[3]

It is enough to read the prayer which closes his Rule of 1221, where he seems to let himself go, piles words one upon the other in his attempt to give substance to a Being that has no substance. In spite of all his efforts, he cannot grasp the unfathomable mystery.

He prayed with his whole body. He could dance in ecstacy while he sang out his devotion. "When he prayed in solitude," Celano tells us, "the woods echoed with his sighs, the ground was wet with his tears, he beat his breast and, as if in the most private corner of a house, held endless conversations with his Lord."[4] These emotions spring from a sense of impotence. Struggling with the infinite, he is unable to express with his body what he feels with his mind.

This is in complete contrast to his "mystical" prayer, which we will speak of later. "He didn't even move his lips. It was as if every fiber of his being was turned inward, concentrating on that divine reality. This was not a man at prayer, but a prayer made man."[5]

This constant loving communion with God was not something that Francis arrived at easily. It cost him blood and tears. Those who see him as the carefree vagabond, who rambles through the woods playing with the animals, know nothing of the relentless, unmerciful asceticism which accompanied him all his life.

His biographers describe this in such gruesome detail that we of the twentieth-century can see in it nothing but senseless masochism. At times he was so exhausted by fasting and vigils that, Pius XI said, there was just enough body left to retain the soul. It remains a mystery to us why so many Christians, who already led such truly heroic lives, felt called upon to torment themselves so. But one is forced to admit that such practices in no way diminished their missionary zeal.

Today we take a different view of asceticism. F.O. Cremer, himself a Franciscan, goes so far as to maintain that the asceticism of St. Francis was an impediment to his mysticism, but that his mystical nature was stronger than his ascetic teaching. We must admit that he went too far and that it would be senseless for us to follow his penitential practices. Francis is not a model, but a child of his day. People docilely accepted the half-truth that the more one tortures the body, the more freely the soul is able to fly to God. But for anyone who knows how Francis loved all God's creatures, indeed all creation, it is clear that this is no Manichean hate of the cosmos. His writings show that the meaning he gives to penance is less harsh than that which the word usually evokes. Penance, to him, is the way which leads through inner denial toward true freedom.

Fortunately, Francis never bound his asceticism to rigid doctrine. One night, years later, in ramshackle Rivo Torto he hears a brother sigh, "I'm dying of hunger." Francis immediately gets up and prepares a meal. Then he gathers the whole community around him and, joining in, helps the hungry brother overcome his lacking. And afterward comes this strange admonition: "Brothers, forget this meal, but never forget charity."[6]

Today we set greater store by earthly values than Francis did. Voluntary penance has disappeared and Christians find their asceticism in life itself. Penance has been integrated into the everyday cares, *malheurs,* and disappointments of the human condition. Indeed, we have only to look around us to see that our world offers more than enough opportunity for this type of penance.

During my visits to the hermitages where Francis spent his solitary vigils, it occurred to me that there is a certain similarity among them. Alverna and Subasio, the caverns of the Rieti Valley, and the caves of Subiaco present views of peaceful valleys fading into a far horizon. This is the kind of religious landscape one sees in the work of "primitive" schools, and which Francis intuitively felt was right for him.

His relationship with the cosmos is actually one of respect. He respects the stones he walks upon and every living thing that crosses his path; he refuses to snuff out a flame; and when chopping down wood he will not pull out its roots. This is his way of honoring the Light and the Life which to him are present in all these things. In them, Francis celebrates the immanent and all-surmounting God. This praise of God in his creation is in sharp contrast to our pollution-plagued world. Later, his Canticle of the Creatures, that sublime hymn to water and air, will reflect the purity of his heart.

It is becoming increasingly difficult for Christians of our generation to follow Francis in his experience of God. We seem to see God retreating further and further into mystery, becoming more and more the invisible, unspeakable, unattainable God. Many a discouraged searcher has ceased to look upward into obscurity and now gropes among more tangible, down-to-earth things. He no longer wishes to give God a name, to allow him to enter his consciousness. He cannot know God, he feels, but he *can* know his fellow man, oppressed, downtrodden, and without hope.

This contrast with the religious experience of Francis

struck me with particular force during a recent visit to Italy. While I was walking along the same roads which Francis traveled, from Porziuncola to San Damiano, then over Subasio to the Carceri, his beloved cave, a convention was being held not 15 miles away, in Perugia. Philosophers and theologians from all over the world were discussing "The Future of Christianity." There were those who argued for a "disengagement" between God and the cosmos. "It is no longer possible to speak of God," said one speaker. "Let us therefore resolve not to do so. Religion must no longer look upward; it must be directed horizontally, toward one's brothers, one's fellow men. We must be responsible one for the other, the true communion of the living and the dead. We must discard the hierarchy, the myths, the authority. Religious life is giving without asking anything in return—not even salvation! "Jesus Christ can be a source, perhaps even *the* source, of this one true ecumenical attitude. Progress toward this goal is the only acceptable resurrection."[7]

This speech dates from the period in which, according to some theologians, God began to "die" and "horizontalism" was greeted as *the* solution to the religious crisis.

Francis is not the type to think on a strictly "horizontal" plane. His religion radiates in all directions, toward God, toward the cosmos, toward his fellow men. One thing that this free-and-easy religious genius has never respected is one-way spiritual traffic.

The day came that Francis decided to end his total isolation. Up to now he had worn the garb of a hermit: cowled robe, cord, and shoes. He lays this aside and makes himself a kind of habit, held together by a rope.[8]

A copy of this first habit can be seen in the sacristy of Sacro Convento in Assisi. Not far away, the museum in Perugia displays the garments worn by wealthy citizens in Francis' day, in contrast to this simple habit. Here are the symbols of the spiritual class struggle which Francis is to initiate.

Footnotes

1. The difference in height between the floor and the arch in the little church shows that construction was carried out in different periods. The crucifix stood on the altar, where it was seen by Francis.

2. *Porziuncola* means "a little piece" and apparently refers to that section of the woods. The chapel which stood there was called S. Maria degl' Angeli. The name *Porziuncola* is first mentioned in a deed dating from 1054, which was connected with the sale of a piece of land, "*il cerretto* (little wood) *a Porziuncola.*" The church has not been altered since Francis' day, except for the painting. The window ledge and the side door are mentioned in early sources. There are even a few parts remaining of the house which the city of Assisi built (against Francis' will) to accommodate some of the thousands of brothers who attended the chapters.

3. Mt 6:9.

4. *II Celano* 94; *Omnibus*, pp. 439–440.

5. *II Celano* 94; *Omnibus*, pp. 439–440.

6. *Leg. Major* V, 7; *Omnibus*, pp. 667–668. See also *III Celano* 22; *Omnibus*, pp. 380–381; *Leg. Perugia* 1, *Omnibus*, pp. 977–978; *Spec. Perf.* 27, *Omnibus*, pp. 1154–1155.

7. According to reports in the Italian press, May 1967.

8. According to Terzi, op. cit. (p. 19), this occurred on Feb. 23, 1208, the feast of St. Matthias.

4

The Prophet Finds
His Mission

Two years elapse between Francis' confrontation with his father and his return to public life. These are the "desert years," during which so many reformers have prepared themselves for their task; they are indispensable to inner transformation. "Anyone who wishes to live as a Christian must first have experienced, through Christ, a direct and personal relationship with God. He must 'die to himself'," Urs von Balthasar tells us. "That is why all the great missionary figures emerge in some way or other from the desert. Christ himself comes to public life after thirty hidden years and forty days of intense communion with God in the desert. The Baptist comes out of the desert, and Paul has . . . spent three years in Arabia."[1]

This direct encounter with God made Francis a man of prayer and a mystic. He returned from the desert a prophet and, like all prophets, he is a challenge to society.

Francis' actions have something of the revolutionary, but a very special kind of revolutionary. He wants to reinstate

the old religious values, radically purged, and his method
of making this known is nonconformist, to say the least.
His disreputable clothing and disheveled hair, his thinness
and his upturned beggar's hands are affronts to the material-
istic bourgeois respectability of his father and his former
friends. He is an insult to their way of life, to the carefully
woven cultural patterns which Church and state, class and
status prescribe for a respectable young man. But Francis
is no rebel, no instigator of revolt who, in Sartre's words,
"carefully preserves the abuses he abhors, in order to revolt against them." The ideals which he offers do not an-
esthetize, they rouse to action.

Francis was young, about 26, and it must have been an
unusual experience for the former *podestà* of the party-go-
ing youth, son of the wealthy Bernardone, to address his
listeners in his poor excuse for a habit. Yet he stood before
them: fellow citizens, friends of his youth, girls he had
danced with, acquaintances who had followed the drama
between him and his father.

Celano notes that Francis is a good speaker—and when
one Italian says this of another the compliment must not
be underestimated. But if his style of speaking was anything like that of his written texts, we are safe in saying
that he did not captivate his audience by the use of literary
turns. His must have been an extraordinary charisma, for
within a few years this unimposing figure, so unlike the
orators of the day, had become one of the most beloved
preachers of all Italy.

At first he remained in Assisi, preaching and begging alms
during the day and returning to the woods of Porziuncola
in the evening. His mission was not immediately recognized.
Even his own brother, Angelo, jeered at him in the street.
But there were others who, having once met this singular
figure, found their thoughts turning inward. They at least
understood the challenge; something inside them, some slumbering protest, had been awakened. They were struck by
the sight of a reformer who had the courage to begin with

himself.

Such a man was Bernardo da Quintavalle. He was a man of distinction in Assisi, who had traveled widely and completed his study of law at the University of Bologna. Francis' whole way of life was a silent reproach to this wealthy businessman, and to Pietro di Cattaneo, who had a doctorate in law from Bologna and belonged to one of the city's most influential families.[2]

Their request to join him presented Francis with a new problem. He is now the leader of a small community. But one of Francis' most distinctive qualities is that he never worries about practical details; he prefers to improvise. Shortly after their request he takes them to the dark interior of the church of San Nicola, on the very square where his father's house stands.[3] In the midst of this turbulent city, while the Umbrian towns are torn by strife, Francis calmly opens the Bible on the altar, and with the simplicity which characterizes all his actions he finds there the solution to every religious and social need. He shows his two disciples a world of humility, sober plainness, and the equality of all God's children, and he charges them to go forth and live this mission to the letter.

There was no formal ceremony. No formula was used, no vows were taken. These men commenced their undertaking simply, earnestly, turning Francis' words into deeds. Just as he had thrown his whole fortune at his father's feet, these men must bear witness to their poverty. The whimsical element is seldom absent when Francis acts on impulse. The scene he chooses for this public happening is one of the busiest spots in the city, the present Piazza Santa Chiara, with its magnificent view of the plains of Spoleto. Here were the dim workshops with their looms and olive presses, the tiny bakers', butchers', and ironmongers' shops. With its busy stalls, the square was vibrant with the teeming life of a crowded city.

In this square Bernardo and Pietro, prominent citizens of Assisi, began to give away their money to anyone who would have it, while Francis provided a running commentary on this remarkable spectacle. There is a certain wry humor in the thought of Pietro Bernardone, traveling all over the world to exchange woolen cloth and damask for solid currency, which he then invests in new goods, while his son wanders around the marketplace, in disreputable rags, encouraging his friends to throw away their money. It was the kind of sermon the ribald shopkeepers did not understand, neither the gesture nor its symbolism. This was the second display of a theme which runs throughout the whole of Francis' life: divesting oneself of one's wealth. This theme was fed by his experiences in the solitude of the desert.

In the little chapel of Maria degl' Angeli near Porziuncola, to which he had retreated, Mass was sometimes said by a visiting Benedictine monk. On a certain feast day, Francis was serving Mass. When the Gospel was read, he only half understood what he had heard and asked the priest for an explanation. Celano says about the episode: "The priest explained the text, point by point. And when Francis heard that the disciples of Christ were allowed to possess nothing, neither gold nor silver nor any coin, that when they traveled they were to carry neither purse nor baggage, nor bread nor walking stick, and that they were to preach the kingdom of God, he was filled by the spirit of the Holy Ghost and cried out, 'This is what I want, what I have been searching for, what I've been yearning, burning for in the depths of my heart!' "[4]

This is a typical sample of Celano's rhetoric. But what is so striking about the story is that the hermetic, ascetic Francis is apparently hearing these words for the first time. At least this is the first time he has consciously listened to them. Even if he had never opened a Bible, he must have come across the text more than once in his life. But until now it had meant nothing to him, because he was not ready to accept it. But now that he had thrown away his purse and owned neither baggage nor walking stick, this text flashed through him like a streak of lightning. "This is what I want. This is what I've been searching for."

Francis had an "inner" relationship with the gospel which is difficult to comprehend.[5] He loved the message of the gospel; but Francis wouldn't have been Francis if his love had not gone out to the book itself as well. The beautifully illustrated medieval Bible was sacred to him. When he entered San Nicola with his two companions and opened the book on the altar, this in itself was a religious rite. We see here respect for the written word which has become rare in our world, filled to overflowing with advertising. Francis' eccentricities take on a deeper meaning: he never allowed a single word of the letters he dictated to be crossed out, even if the word had been misspelled. He picked up every tiny piece of parchment that he found on the floor. Someone once asked him why he was concerned about the work of pagan writers, and his reply was surprising: "Because their work contains the letters which form the glorious name of our Lord."[6] No fewer than five times in his writings he alludes to this conviction, that the words of the gospel must be respected wherever one finds them. He understood the psychological value of this symbolism. He will later write to the chapter of brothers: "We must carefully nurture everything which contains the sacred word of God. The sublime message of our Creator and our dependence upon him will penetrate our souls."[7]

The difficulty we experience in trying to understand how Francis read the Bible lies not in the distance between the medieval culture and our own day but in the singular fact that this reader was a man as the Bible wished him to be. He looked for no loopholes or excuses. With heroic candor, Francis accepted the text because, long ago, he had felt its irresistible attraction. He may have overemphasized the gospel, but he never underemphasized it.

A man of God follows his intuition. Many great composers have had to wrestle long hours with music theory before composing a masterpiece; but it is possible for a youthful Mozart to reach out a chubby hand, grasp a sheet of paper, and write a brilliant composition. A biblical scholar can bare a text, like the newly discovered ruins of a long-lost city, and discover unsuspected evidence which throws new light on a certain sentence or phrase. And it is also possible for a simple, unlettered man to open the Bible, read past all the historical facts, and penetrate to its very core. The man who reads the Good Book in this way may never contribute new theories to enrich the field of biblical research, but he can use the Bible to reform the world. This is not a plea for conservatism in exegesis, but it is a rare gift to be able to read through the literal text intuitively, believingly. Francis was forever mistaken exegetically but almost never biblically.[8]

The Bible was to him—and here he approaches the existentialist thinkers of today—first and foremost a book that brings salvation, that is directed toward man's final destination. And that final destination was revealed to Francis in the Bible as nowhere else. Whenever he had a question he opened the book. It was as if he were opening the doors of a room where God awaited him.

Is it really necessary to ask if Francis' interpretation of the Bible is still of value to us? Every religious revolution is accompanied by a search for what is authentic in the Bible, and for what has not stood the test of time. And in every period it is the truly great Christian who recognizes authenticity. No great genius is necessary to improve a piece of text or place one's finger on weak spots in obsolete Church structure: but when we are discussing eternal values, intuitive insight into one's faith is indispensable. It is not so strange that a man like Francis, who had, as it were, abdicated from his society in order to live the gospel to the hilt, would discover something that transcends every culture and every society. Great figures are not ahead of their time, but above it.

Footnotes

1. See *Concilium* (November 1967).

2. It was not until later that Bernardo was given the name "da Quintavalle." His house still stands, in the street which bears his name and which has retained its medieval character. Pietro di Cattaneo was a man of exceptional culture, breeding, and knowledge, who, according to Celano, was always addressed by Francis as "lord." It is now certain that he is the same man who will succeed Francis as minister-general.

3. This church no longer exists; it was situated near the entrance to the Via S. Paolo (near the present post office).

4. *I Celano* 22; *Omnibus*, pp. 246–247.

5. By "gospel" Francis sometimes means the Four Evangelists, sometimes the whole New Testament, and sometimes even the whole Bible. This is evident from his rule, which is based on the gospel but contains texts from the whole Bible. However, Francis had a very special regard for the Four Evangelists.

6. *I Celano* 82; *Omnibus*, p. 297.

7. See *Omnibus*, pp. 107, 101.

8. The question still remains, whether Francis took the Bible as literally as we are told. A Dominican, with a doctorate in theology, once evinced enough confidence in Francis to put to him an exegetical question. It involved the words of Ezekiel: "If you do not warn the godless about his [their] behavior, then I shall demand a reckoning of your soul." The Dominican's problem was that "I know many people who are living in a state of sin, yet I do not always warn them. Shall I be called to account for the state of their souls?" In the first place, we may wonder how this man ever got his doctorate! But perhaps he was only testing Francis, who replied that he felt more inclined to ask for than to provide explanations. But he acquiesced, and resolved the problem as follows: "Interpreting the text freely, I would take it to mean that the servant of God must exhibit such devotion that the holiness of his life is to others a constant warning and reminder of their sinfulness." See *II Celano* 103; *Omnibus*, p. 447.

5

The Religious Experiment

The "organization man" plays an important role in the modern Church. He works according to a plan, researches projects, addresses conferences, periodically produces bulky reports complete with graphs and statistics. One might say that modern Church life functions by the "grace" of the reports it produces. And while no inspirational tongues of fire rise from the carefully written pages, we must admit that many a Church enterprise has gone amiss because it was not considered necessary to consult the reports and statistics of the organization man.

Francis probably would not have been much good at writing reports. Nor would he have shone at committee meetings. We can imagine him embarking on a prophetic dissertation while an urgent report awaits discussion. Cool and logical reasoning was not his forte , and his motto might well have been "after me, the organization." What interested Francis was the present, the here and now. And when all is said and done, who knows how long his impulsive acts will continue to influence the world, when the multitude of reports produced by our generation will have

41

long since been forgotten?

The prophetic leader of a religious movement is seldom strong on planning. His thoughts are on other things. He touches his torch to the flame of one great idea and then goes about starting new fires everywhere. That is why the flame of such a movement blazes strongest in the beginning. Then it subsides, only to flare up later. It follows that Christian revival is an absolute necessity if this flame is to endure, and to rediscover its source in the glowing heart of the gospel.

Such an idea must be possessed of indestructible force, for on the heels of the first generation, which brought it forth, comes the second generation, which encounters it complete and entire. The second generation is always tempted to incorporate this idea by means of rules, laws, and structural definitions. Only the truly original thinkers return to the source and bring new life to the old structures—only to discover that the movement can no longer entirely do without the new structures. This is the eternal conflict between creation and evolution, gospel and Church, which Francis is to experience so painfully in later life.

What is this compelling central theme which Francis discovered in the gospel and which is to give the movement its special character? According to biographers, it is embodied in the gospel texts which Francis found in the chapel at Porziuncola and in the church of San Nicolà.[1] Hard words which penetrate to the very heart of Jesus' way of life. "If you seek perfection, go, sell your possessions, and give to the poor."[2] "Take nothing for the journey."[3] "If a man wishes to come after me, he must deny his very self, take up his cross, and begin to follow in my footsteps."[4] These texts all reiterate one theme, which is meant to be taken in its most literal sense. The whole weight of emphasis is on *renunciation*.

When, later, Francis writes in his Testament "*Et exivi de seculo*"[5] (I have left the world), by "world" he means everything that was dear to him, not only his family, his home, the friends he had sung and danced and drunk with, but also the gifts which prosperity had so lavishly bestowed upon him: position, power, social status and, especially, wealth. Only when he has cast aside all this does he understand the gospel texts which he had overlooked before.

It may seem strange that a man who showed such loving respect for all of God's creation should suddenly turn his back on it. To Francis, however, this is not a leave-taking but a release, which will enable him to love more freely. Suppose a man has a cherished hunting dog that he usually locks up at night, and now the time has come to set him free—not because he loves the dog less, only differently. With a love that does not dominate, but rather gives. It was with this kind of love that Francis and his brothers approached their fellow man and the world.

Francis and his followers had taken possession of a few shacks around Maria degl' Angeli in Porziuncola. Gradually their number increased. It is characteristic of this revival that most of this first group left behind not poverty but prosperity. Most of them were men with successful careers, men of nobility and wealth, members of the *maggiori* of Assisi and neighboring towns. The archives of the city tell us about their positions and social standing.[6]

Anyone who is caught up in a network of family ties and social obligations will realize what it cost these men to renounce that life, to give away their possessions, and to set off, without a decent set of clothes, for the hovels of Porziuncola so as to ally themselves with a man who was considered not quite right in the head.

Such faith is uncommon today. We are more inclined to stay put, to try to influence our environment, to attack unethical practices in the business world, to rid society of some of its aggressiveness, to do "good work" of some kind or other. But Francis and his followers broke with all their cultural patterns in an almost grotesque manner. They cut themselves off from position, the labor process, and day-to-day life. They firmly believed that they could save the world simply by preaching the message of the gospel.

The little town of Assisi became the scene of an adventure that might justly be termed senseless and antisocial, were it not that seven centuries have borne witness to the contrary. It is characteristic of Francis that he completely fulfilled the needs of these cultured and deeply religious men. They did not go to the nearby Benedictine abbey on Monte Subasio, but were drawn to join this 26-year-old youth, part mystic, part troubadour, part vagabond.

Francis was not a learned man in the bookish sense of the word. He had learned to read and write and was acquainted with the fundamentals of Latin. At one point the biographer calls him *"idiota"* (unlettered), to stress the contrast between Francis and the scholars of the University of Paris. Moreover, his inherent good breeding undoubtedly impressed his cultured followers. But throughout his life Francis evidences a special kind of intelligence which is sometimes lacking in the most brilliant scholars.

One gets the impression that this first group, in spite of the asceticism they had in common, was characterized by a certain quality of engaging charm. Francis, as the man in charge of welcoming, was courtliness itself. Describing what was probably his own reception into the group, Celano says: "His nobility of spirit and his rare sense of occasion enabled him to receive them [the brethren] with dignity and grace, giving to each his due."[7]

It is impossible to consider the movement initiated by Francis without considering the cultural background of medieval times. Then, too, there were youth movements, trying to bridge the generation gap. They rejected the cultural status quo and the "establishment" in their search for a new meaning to life. It is not difficult to draw parallels between the Franciscan movement and our present-day hippies, dropouts, and beatniks. All flee a society in which status, success, and comfort threaten to choke the deeper values of life.

Both the medieval and the present-day movements view

Both the medieval and the present-day movements view the Church with a critical eye, but there is one difference. Francis rebuilt the Church of his day, while the majority of our young people would rather see it razed to the ground. That doesn't mean that the youth of today lack religious involvement—as long as the Church is left out of it. Whether it speaks or remains silent, the Church has disappeared from their field of vision, at least as far as the old, institutionalized Church is concerned. Religious ideals today are directed toward solidarity and peace in the world.

But there's more to it than that. These young people hunger for honesty, but they forget that casting aside all sham and pretense makes them terribly vulnerable. They are unprepared for the serious conflicts which this causes within the home, in society, and even among themselves. They yearn for a certain security and intimacy. This drives them into various forms of communal life, where they often discover that a deeper intimacy is difficult when the members share no basic view of life beyond the cares of everyday survival. Once in a while they feel intuitively that something is lacking—that without permanence or vision, life is void and meaningless.

It is hard to say what will become of this generation when it comes of age. Some modern version of Francis' apocalyptic message would certainly appeal to these young people, searching for the same things Francis wanted: simplicity, soberness, love, honesty, and frankness in the midst of a threatening world. They are not impressed by the trappings of status. But a man who has the courage to discard everything he owns, to stand in rags while preaching a message without having all the faults and failings of the Roman Catholic Church thrown in his face. The figure of Francis on the street corners of our cities, with his radical call to imitate the Master, might be seen by passersby as some kind of idealistic madman. But it is just possible that some long-haired dropout might suddenly see in him the leader he has unconsciously been searching for. Indeed, the very same

thing happened to Bernardo and Pietro when they saw the
son of Bernardone standing in the *piazza,* the laughingstock
of Assisi.

One of the most fundamental reasons for the continued
influence of Francis' movement throughout the centuries is
the simple fact that he was a new type of man. I am not
prepared to accept unreservedly the view of van Niftrik that
the figure of Francis marks the beginning of the Renaissance,[8] but one thing is certain: he represents what might
be called the first Franciscan—a man with a new view of
life and a new spirituality, which, according to H. Thode,
reconciles God and the cosmos by its ability to see the
reflection of His being in nature.[9] Moreover, a man who
has the courage to take the most radical gospel texts and
live them, to take a stand at the side of his fellow man in
need. It is not only twentieth-century man who maintains
that "my aim in life is to be a true and complete man, to
develop my humanity to the best of my ability by helping
others be happy and by making the world around me a
better place to live." A Franciscan subscribes to every word.
But he might be taken aback by the following: "Then perhaps I might begin to approach the created image of man,
might be able to stammer just one acceptable word or
thought about the Creator"!

And what of those Christians who did not "stammer" a
single word about God, but rather crushed his mystery under the sheer weight of their eloquence? Who could find
no better solution for the needs of the world than to speech-
ify on the kingdom of God somewhere beyond the horizon?
In the huts of Porziuncola, however, the Franciscan brothers
lived the "humanity of Christ" so completely, so radically,
that if we had men of their caliber today we might see the
world's most pressing problems solved in our own generation. The program which Francis laid before them was not
contained in words alone. A man like Ernst Renan, who
left the Catholic Church after a painful conflict, had to
admit that "one may safely assume that after Jesus, Fran-

cis is the unique, perfect Christian. His true originality lies
in the fact that he dared to practice the Galilean's precepts
with boundless love and boundless faith."

Francis is indeed an original figure, so unlike the monks
of his day upon whom he consciously turned his back. No
class recognizes him, no guild claims him. He moves through
the society of his day with striking ease, living the eternal
dimensions of the word of God. What we are talking about
here is the very core of religion. Such a figure cannot be
confined by the rigid rules of the time-tied. When he walked
in prayer over the Italian fields, spoke to the sun and
clouds in mystical union with the cosmos, every bond with
time disappeared and he was caught up in the immeasurable
realm of God's spirit. Neither did he wish to bind his
followers to a strict set of rules. Shortly before his death,
he returned to the subject: "He spoke a few words to them
on patience and poverty and ordered them to place the
gospel above every constitution."[10]

The conflict between freedom to act according to one's
conscience and the discipline of Church restrictions will
continue to plague Francis throughout his life. It is possible,
as the biographer Sabatier suggests, that it was this conflict which finally broke him. If so, he kept the secret well,
for he remained faithful to the Church which had given him
the gospel.

It is in his freedom and under these restrictions that
Francis brings up his brothers. For all his humility, he remains the absolute master. The former *podesta* has renounced his possessions, but he has relinquished nothing of
his character. His vibrant personality will put its mark on
the rule and the spirituality of his order for centuries to
come.

He instructs not only with words but with his special
talent for "acting out" what he wants to say, even to the
point of miming Christ himself.[11] Only a medieval man and
a Mediterranean could really understand this phenomenon.
The man who inspired by the words "most high, all-power-

ful Lord," takes two twigs and begins to play the violin displays a simplicity and a gift for mimicry which few modern men of colder climes would understand. Francis not only exhorted his brothers to live according to the gospel, he showed them how, playing their role for them, wordlessly, movingly.

The first two years of the movement are no more than an experiment, like so many others throughout the years. The most notable characteristic of the Porziuncola group is the carefree attitude and lack of planning with which each member lived his own, personal religious experience. The strength of the movement lay not in the organization but in what might be called the glowing heart of the gospel. The brothers make no earth-shattering proclamations; they have no futuristic vision of coming generations, as did the prophets described by G. K. Chesterton—those who saw the future "all quite clear, all quite keen-sighted and ruthless, and all quite different."[12] The movement, which was to evolve into a worldwide brotherhood, was not even certain of its own immediate future, as witness the fact that this little commune of twelve men separated and set out to travel the world. Francis and several other brothers went to Ancona and the Marken and then withdrew to the Rieti Valley. Bernardo and Egidio, without a penny and with no caravan for protection, set off over the Alps and Pyrenees for the famous pilgrims' refuge, Compostela, but got no farther than France.

In their travels the brothers slept in barns and haystacks, did farm work, and proclaimed in city squares and crowded marketplaces the message that filled their hearts. The spirit of this first community is described by the Three Companions, who for years worked alongside Francis. "They got up at midnight for prayers. They were each other's servant. If they came upon a beggar along the way who asked for alms 'for the love of God' and they had nothing to give, they sometimes tore off a piece of their habit, to fulfill the scriptural admonition to 'give to those who ask you.' "[13] This was written more than twenty years after Francis' death, and the first stirrings of the later poverty conflict are already audible. But it barely touches the deeper reality, the relentless, radical living of the letter of the gospel. This same depth characterizes every period of spiritual renascence which the Church has ever known.

Francis and his first brothers experienced what Karl Rahner calls "*die Erfahrung des Geistes*", the last and most fundamental experience, when man is confronted with a silence tense and meaningful, the silence of God. He asks, "Have we ever kept silent when we had been treated unjustly and longed to leap to our own defense? Have we ever tried to love God, when we were not riding the crest of a wave of emotional enthusiasm, when the only feeling was one of 'dying of love,' death and absolute denial?"

"This," says Rahner, "is the realization that man's *raison d'etre* has nothing to do with worldly happiness."[14] It is an adventure which Francis and his brothers share with religious men of every generation.

Rahner's trenchant view of life in Porziuncola warns us not to see this episode as a romantic adventure in which the troubador Francis travels the length and breadth of sunny Italy with a song on his lips and not a care in the world. If the movement were no more than that, it would long ago have passed into the realm of forgotten episodes. Of course, Francis knew the ecstacy of the mystic. But he and his brothers had also gone through doubt and desolation, through the dark night when the mystic almost dies from "the lack of God." In the stillness of Porziuncola they struggled through the darkness toward an indissoluble union with God: "from shades and images to the truth," as in the magnificent epitaph of Cardinal Newman.

Footnotes

1. See *Leg. Major* III, 3; *Omnibus*, pp. 647–648.

2. Mt 19:21.

3. Lk 9:3.

4. Mt 16:24.

5. See *Omnibus*, p. 67. This *exivi de seculo* is the object of a study by Fr. R. Koper O.F.M. in *14th Heft von Franziskanische Forschungen: Das Weltversständnis des H. Franziskus von Assisi* (Werl./Westf., 1959) (also published separately in 1959).

6. The identity of the first followers of Francis has been established and research into the archives of Assisi has thrown more light on their origins. This will undoubtedly put an end to the widespread view that these brothers were for the most part pious but somewhat naive men—a little like Brother Juniper, who snatched whatever he could find to give to the poor. Besides Pietro and Bernardo, the first group of eleven followers was made up of Philippus, a remarkable personality, and Aegidius or Giles, who as a mystic was certainly the equal of Francis and about whom a whole body of literature has arisen (among others, a biography by Brother Leo). Then there was the fabulously rich Morica, son of a consul of Assisi, whose family owned several castles, and John a Capello and Angelo Tancredi, both members of the nobility (Angelo was also the first soldier to enter the order). And finally Bernardo di Vilgilante, who came from a wealthy family, and Sabatino. Some sources also mention the priest Sylvester of Barbaro. In any case, this group towered over the average citizens of Assisi, not only in education but in material prosperity. Later, the same will be true of the Poor Clares.

7. *I Celano* 57; *Omnibus*, p. 276.

8. G. C. van Niftrik, *De Vooruitgang der mensheid* (Nijkerk, 1966), chap. III.

9. H. Thode, *Franzi von Assisi und die Anfange der Kunst der Renaissance in Italiën* (Vienna, 1934), pp. 78-79.

10. *II Celano* 216; *Omnibus*, pp. 535.

11. Auspicius van Corstanje O.F.M., "Francis of Assisi, Christplayer," in *Third Order for Our Times* (Chicago: Franciscan Herald Press, 1974), pp. 29-39.

12. G. K. Chesterton, *The Napoleon of Notting Hill* (Middlesex, 1948), p. 10.

13. See *Leg. 3 Comp.* 41, 44; *Omnibus*, pp. 928, 930.

14. Karl Rahner S.J., *Schriften zur Theologie* (Cologne, 1956), III, 106-107. Eng. equivalent: *Theological Investigations* (Seabury, Crossroad Books), vol. III.

6

Pope-King and Church

If we were to look upon the Church as a body, Church structures would be the skeleton of that body. A skeleton, however, is unattractive. It may never intrude, but must quietly and unobtrusively make itself useful by supporting the body. When it ceases to do so the body becomes a carcass. It is the task of the Church to see that her structures do not interfere with the free movement of the body, nor of the religious idealists within that body.

Francis knew this when he composed his first rule. This rule has been lost,[1] but Celano, who lived under it for five years, says that it was simple, was expressed in few words, and consisted mainly of gospel texts to which a few regulations were added.

The simplicity of this rule shows a rash confidence in humanity. Francis' followers were brought face to face with the glowing fire of the gospel. These were heroic words, unaccompanied by moderating footnotes: "Sell all you possess and give to the poor."[2] "My followers must deny themselves."[3] "No greater love has any man than that he lay down his life for his friend."[4] They were expected to *live*

51

these words, no more and no less.

In the midst of his early, fiery enthusiasm, untempered by the voice of Church authority, Francis was led by a spirit he heard speaking to him directly. His rule was the product of a religious experience, not the joint effort of a committee. Once released from the rigid explanatory texts in which it has been enshrined, the gospel is free to shed its original light upon the world. As always when this light reaches the furthest corners of the Church, old forms are threatened, seemingly eternal structures crumble. This is invariably accompanied by a period of crisis and confusion, rebellion and new inspiration. These are the most hazardous but often the richest hours of the Church.

Such an hour awaits Francis and his brothers. The few brief pages of their rule are about to fill the papal-royal Church of the Middle Ages with a new breath of Christian life, on the strength of those few gospel texts.

Again and again we must return to Francis' Testament: "After the Lord had entrusted brothers to me, there was no one to tell me what I should do. But the Most High himself revealed to me that I should live according to the norms of the holy gospel. And I had this written down in a few simple words, which were confirmed and approved by the pope." These are strange words. Instructions from the Most High are laid before the authorities in Rome for approval!

It is indeed a decisive moment in the history of the Church when, in one of its most hazardous but richest hours, a man submits to the authority of the pope the new freedom he has discovered in the heart of the gospel.[5] These simple words from Francis' Testament take on deeper significance when we see them against the background of the time. In those days it was not customary for someone who believed he had heard a voice, calling to him from on high, to pack his bags and hurry to Rome to ask the pope to pass judgment on the veracity of the message.

God's spirit does not reside permanently in Rome but

roams according to His will. It is not uncommon for Him to work from the ground upward, only later stirring the higher echelons of the hierarchy. Popular religious movements have always viewed with a critical eye the pronouncements laid down from above, and in the twelfth and thirteenth centuries the conduct of Church officials was judged against the scriptures, according to straightforward but no less correct norms. The man in the street, seeing the magnificent palace of his bishop and the luxury, hypocrisy, and dishonesty which surrounded his prelates, might be led to philosophize on this remarkable interpretation of the evangelical message. He needed no course in biblical studies to conclude that something was amiss. And when an eloquent itinerant preacher treated him to a more detailed view of the private lives of some of the better-known members of the Curia, monks, and other Church personalities, he proceeded to take practical action with little regard for the infallible magisterium, or the fine distinction between authority and the person exercising that authority. He had seen enough. Or, if he were a devout man, he might look around for a community where there were fewer miters and more true shepherds. This explains why (with the exception of the Cathars) the heresies of this period were little concerned with dogma but evidenced a passionate desire for a more literal interpretation of the gospel, the "true" gospel as retrieved from the debris.[6]

This conflict recurs again and again throughout the history of the Church. On one hand the poverty preachers, with the people behind them, and on the other hand the authorities, bent on protecting the established order. Even in our day there are parishioners who refuse to tolerate the removal of their pastor, because he is to them a true Christ, a man who fights obsolete situations and dares to proclaim that man does not exist for the Sabbath. In the midst of such conflicts the people rise way above themselves, intoxicated by the exhilaration of being able to preach the gospel themselves. Many a man who scarcely knew where his parish church stood a year ago is prepared to hear Mass in the middle of the street in protest. Those who never before lifted a finger to help their pastor are suddenly prepared to defend his door like bulldogs.

This is not due entirely to evangelical inspiration. Something has suddenly come alive in the religious pauper which makes him realize that he does indeed possess Christian convictions. Certain groups, such as young people and artists, are more inclined to lend their support to an evangelical ideal the more it runs contrary to the establishment. And what of those youths who not so long ago assembled before the papal residence with their banners and slogans: "The Church can no longer promote the interests of the few and refuse the masses its support" (*La chiesa non può sostenere i privilegi di poche e sopportare la sofferenza di molti*).

These conflicts go back as far as the eleventh and twelfth centuries, when the Waldensians, Humiliati, and many other poverty preachers turned to the Man who possessed nothing in a world where even the fox had its hole and the ravens their nest. The gospel never speaks louder than when its voice is suppressed. The Church cannot do without these movements. She would perish from comfort and overindulgence if certain biblical texts were not bruited about by the people from time to time, albeit in a clumsy and unexegetical manner. We might revise St. Paul's dictum, "The Church needs her heresies," to read "The Church needs authorities who scandalize." A flock led by a mediocre, well-meaning shepherd may doze off during the sermon, but let him make one false move and they awake with a start, to seize the gospel with both hands. Thus in many dioceses, and around the great convents of the day, simple folk were startled out of their sleep and found themselves reaching for the Bible. The tragedy of many of these poverty movements was that they unconsciously crossed the borderlines drawn by the Church and found themselves in heresy.

It would be unfair to maintain that the entire medieval

hierarchy was suffocating in luxury and devoid of understanding. There were, of course, two sides to this controversy. When Peter Waldo, founder of the Waldensians, was threatened with excommunication by the bishop of Lyon, he fled to Pope Alexander III, who embraced him and spoke loving words of comfort and encouragement. And in the very year that Francis initiated his movement (1206) the bishop of Osma, Didacus, protested at a conference of Cistercian monks against the advocates of orthodoxy. He pointed to the dismal contrast between these men and the popular preachers of the poverty movement who, as he said, went from village to village, content with a crust of bread but impressive because of their ascetic appearance and their dramatic example of evangelical poverty.[7]

In general, the Church has not been strong enough to guide such movements into the right channels. There is not much use in trying to combat such proponents of rigorous poverty from the comfortable armchair of the establishment, no matter how many theological studies and papal encyclicals one has on one's side. This, then, was the situation when Francis decided to submit his "mandate from the Most High" to the judgment of the bishop of Rome—when, in the sunny spring of 1209, he and the eleven brothers set off through Umbria and Sabina for Rome, *caput rerum,* the source of all spiritual and earthly influence. A greater contrast can scarcely be envisioned than that between these twelve holy vagabonds and the man in whom all the powers of the Holy Roman Empire were united, the representative of Christ, Pope Innocent III.[8]

Those who are incapable of reasoning in any but modern, Western-orientated ideas and ideals will never be able to understand the Church as it was in the feudal era. In spite of all the abuses, the ordinary faithful did not cringe under the crack of the slavedriver's whip. The feudal Church was no more offensive to them than the feudal society in which they lived. The crisis in which the papacy finds itself today is due largely to the fact that the spirit of democracy developed more rapidly in civil society than within the Church. But in the thirteenth century it was of no great concern to the people that the lord high pope was a dignitary capable of bestowing or refusing royal crowns. The medieval man in the street had other things on his mind.

Moreover, he had been told from earliest childhood that the visible head of the Church reigned as "vicar of the King of Kings, Lord of Lords." When, through a combination of teaching and preaching, a certain view gains a foothold within the Church, nothing short of a revolution is capable of expelling it, especially when this view is shrewdly rooted in theology and jurisprudence. And the kingship of the pope had for centuries the authority of a semidogma, bringing with it all the trappings of title, ceremony, and royal purple. The gospel has been dimmed and blurred by such a show of supermundane glitter, but it had become so matter of fact that one wonders if, in his heart, Francis really rejected all the glamor. In any case, he never protested against it.

What we are about to recount concerning Innocent III and the Church of his day is more than a historical survey,[9] for modern man cannot help but recognize the silhouette of his own Church against this historical background, with all its cares and queries, good will and failures. Though there is only one gospel, there will always be this struggle between insight and error.

Innocent has been called the greatest pope of all, which does not mean a great deal (a pope can be "great" when the faithful would have preferred him humble). When one places Innocent at the top of the list of popes, one is commending him for his talent as organizer, jurist, and politican, and in these areas he is indeed unsurpassed. But if we take this to mean that he was a man with a lust for power, we are mistaken.

From the day he was unanimously elected pope, as a 38-year-old cardinal-deacon, he labored for the reform of the Church. He had little experience in pastoral work, but he was a friend of the noble families of Colonna and Orsini, and of many others who exercised great influence over Roman life. A brilliant lawyer, he knew which roads led to power and he was a match for the European monarchs, with their diplomatic and political intrigues, as perhaps no other pope before or since.

In private life, however, Innocent was an ascetic who did not deserve the notoriety of the gossip columns of the Vatican, a man of courage who, contrary to the general tendency of his day, was noticeably lenient in his treatment of heretics. It was not rhetoric but deep conviction when, at the opening of the Fourth Lateran Council, he cried out: "It is quite common that bishops because of their lusts and bellicosity, and even more because of their lack of training and pastoral zeal, are powerless to preach the message of God's word and guide the people."[10]

As a deacon, he had published a work on the contempt of the world and the wretchedness of human existence, in which he attacked priests who spent the night in Venus' embrace and the next morning paid tribute to the Virgin Mary. But even his enlightened mind could not stem the almost invincible tide of generally accepted patterns and norms. He did not reject the views of his predecessors on the exercise of power, but strengthened them. He saw himself as a ruler over Church and princes, even though he knew in his heart that one day Christ would say to him, "In spite of all you have done, you have been a worthless servant."[11]

Historians have not yet established the juridical foundations of his policies, but his political views have a depth and certitude which no other pope displayed. An admirer of Bernard of Clairvaux, he adopted not only his ideas but also his failings. He was capable of condemning the power-madness of his bishops while, at the same time, writing to Kalojan, prince of Bulgaria: "You have come to me to ask a king's crown, because you have come to realize that St. Peter not only received the key to power, but also has been placed above nations and empires."[12]

The basis of his view was the primacy: the pope, just as Melchizedek, is priest and king. He possesses the pontifical power of the sun and the royal power of the moon. The latter power is also delegated to earthly kings, with the reservation that the moon cannot shed her light if she is not shone upon by the sun. And this sun illuminated almost all of Europe.[13]

Innocent thought in terms of power and ascendancy which were religious in nature and directed toward an ideal world Church, but the manner in which he made his moves on the chessboard of Europe is mind-boggling. A sound set of moves made him regent of young Frederick II of Sicily, grandson of Frederick Barbarossa. He chose to support Otto of Brunswick in preference to Philip of Swabia, and then was forced to make peace with Philip. He crowned Otto IV emperor but later issued a ban against him, and released his subjects from the oath of loyalty. He declared King John's rights to the English throne null and void but condemned the Magna Carta, which curtailed John's rights, and again made him a vassal of the Church. When one sees how he wielded his power to excommunicate kings and to issue interdictions against cities and whole nations, how a deathly stillness settled around the altar and church bells fell silent, one must admit that Innocent transformed the whole Christian world of his day into a theocratic state.

This does not mean that he did not meet resistance. Philippe Auguste of France, for one, always had great influence over the events of his day. And when Frederick II came of age, he was one of the most intelligent and elusive opponents of his former regent. This scion of the Austrian Hohenstaufers, who spoke nine languages (among them Arabic), who was accompanied on his journeys by philosophers and beautiful women, by astrologists and an exotic menagerie, strode forward to meet the pope-king as the king-pope. In his *Liber augustalis* this agnostic (and fervent hater of heretics!) proclaimed "that it was a sacrilege to enter into discussion on the judgments, decisions and interdictions of the emperor." As head of state, Frederick was infallible too.[14]

This gives us some idea of the enormous struggle for power between the pope and worldly princes. In theory it was a theological-juridical question, but it was settled on the battlefield. It is difficult for a modern Christian to understand how such a pope, with his countless theological advisors, could fail to see that every page of the gospel contradicted his policies.

Innocent III was an intelligent realist, but he lacked the prophetic intuition to see through the formalities of Church structure in which his education and talent had imprisoned him. The greatest rigidity in the Church is found where one's own status is linked to the established order, and the danger is greater for a prelate than a layman, for the Curia than the episcopate. And by the very nature of his office, a pope will never (perhaps *can* never) belong to the most progressive group. A pope who is capable of seeing beyond the present will do so by his personal charisma. He will have to disengage himself from protocol, of the Lateran or the Vatican, from conservative advisors, and from an endless succession of decrees laid down by his predecessors. Their words belong to another age, and they, too, were hampered by obsolete structures. Thus when he ascended the throne, Innocent was already imbued with the idea of papal predominance, rooted in a long period of Constantinism dating back to the fourth century.

And though he might also consult the gospel, it would nevertheless be the gospel as interpreted by preceding pope-kings—a gospel that had nothing to offer an original and intuitive thinker such as Francis. In fact, one suspects that Innocent had the jurists of Bologna search the Bible for just those arguments that were calculated to support his own, previously established view of the papacy. This is the "martyrdom of the word of God," no longer leading but led, which recurs again and again down through the ages.

The spirituality of a pope cannot but suffer when he commands armies, seeks victory on a bloody battlefield, and makes compromises with bankers and princes. The fact that this man also found time—and a considerable amount of time—to devote to Church affairs makes him a marvel of energy and vitality. But such marvels are not capable of reanimating declining dioceses, turning extravagance into soberness, calming heretical storms, or bringing dead ideals to life.

The popes of the twelfth century set great store by the centralization of Church authority. Innocent, too, concerned himself with affairs which any bishop could have taken care of, but which were brought by special courier to Rome for his consideration. The construction of a chapel, the appointment of a canon, a sick pastor who wished to resign his post, and thousands of other minuscule questions claimed the time and attention of a man who was weighed down by the problems of a world which stretched from Scandinavia to the land of Islam. He called upon Christ and St. Peter, whom he was fond of calling "the Prince of Apostles," and let no opportunity pass to impress upon the bishops the extent of his authority. And under Innocent, centralization within the Church had yet to reach its pinnacle.[15]

It is never the Church as a whole that dons sackcloth, ashes, and the spirit of reform. And in this case there was no world episcopate yearning for metanoia; rather, one powerful figure was about to submit his plan to the people. Admittedly, he had the enormous information and help of the Curia behind him, and he relied on the spiritual resources still present within Christianity, but he led the reform as a spiritual *imperator,* maneuvering his forces and resources like a general. According to his letters, he also spent many nights in prayer, with all the sins of his Church before him. His solicitude was not primarily for the religious life of the Church, for at that time there was no question of a crisis. Many a modern pope might envy Innocent the dogmatic peace and quiet of the times, disturbed only by a group of Cathars. The Church did not yet find itself in the situation so acutely analyzed by Karl Rahner, in which spiritual backgrounds have moved so far apart that there is scarcely a single mystery of faith which can be so formulated as to be correctly understood by everyone. All Christianity thought in the same terms then, and philosophers employed the same ideas and concepts.

But there was, nevertheless, sufficient cause for concern, and it is a tragic irony that the Crusades were the cause of moral decline. Ships loaded with knights and soldiers, eager for war, set off for Eastern shores; they returned laden with gold and spices, perfumes and dark-skinned women, and considerable experience in the enjoyment of all these pleasures. The noble ladies who had been left behind were forced to seek their entertainment in the form of jugglers and troubadours who visited the various courts, singing the praises of the worthy knights of the Crusades. The French tales, the *fabliaux,* paint a vivid picture of the amusements of the people, and the feminine portraits taken from the *Livre des Manières* by Etienne de Fougères form a fascinating but scandalous gallery.

As regards the clergy, it is difficult to distinguish fact from fiction in the descriptions of immoral practices which have come down to us. However, constant accusations of exaggerated enjoyment of food, of drunkenness, and the practice of maintaining mistresses on the "inheritance of the crucified Lord" are confirmed by papal bulls. In addition, the condemnation of extortion and the sale of marriage annulments points to corruption among some of the clergy. The state of church buildings and accouterments must have been horrendous. Quite probably, Francis' simple complaint about disrespect to the Holy Eucharist is an even more reliable indication than the emotional language of the Lateran. He mentions the defilement of altar linens and chalices, the profane places where the sacred Host was kept, and the disrespectful distribution of Communion. How-

ever, the whole body of religious was not guilty of such
practices. Celibacy was generally observed in those areas
covered by the Gregorian reform—though one might wonder
at a question put forward by the archbishop of Lund in
Sweden: whether it was considered bigamy if one had two
consecutive concubines!

The sumptuous life of some of the clergy was flagrant.
They went about in silk robes and their horses had bits
made of gold. It is a telling commentary on the general
view of holy services that in Avignon, for instance, it was
necessary to ban erotic dance and song on the eve of Church
feasts.

Such practices among the lower clergy are a reflection on
the bishops, but there is, nevertheless, a certain danger in
judging the entire episcopate on the basis of a limited number of actual cases. It would have been easy for the preachers of penitence to represent abuses in such a way as to
cause an entire congregation to leave the Church, overcome
by shock and horror. But this is not the sort of material
on which one bases a historical judgment. The temperament
of the Italian orator often leads him to stretch the truth in
order to produce an impressive antithesis, as Adam de
Perseigne did when he said of the bishops: "The poverty of
Christ has enriched them, his humiliation has become their
glory, his indignities have showered honors upon them, his
abasement has ennobled them, his degradation has exalted
them." The words are exaggerated, but they have the ring
of truth.

The Curia had not yet sufficiently recovered from the
period when it was described by Bernard of Clairvaux as
a "robbers' den, where the booty stolen from the travelers
lies piled up." The monks themselves vehemently denounced
the abbots, whom Innocent urged to spend less time at court
and more time sharing the life of their monks.[16]

In this light we can understand the despair of Innocent,
and so many other popes since him, "when in our modern

era human wickedness seems to have exceeded all normal proportions."

Footnotes

1. Attempts have been made to reconstruct this First Rule—for example, by deleting from the Rule of 1221 everything that could not have been contained in the First Rule. Others, such as de Beer, have tried to analyze the problem which probably faced Francis and his brothers after Innocent III had approved the First Rule, such as the poverty question and the apostolate. See F. de Beer, "La Conversion de S. François," *Ed. Franc.* (Paris, 1963). Yet these reconstructions are difficult to reconcile with what Celano tells us about this rule.

2. Mt 19:21, Mk 10:21, Lk 18:22.

3. Mt 16:24, Mk 8:34, Lk 9:23.

4. Jn 15:13.

5. See *Omnibus,* p. 68.

6. For details of these movements see H. Grundmann, *Religiöse Bewegungen im Mittelalter* (Berlin, 1935); J. B. Pierren, *Die katholischen Armen* (Freiburg, 1911).

The poverty movements were not all heretical. They opposed the wealth of the Curia, hierarchy, and part of the clergy which contrasted sharply with the simplicity of the gospel. Some of them, however, crossed the boundary of orthodoxy and became contaminated with Manicheism.

Manicheism was founded by Mani (third century) and has Eastern (Buddhist) as well as Christian elements. It is a religion which endows man with a kind of dualism: on the one hand the divine (God) and on the other evil (material). Manicheism became quite widespread, in the Western as well as the Eastern world. In Francis' day it was closely associated with the teaching of the Cathars, which the Crusaders had introduced. Under the name Albigensians, they settled mainly in the south of France. Manicheism is the only dogmatic heresy of this period.

7. F. Mandonnet, *Saint Dominique: L'Idée, l'homme et l'oeuvre* (Paris, 1938), I, 85.

8. Innocent III (1160/61–1216)—Lotario, son of Count Trasimondo de Segni—belonged to the old nobility. He studied Church law in Paris and Bologna and was an expert in Roman law. In 1187, under Gregory VIII, he was ordained a deacon. Several months later he was elected pope, and not until one month later was he ordained as priest and bishop.

9. Perhaps Innocent III occupies too prominent a place in the following chapters, but I felt a need to place this great exponent of the papacy opposite the figure of Francis.

10. He was charitable to heretics—in any case, compared to the prelates of his day. Thus he defended the Humiliati against the criticism of many bishops. See A. Luchaire, *La Croisade des Albigois,* p. 105.
     The political view of the world which Innocent III displayed was of a depth and surety which no other pontiff has ever attained. He was a spiritual man, a theologian, and probably the greatest authority on canon law ever to wear the papal crown. And yet it is extremely difficult for historians to fathom the legal grounds on which his policy was based.

11. See Mt 25:26.

12. Innocent truly considered himself *vicarius regis, regum, domini dominantium* (representative of the King of Kings and the Lord of Lords). The theological basis of his power was as follows. Heaven and earth belong to God, and God has appointed Peter and his successors to be his representative and placed them "above the peoples and the nations" (*Ecce te constitui super gentes et regna* [Jer 1:10]). Thus with the following words Innocent bestows a royal crown on Kalojan, prince of the Bulgarians: "As you have come to realize that Peter has received not only the power of the keys but also power over peoples and kingdoms, you have come to ask for the royal crown" (a year before his crowning). Kempf remarks: "Der Pabst, Stellvertreter Christi, vereint also in sich die beiden hohen Würden des Herren, dan Königstum und das Priestertum. Er steht an der Spitze der Welt." This would lead us to believe that the pope possesses direct power over the king. But elsewhere, when he maintains that the priesthood and kingship are united in the pope as body and soul are united, Innocent says: "Die Herrschaft des heiligen Stuhles uber die Könige ist also lediglich geistlicher, kirchlicher Natur. Wenn sich ein König daruber hinaus der weltlichen Herrschaft des Papstes unterstellt, tut er gut aber er ist niht verpflichtet" (Kempfc, p. 290). Does this then mean *no* direct power? The dualism remains insoluble.

13. In the end, even Frederick II was no match for the powerful pontiffs of his day, and in 1245, during the Council of Lyons, he was deposed. Innocent IV, even more absolute in his pope-king convictions than Innocent III, says in the official document: "We have determined that anyone who in the future advises, helps or supports [Frederick II] will be excommunicated. Those empowered to elect the emperor will find no difficulty in appointing his successors. We ourselves will make a decision concerning the kingship of Sicily after consulting with our brothers." The pope and the council fathers threw their lighted candles onto the stone floor of the basilica, as a sign that the fire of Frederick's glory was extinguished. Then they all burst into a *Te Deum*.

The Roman Curia began to introduce more and more terms borrowed from the emperor's chancellory. To lord it over the emperor, Boniface VIII donned the double tiara, laying aside the simple bonnet which he had worn until then. Benedict IX later made it a triple tiara.

14. We are inclined to believe that Innocent desired a certain decentralization, especially in administrative affairs. He requested the bishops not to apply to Rome for every minor offense, and he never sent legates to a diocese when neighboring dioceses were in a better position to pass judgment than Rome.

15. See L. Bourgain, *La chaire Française au XIIIe siècle*, p. 275.

One of the most notorious ladies' men in this period was Cardinal Ottaviano degli Ubaldini. His chamberlain was a faithful accomplice in all the prelate's undercover activities, and Ottaviano rewarded him for his loyalty by making him archbishop of Milan (see H. Nolthenius Duecento, *Zwerftocht door Italië's Late Middeleeuwen* [Utrecht, 1951], p. 140). Dante names Ottaviano and Frederick II in practically the same breath, relegating them to the fires of hell. In the *Inferno,* apparently, *"il Cardinale"* could only refer to Ottaviano, the bishop of Bologna. (*"Que dentro ê lo secondo Frederico e il Cardinaly, e degli altri mi taccio*—Frederick II and the cardinal are down there; I need not mention the others" [X, 116].)

16. In 1202 Innocent was greatly concerned about rumors which had reached him concerning the Cistercian abbeys. They were in danger of losing their original character because "many of their members had wandered from the path of virtue and had renounced the original spirit of simplicity" (Epist. V, 109). Abbots had been known to allow their sons and daughters to share in the wealth provided by their abbeys. It was known that many convents were in the midst of a crisis. Local councils devoted a great number of canons to convent abuses during this period. See Fortini, op. cit., p. 15.

7

The Dream of a Pope

It was this pope, Innocent, whom Francis and his brothers were now on their way to see. The road led for 200 kilometers through Umbria, Sabina, and Latium, and entered the city by the Via Flaminia. Under his habit Francis carried a piece of parchment, containing the rule upon which Innocent was to pass judgment. The first man whom the brothers met in Rome was none other than their bishop, Guido, who was dumbfounded to see them. And it does indeed seem strange that a band of faithful should be about to lay before the pope a rule of which their own bishop knows nothing. The latter "took the matter quite seriously" (*graviter tulit*).[1] And when Celano says of a hothead like Guido that he *"graviter tulit"* something, we can assume that he was in a towering rage.

The bishop probably felt that his authority had been flouted, but there was also the fear that these men, for whom he had a strange kind of admiration, might decide to leave his diocese. Francis apparently reassured him on this count, for Guido offered to speak on their behalf to an influential prelate of his acquaintance, Cardinal John of St.

Paul. This cardinal was a member of the famous Colonna family, and belonged to the Benedictine convent next to the basilica of St. Paul. The beautiful inner courtyard behind the basilica is still open to visitors, and anyone who has seen it will readily believe that this convent was a cultural center in which the talented diplomat, John of St. Paul, felt completely at home.

During this period the Benedictine Order was at the height of its influence, and also on the eve of its decline.[2] The order lived according to a rule which had stood the test of centuries. Monte Cassino had produced men who, in the most culturally destitute period of Church history, had shed the light of scripture and science over Italy. But the abbots of the thirteenth century were often more interested in the excitement of the battlefield than the quiet of their abbey. Inheritances, legacies, donations were showered upon the convents, which often looked more like castles, peopled with servants and soldiers. Undeniably, the monks did much to further the cause of civilization. They reclaimed swamplands (among them the fertile plain of Assisi) and built orphanages and leper hospitals. But when the enemy showed signs of advancing, they readily exchanged their habit for a suit of armor.

They seemed not to notice that the intellectual life of the cities was beginning to flourish and that the universities were gradually taking over the cultural work of the monks. The bond between the convents and the nobility was the cause of a growing rift between the Benedictines and the people. Popular religious life was sorely in need of a new spirit, which could scarcely arise from remote convents of monks who had no knowledge of a changing world, which was even then embarking on the road toward humanism and the Renaissance.

It is significant that a simple man like Francis stubbornly resisted the efforts of John of St. Paul to persuade him to join one of the existing orders or else continue life as a hermit. No pressure was put upon him, as was later done in the case of the so-called Poor Catholics. John of St. Paul was a friendly and deeply religious man. Celano, who never dared to criticize the situation within the Church, says of him in passing that although(!) he lived among the princes and prominant personages of the Roman Curia, he had the reputation of one who "despised earthly goods and reserved his love for the things of heaven," then considered the ideal Christian attitude of life.

We can safely assume that Francis was not greatly concerned with the economic and cultural changes which were taking place. But an intuitively gifted and truly religious man knows that the outer packaging of a religious ideal can change and cease to appeal to the faithful. We cannot resist a comparison with our own day. The great surge toward *aggiornamento* was not introduced by some impetuous progressive; it was a theologically orthodox pope who in a flash, as he himself described it, realized that a revival of the whole Church was necessary. When Pope John XXIII, directly after his election, broke with an unimportant but centuries-old tradition, or visited the prison of Regina Coeli and confided to the inmates that his uncle had "done time," these occurrences were in themselves insignificant, but they show John's deep insight into the minds of the people. He felt that they had had enough of ceremony and tradition and all the pressures emanating from Rome, which threatened to stultify any new idea which might arise. Do not many bishops, theologians, liturgists, monks, and other Christians feel that they too are confined in some kind of Roman prison? But which Roman prelate would dare admit that his uncle had suffered the same fate?

Francis was not the type of Catholic we would today call ultraprogressive. He dutifully conformed to the theological precepts of his day, obeyed any man who, according to his belief, had authority over him. Many a prelate must have taken him for a docile and harmless follower of the Curia. Few people understood that this humble facade concealed a brilliant mind, which realized better than anyone else what was needed to free the Church from "imperialism" and spiritual poverty. Francis never rails, he does not preach against the abominations of serfdom, and he organizes no protest march on the palaces of the nobility. A direct reference to heretics will not be found in his writings. But he is preparing a new spirituality, so deeply evangelical that respect for the human person and love of soberness will eventually strike at the very heart of slavery, extravagance, and heresy. His heroic example is a sermon on nonviolent revolution. He was one of those rare prophets who are not enveloped in supernatural clouds but are one with their listeners in all their human misery.

This man finally gained access to the throne room of the Lateran Palace.[3] He appears before Innocent in the company of eleven poor, emaciated figures, humble and unassuming, straight from the forests of Umbria. They have with them a few pages of text on which the pope must pass judgment. Few details are known about the protocol of papal audiences in those days; we know only that the sovereign of Church and state was prepared to interrupt his many activities to receive this little band of poorly clad Umbrians.

The first meeting was short and not particularly successful. While reading Francis' rule, Innocent is said to have shaken his head in amazement at such a reckless adventure. "Your life seems to us too hard and rough. We must be sure that the road you have chosen is not too difficult for those who will later follow you," the Legend of Three Companions has him say.[4]

His answer to Francis and his Umbrian company is negative: the rule is too severe. But he advises Francis to consider well what he is about. Celano, in his polished style, tells us that Innocent said, "My son, pray that Christ may make known to me his plans for you. As soon as I know more I will feel more sure of myself in granting what you, in your nobility of spirit, so desire."[5] But these words cannot obscure the conflict which is arising—which the Church has often known before and since—the conflict between common sense and heroic idealism.

In the Lateran Palace, a fine diplomatic and political balance has been established: envoys are sent back to their princes with clever compromises, plans to improve the Church are tempered by evangelical inspiration and psychological discretion, while the pope steers a careful course between tolerance and reproof of the prelates. He reads Francis' rule and deems his interpretation of the gospel too severe. Before him stand twelve idealists who believe they have discovered that the gospel can be lived without compromise. Ragged and humble, they stand in the papal throneroom, asking to possess nothing but to be allowed to labor quietly for the reform of a Church which seeks to possess all. They are pleading for recognition that Christ was not preaching folly when he gave us the gospel.

Strangely enough, modern man is inclined to admire Francis while taking Innocent's side. The figure of the hero arouses our admiration, but he can never be the cornerstone on which to establish a community. And Innocent shows himself to be a compassionate father, who does not wish to relegate the brothers to a life which would gradually become unendurable. In spite of his book, *The Contempt of the World,* he still wishes to retain something of the world, to soften the hardships of life. Apparently, he never dreamed that a group of men might come along who would take his book *too* seriously.

Celano gives us an impression of Francis' second meeting with Innocent. We hear of the famous dream which Innocent was supposed to have had several days before this encounter. He saw the Lateran basilica, mother church of Christians all over the world, about to crumble and fall. Walls tottered, pillars cracked, the supporting beam on one side of the colonnade almost touched the ground. Then a small, habited figure took the beam upon his shoulders, supporting the basilica and saving it from collapse.

We can see in this dream a symbol of Innocent's long-felt fear, as well as an unconscious wish for an evangelical move-

ment which would save the Church from disaster. This man,
whose papal policies were based on the Crusades and a
constant quest for power, was still too much of a Christian
not to realize that without inner reform a Church which
captured the most sacred places of the Holy Land would at
that very moment desecrate them. He had been well dis-
posed toward the poverty movement of the Waldensians,[6]
and now he saw before him a man who had made a greater
impression on him than he first realized—a figure whose
like could not be found among all the members of the
Curia, fresh from the desert, unaware or uncaring of all
the things they considered so important. Poor and un-
pretentious, emaciated by fasts and deprivation, with a
selfless love for the Church. Innocent understood that
a Church which rested on cracked columns needed the
support of this pillar. He charged Francis and his brothers
to "preach penitence to all, as God inspires you. And
when by the grace of the Almighty you have increased in
number and in grace, inform me of this and rejoice, for I
shall confidently entrust to you even more important missions."- Then, according to the Three Companions, they
were tonsured, indicating their entry into the ranks of the
clergy.- The impression remains that Innocent did not relax
the rule and that Francis left the Lateran as victor.

When, in his *Vie de S. Francois d'Assise,* Sabatier describes the meeting between Francis and the Curia, his tone
is sharp. This Protestant, whose writings have fascinated
thousands and who has resurrected the shining figure of
Francis from the dusty records, clearly suspects these Roman
prelates of the most infamous intrigues. What he most ob-
jects to is that Francis and his friends are drawn within the
circle of the clergy by the tonsure. The official Church is
quick to take possession of these unsuspecting but highly
useful men.

No historian would deny that the Roman Curia of the
thirteenth century was capable of such intrigues, but does
Sabatier possess enough information to support his hypo-

thesis and to make it acceptable to the historian? My view is that he does not. The primary sources give no information whatsoever on the subject. Sabatier's text is as follows:

> Francis and his companions were not sufficiently acquainted with the phraseology of the Roman Curia to realize that in effect the Holy See did no more than to suspend judgment on the sincerity of their intentions and the soundness and purity of their faith. . . .
>
> Thus Francis' creation, originally an organization for lay persons, became an organ of the church whether he liked it or not. Before long it would be reduced to an ordinary religious institution. Unwittingly the movement had betrayed itself. The prophet had allowed his hands to be tied by the priest.[9]

I consider it extremely unlikely that students of law, such as Bernardo and Pietro de Cataneo, or indeed Francis himself, with his intuition, would so easily allow themselves to be hoodwinked by the Curia. Some of the brothers were well acquainted with Roman phraseology, and they were not strangers to the workings of Church diplomacy. But this first encounter between the Franciscan movement and the Curia was of great significance for reasons other than those put forward by Sabatier.

It is not surprising that such artists as Giotto, Ghirlandaio, and Gozzoli have portrayed this scene, for it is a truly dramatic happening: on one hand, the representative of earthly power and luxury, and on the other a man who surpasses the whole of the Lateran in the power and richness of his nature. A man who illuminates the evangelical paradox: the power of the weak and the weakness of the powerful. While Innocent may have realized what scandal was given by extravagant prelates, this pope-king was unable to offer the people the powerful challenge of his own, personal example. Even if one assumes absolute good faith, it is well-nigh impossible for a man to defend his extensive properties by armed force while, at the same time, preaching a doctrine of gentleness and charity. How can a pope call himself the representative of Christ, who came to serve, and yet not shrink from accepting the deference of crowned heads? And how can he appear before the people in the midst of a Curia which cannot escape criticism even from the docile Celano?

Francis and Innocent have one thing in common: a passionate desire to serve the Church. Innocent, the pope, the high priest and supreme official of the Church, is fascinated by a vision in which all mankind is brought together in an *imperium* stretching to the ends of the earth. Francis, the prophet, the charismatic leader, wants to give himself completely to that Church. But he is scarcely interested in the Church as institution. His love and devotion go out to the Church of the poor, the Bride without diamonds, for whom he would give his life.

Undeniable drama lies in Innocent's conviction that he was bound in conscience to act as he did. There is no greater catastrophe for the Church than a pious pope who misunderstands God's message. An erroneous decision is defended with all the fervor of a clear conscience. When, later, a Borgia—such as Alexander VI—scandalizes the Catholic Church and the world, he will know why. But the Innocents of this world have affirmed and strengthened earthly power *in nomine Domini,* just as they preached the Crusades with a simple *Dieu le veut.*

God's message is often understood far more clearly by a man or woman of the people. Here stands Francis, equally convinced that he has been sent by the Almighty. How, then, is the Spirit to make known to the Church his secretmost wishes? From above comes a clarion call to arms, and out of the depths a desperate cry for radical poverty and peace. The brilliant lawyer, Innocent, and the entire University of Bologna find in the Bible a justification for the royal might of the pope. Francis opens the Good Book and reads that his Master had no stone on which to rest his head.

It would be an oversimplification to condemn the imperialist tendencies of a pope on the basis of a few Bible texts. His entire hierarchical and feudal background cried out for monarchs. As a child, he was indoctrinated with the idea that the pope stands above the rest of humanity, as king of Church and the world. It is only natural that, as Innocent III, he will translate the gospel into his own cultural pattern. He knew that the gospel preaches a doctrine of simplicity and poverty, but he believed there is a difference between subjective profession and objective policy. This same distinction can be seen in the Church of today, where there is prosperity, even affluence, at every level, while true Christianity cries out for a poor Church.

In the Lateran, Francis is confronted with a phenomenon common to all ages. Only the mystic is capable of thinking in the timeless terms of God, divorced from his own culture. If Innocent had entered a convent instead of the university and had emerged as an intelligent ascetic, he might have condemned the policies he now feels bound in conscience to follow. But there are few men to whom it has been given to break the traces of a time-tied culture, though they are well aware of the existence of slaves, Great Inquisitors, and pope-kings. It is no simple matter to divest the gospel of its myths without becoming entangled in the myths of one's own day.

This dramatic conflict took place in the Lateran Palace, once bestowed upon Emperor Constantine and later given in loan by him to the popes, to which they moved after twelve centuries of simple housing. It is a conflict between power and simplicity, and it will continue throughout the history of the Church because it is the story of man and the gospel. It is no coincidence that the painters and sculptors of the Renaissance and Baroque periods were intrigued by this conflict between Innocent and Francis.

The phraseology and the intrigues which Sabatier describes are pure hypothesis, but this conflict between power

and poverty was very real. How many of us, fervent admirers of Francis' simplicity, have not followed Innocent in
his quest for power?

Footnotes

1. *I Celano* 32; *Omnibus*, p. 254.

2. San Paolo fuori de Mura replaced an earlier church which had
been built by Emperor Constantine (during the fourth century) on the
spot on which tradition has it that St. Paul died. The colonnade
behind the basilica was built from 1193 to 1214 by Pietro Vassaletto,
during the lifetime of Cardinal Giovanni.

3. Today the rear wall of Innocent's throne room is still visible
against the side wall of the Scala Santa. This is in all probability
the room in which Francis and his brothers were received.

4. *Leg. 3 Comp.* 52; *Omnibus*, p. 936.

5. *II Celano* 16; *Omnibus*, p. 376.

6. The Waldensians were founded in the twelfth century by Waldes,
a Lyons merchant. After reading the gospel, he was seized by an intense desire to experience and to preach true evangelical poverty. He
sold all his possessions and founded a movement which, in the end,
transgressed the bounds of orthodoxy, denouncing tradition, the
hierarchy, indulgences, etc. Innocent retained a certain sympathy for
him, but in later years Waldes' followers were often the victims of
cruel persecution.

7. *I Celano* 33; *Omnibus*, p. 255. See also *Leg. 3 Comp.* 52; *Omnibus*, p. 936.

8. According to Wadding (*Annales*, adn. 1210), it was on this occasion that Francis was ordained a deacon. He bases this assumption
partly on a letter addressed to the clergy, which begins "We of the
clergy," and says that the Lord "has placed himself in our hands,
and we touched him." See *Omnibus*, pp. 100–101.

9. It is not until p. 114 of his *S. François d'Assise* (1933 ed.) that
Sabatier permits himself to utter sharp criticism of Rome. Today,
one cannot help wondering why this magnificent work had to be
placed on the Index of Forbidden Books.

8

Reform in Crown
and Cowl

There is a story that Francis once emerged from the woods at Porziuncola, where he had been praying, and was met by Brother Masseo. "Why you, why you?" the brother said, shaking his head. When Francis asked what he meant, Masseo answered, "Why does the whole world follow you? Why you? You're not handsome, not clever or educated, and you don't come from a noble family. How do you explain it?" According to the story from the Fioretti, when Francis heard this he spent some moments gazing up to heaven and his heart was with God. Finally he said, "You want to know why the whole world chooses to follow me. It is because the Lord could find no more miserable creature for the miraculous work he wished to accomplish—that is why he chose me. To put to shame nobility and greatness and power and beauty and wisdom."[1]

This anecdote not only reveals the extent of Francis' influence but indicates the manner in which he experienced this influence. He recognized it, accepted it, but in all

humility. It is in this light that we must see the reform
initiated by Francis. It is quite possible that Francis never
considered himself a reformer, so great was his humility.
Indeed, he lacked one of the prime assets of a reformer:
strategy. His visit to Innocent was not the first phase of a
carefully worked out plan. Even when he left the Lateran
with his companions and set off through the magnificent
countryside around the foot of the Apennines on the way
back to Umbria, his thoughts were so far from reform that
he wanted to settle in the first pleasant valley he came upon.
He was not quite sure whether he was the leader of a
band of apostles or hermits. If Francis wanted to reform
anything, it was simply himself and, with him, his brothers.

It was not until the following period, as he and his brothers (among them lawyers, members of the nobility, sons
of consuls) began to travel about, working on farms and
caring for the poor souls in the nearby leper hospital,
that it occurred to him that he would often be called upon
to forsake his hermit's existence for a life on the road, if
he were to bring to the Church a religious reform, a reform of the spirit.

We must not forget that even a St. Francis of Assisi can
not effectuate each and every aspect of a reform. And
certainly not one which is to usher in a new period in the
history of the Church "in head and in members," in
theology, legislation, structures, and above all in spirit.
All this cannot emanate from the head and heart of one
figure, but is borne by the whole community of the faithful. These are the reforms which take place at the turning
points in Church history[2] —the papacy of Gregory VII
in the eleventh century, the Reformation, and our own
chaotic times. Francis made the way clear for a reform
which was to make itself felt for centuries, right up to
the present day. His reform of the spirit was accompanied
by another reform, that of the structures. And again we
are confronted with that organizational genius behind the
scenes, Innocent III.

We must take care not to exaggerate the contrast which
is evident here. The dialectic between spirit and structure
does not take place between reformers but—ideally—is fought
within the reformer himself. Innocent is also aware of this
problem. The reform of spirit is not foreign to him, though
Francis is the defender *par excellence* of the "primacy of
the spirit," Spirit and structure are interdependent where a
community is concerned. If the spirit cannot survive within
certain forms, other forms will have to be found. Congar
points out that the so-called *Devotio Moderna* movement
(Thomas à Kempis) died out because it did not find the
proper structures.[3] Present-day groups are subject to the
same danger, no matter how alert they are to it, especially
in the second generation. And the movement which Francis
initiated would have been no more than a highly interesting
episode in medieval history if it had not finally found
refuge in the modest structures of an order. It is unrealistic
to assume, as some people appear to do, that had he been
completely free to follow his own inclinations, Francis'
spirit would have conquered the vicissitudes of more than
seven centuries and retained greater force and influence than
it has. Had no order been founded, that spirit would sooner
or later have faded away like a fresco on a crumbling wall.

Innocent III has gone down in history as a controversial
figure. "His religiosity," says Sabatier, "was more that of
the Bible than of the gospel. He may at times remind us of
Moses, leader of his people, but he has nothing in him of
Jesus, the shepherd of souls."[4] This is an exaggeration, of
course. And this view is clearly inconsistent with the personality of Innocent as revealed in his enormous correspondence, very little of which had been published in Sabatier's
day. The 6,000 bulls are certainly no fountain of poetic
eloquence, but here and there among these straightforward
documents one catches a glimpse of the priest, who continually asks himself how he can guide the Church to moral
greatness (while not losing sight of world political power!).
He became more of a statesman than we might have wished,

but in any case he used his political power to further his religious ideal, which cannot be said of all his successors.

As a reformer, he always turned a critical eye first on the Curia, where he exposed the practice of trafficking in false documents and privileges, and he forbade members of the Curia to accept any gratuities above and beyond their salaries. He did not shrink from removing incompetent bishops, on the reasonable grounds that the bishops exist for the Church and not the Church for the bishops. In his battle against demoralization, he exhibited remarkable charity for women of the streets, and encouraged the faithful to remove these women from their evil surroundings and help them find good husbands. He fought against usurious practices in the convents, and marital infidelity (even among princes), and understood that the mendicant missionaries could be of great importance in influencing the clergy, spoiled by lives of luxury and rigidly territorial in their thinking.

His work of reform was crowned by a general council, an event which he had looked forward to for years. On November 11, 1215, in the presence of 400 bishops, 800 abbots and convent superiors, and representatives of the emperor in Constantinople and a dozen or so kings, he delivered his opening address, which began: "It has long been my fervent wish, before I die, to share with you this paschal meal." Reading between the customary lines of rhetoric, we discern the emotion which gripped this man, with his passionate desire to arm the Church with ironclad structures and to make it into a religious body which need fear neither king nor heretic nor Saracen.

At the Fourth Lateran Council it was not a question of creating new structures to meet the challenge of a new and modern age just around the corner. It was more an attempt to buttress the old and tottering figure of the Church. Innocent was not the type of shepherd who walks behind his flock, allowing it to search out new pastures under his watchful eye. Innocent did not follow, he led. There was opportunity for discussion during this council, but no clash of ideas. Three sessions in the space of three weeks were sufficient to make the decisions it had taken two years to prepare. Seventy-two legally and theologically impressive decrees shored up the Church like so many piles driven into the ground. A new era was about to begin.

Innocent represents a type of reformer who has always played in important role in the history of the Church: the man who reorganizes and reshapes. The contours of the pattern he laid down have remained visible for seven centuries; and the Church structures which he framed are only now being systematically demolished. It is not easy to gain an insight into the complicated personality of this pope, who wrote a book on contempt of the world and yet made very shrewd moves on the political chessboard, who labored for unity with the Eastern Church but sacrificed Constantinople for Jerusalem, who blessed the Crusades with "God wills it!" and left thousands lying dead on the battlefield. When he took steps they were giant steps, which did not always land him where one would like to see a leader of Christianity arrive.

Looking back, it is not difficult to see where he went wrong. It was not so much in his political mistakes, not even in the remarkable blind eye he turned to the Crusaders who ravaged Constantinople. His political and personal mistakes are all but forgotten. We are critical today of that side of his character which was considered brilliant during his lifetime: he built the Church into a worldwide political power by means of a policy which can find no favor today.

And yet Innocent was one of the greatest of the group of reformers to which he belonged. He is not to be blamed if many of the structures which he established lived on into an era for which they were not suited. We are rebuffed by his authoritarian attitude, but we no longer live in an age where the average priest and even bishop is scarcely better educated than his illiterate parishioners. His powerful grip on the world, though not rooted in the Bible, at least put an end to lay investiture, and for a time freed the Church from royal custodians.

But as a reformer he lacked originality and religious intuition. No radical, he repaired more than he reformed. His aim was to mend the Church, to strengthen the tottering pillars. And he did so with great energy and devotion, making use of his exceptional gifts, from the day that as a young deacon he was elected pope right up to his death, a year after the final session of the Lateran Council.

If a reformer like Francis cannot fathom every aspect of a reform, neither can a pope. If he wishes to live up to his honorary title, Servant of Servants, he must turn an understanding ear to the needs of others, knowing that the Spirit bestows his charismata where he will, including those of the reformer. The visit of Francis and his brothers to the Lateran may have been a fairly unimportant event in the eyes of the Curia, but Innocent interrupted his busy life to receive a group of unknown, unkempt men who wished to embark on a religious adventure, and listened carefully to what they had to say. It was one of the most far-reaching decisions of his life.

The Church is always subject to the tension which arises between the letter of the law and the message of the gospel, spirit and structure, hierarchy and Curia, Curia and pope. But the most intolerable tension, which sometimes charges the Church to the point of explosion, originates when reformers, diametrically opposed to one another, start pulling at the Church.

This kind of strain never arose between Innocent and Francis, mainly because Francis was a reformer who never shouted and never damned. "Beware of those who despise [the clergy], for though they live in sin, no one may judge them, for the Lord has reserved judgment over them unto himself."[5] Whoever builds such a plank into his platform would seem, *a priori,* unsuited to the task of a reformer! And this was a period in which the scandal given by the clergy caused many a son of thunder to call down chastising fire from heaven.

No such prayer passed Francis' lips; that was not his style. In the Fioretti he says, "The Lord could find no more miserable creature for his wonderful work. That is why he chose me."[6] And one wonders if he was not thinking of the hierarchy when he said: "Blessed the servant who, though exalted, ever desires to be the slave of others."

Francis knew intuitively what his age so desperately wanted. He gave the poor a new status, made work respectable, and raised the leper above himself, as a symbol of the suffering Christ, touching the very foundations of medieval life like a premature Karl Marx. But he was a revolutionary without a "bloody banner raised on high."

To the faithful of the thirteenth century, Francis was the real reformer. Innocent's dream, in which the pillars of the Church tottered, might have sprung straight from the imagination of the people. But they knew it was not the pope who had shored up the sagging timbers. The rebuilding of the church was the work of Francis.

Admittedly rather biased, this view of the affair is evidence of a very human tendency to root for the underdog, the little man who turned out to be a match for the supreme power of a pope. But even his critics, and not only those of the Middle Ages, give Francis credit for the spiritual reform.

Men like Renan and Sabatier go even further. They see in Francis a prophet who would have liked to bypass all the existing structures but was prevented from doing so by officialdom. This is reflected in Sabatier's bitter commentary on the meeting between Innocent and Francis: "The priest bound the hands of the prophet." The eternal dilemma arises when the authority of the Church is confronted with personal inspiration.

It is undeniable that in the course of history many a shortsighted official has suppressed the charisma of one of the faithful. This can have the most disastrous results, especially at moments which later prove to have been turning points in history. But in the case of Innocent and Francis I cannot help thinking that Sabatier should have listened more carefully to the wise words of Charles Péguy: "It is the fault of every hagiography to disparage those who surround a saint." A more subtle consideration of historical sources would have led Sabatier to admit that Innocent allowed Francis considerable freedom by saying "Go forth and preach the message of penance as you are inspired by the Lord."[7] Moreover, Francis was not the type to allow his hands to be tied while the voice of the Most High was calling him. His bishop, Guido, wants to keep him within the limits of his diocese, but Francis chooses the world. Cardinal John of St. Paul wants him to remain within the existing orders, but Francis founds a new order. Innocent considers the rule too severe, but Francis leaves the Lateran and proceeds to live according to this unaltered rule in all its radicalism.[8]

He never felt that his obedience was based on the proposition that "orders are orders." And when he obeys, it is because he believes that the Almighty desires this of him. This kind of reformer never marches in step with others, not even a pope-king. "As you are inspired by the Lord," Innocent said, and that is exactly how Francis meant to act.[9] His was the charisma of the prophet.

Anyone who has made a study of prophecy knows that this term has been used to refer to the most brilliant and the most fanatical ideas. The genius and the fanatic both deviate from normal standards, and both are misunderstood. But the similarity ends there. It is, however, possible to use the term prophet in an acceptable sense, as it developed after the apostolic era—as a man who is guided directly by the hand of God. Often he emerges from solitude, as in the case of John the Baptist. He is an "enlightened" man and his voice is heard because his message is honest and original. He often appears just when the enthusiasm of the Church as institution is beginning to wane. Existing forms do not bother him. Creative and inventive, he always makes the gospel seem real and compelling through his personal interpretation. He does not spurn the media of his day, for he knows that God's word was not meant for the desert. But it can be enriched by the desert, by the penance, prayer, and contemplation which prepare the prophet for his reentry into the world. Only then, if he is a true prophet, does God's hand guide him back to his people. It is with a new voice that he brings his message to the faithful.

The prophet does not oppose but rather challenges the hierarchy. He is critical of the establishment; he looks beyond the present into the unfolding future. A prophet, by definition, distrusts the present, which explains why he is either feted or hated. He is by definition inimitable, as Francis was.

For six years Innocent and Francis collaborated in bringing the Church from decline into flourishing growth. Together, they prove that the Church does not live by spirit alone, nor by structures alone. The success of a reform depends on the harmonious interplay of priest and prophet, institution and movement. They must be in perfect balance. When the prophet gets the upper hand, chaos threatens. But a Church without prophets is doomed to fruitless rigidity.

Innocent was without doubt a man of exceptional ability, who labored with heart and soul for his ideal, but he was great only against the background of his day. His reforms are of little use to us today. Francis did not have Innocent's legal prowess and talent for organization, but in those things in which he excelled he was timeless.

Innocent lives on in the history books,[10] whereas Francis belongs to history.

Footnotes

1. Fioretti 10; *Omnibus,* pp. 1322–1323.

2. See Rene Pascal in *Esprit* (January 1968), p. 112.

3. Y. Congar, *Concilium* (March 1972), 3: 38.

4. *S. François d'Assise* (definitive ed., 1931), p. 122. As regards the one-sided interpretation of Innocent's correspondence, see A. Fliche, *Histoire de l'Eglise depuis les origines jusqu'a nos jours,* part X: "La chrétienté Romaine." Many of his letters were not published until after Sabatier's day.

5. *Admon.* 25; *Omnibus,* p. 86.

6. Fioretti 10; *Omnibus,* p. 1323.

7. *I Celano* 33; *Omnibus,* p. 255.

8. It may be tempting but it is nevertheless historically incorrect to speak here of "Francis in Rome before the Pharisees," as Karl Piser does in his *Franziskus der himmlischer Kommunist* (Mainz, 1967). That does not mean that the members of the Curia never feigned an admiration for Francis which they did not feel, but it would have been ridiculous to attack him openly.

9. *I Celano* 33; *Omnibus,* p. 255.

10. Innocent died in 1216 in Perugia, during preparations for a crusade. His body was solemnly displayed in the cathedral. Jacques de Vitry, who happened to be in Perugia at the time, mentions an incredible and horrifying occurrence. One of his letters has been preserved, in which he writes: "Then I arrived at a town called Perugia, where Pope Innocent had just died, but had not yet been buried. That night thieves had stolen his costly garments and left his nearly naked body behind the church, in the midst of the most horrible stench. I went to the church and saw with my own eyes how brief, how vain and fraudulent is the glory of the world." This letter is dated October 1216.

9

"I Already Know Christ"

The secret of Francis' reform was this: he *was* what he preached. He felt intuitively where true evangelical reform lay. Not in the vow of poverty, nor in fasting and penance, nor in a sincere effort to make this world a better place to live in. At the heart of every reform is Christ. Not his words, but the person of Christ.

Words lose much of their force when they are separated from the person by whom they were spoken. And to Francis the gospel was not a book which had somehow floated down from heaven. Behind the parables and the Sermon on the Mount, with its radical call to arms, stood a Person whom he loved and in whom he believed. Like St. Paul, he felt the truth of the words: "Not I live, but Christ lives in me."[1] On his deathbed, the person of Christ will have permeated his being to such an extent that Francis will wave aside the gospel with the words: "I already know Christ."[2]

For centuries people have been drawn to Jesus, even though they were often unwilling to embrace his Church. "Why am I not content with Islam," a Mohammedan

woman writes, "the religion of my forefathers? Why does
it have to be Christianity, that tissue of absurdities, that
fascinates me?"[3] Her answer is contained in these words:
"My mind refuses to accept the dogmas, but my heart
lies at the feet of Christ."

Francis never stood outside the Church, but for a long
time Christ was no more to him than an article of faith.
But when he first truly experienced Christ, it was with
such force that the conscious memory of it remained with
him the rest of his life. From then on he was a Christian,
and he understood Rahner's words: "Who even looks upon
Him shares in the contemplation of God, though as yet
through a veil."[4]

In the writings of Francis we find many references to "the
imitation of Christ." He sees himself as a faithful servant,
who follows his Master, even through the deepest humiliation. With an exegetical simplicity untouched by modern
"discoveries," he finds in the gospel what he must be,
how he must act. Jesus calls Judas his friend—Francis wants
to love his enemies. Jesus became a servant—Francis will
never wish to be more. The Son of Man came not to be
served but to serve—and the entire history of the order will
be charged with the spirit of loving service, which tolerates
no superior, no prior, but only servants and ministers.

It may sound naive, this form of imitation, but Francis
was not out to imitate his Master in details. It was not the
outward similarity he was seeking, but some way to sub-
merge his own person in the person of his Master.

The brothers did not always understand this. Several
decades after Francis' death the exaggerated imitation theme
began to invade Franciscan literature. One cannot help
wondering whether many samples of "imitating Christ,"
attributed to Francis, are not the product of this interpretation, which saw everything in terms of "mirror image,"
"resemblance," and the like. Pious brothers began to search
for striking details, which only detracted from the simple
greatness of their master. At the request of an angel, his

mother bears him in a stable. Later he goes to Rome, not with eleven but with twelve "apostles." And out of nowhere appears a kind of Judas figure, who hangs himself. And finally, crowning all efforts, the *De Conformitate*, in which the author discovers no fewer than forty similarities between Francis and Christ.[5]

These writers were pious men, but they lacked insight. They failed to see the originality and creativity of their master. To Francis, imitation lay more in "being like" than in "acting like" Christ. This cult of imitation led many brothers to emulate Francis in the most narrow sense of the word. One can forgive a brother like Simple John for believing he had found the secret of perfection in kneeling, bowing, laughing, and coughing at the exact moment Francis did—in fact, so pointedly that Francis, with a good-natured smile, asked him to stop. But it would be childish and immature for a movement to concentrate solely on the outward actions of its founder—though this is undeniably a danger to which every movement is prone. In the shadow of great personalities, many followers became imitators, even in the convents. In the eyes of the world, they never felt the excruciatingly painful gap between the example and one's own poor efforts at emulation. They avoided the personal decision; they preferred the photocopy.

His evangelical freedom saved Francis from becoming a carbon copy of Jesus of Nazareth and a superfluous link in the tradition of spirituality. Rahner may have been thinking of Francis when he said, "The true imitation of Christ consists in following Jesus' inner way but doing so in a novel and personal relationship to God."[6]

The figure of Jesus in the gospel displays such a many-faceted richness that it is impossible for a Christian to reflect all these aspects in his own life. As early as the first century we see how the Jewish Christians, for instance, stress the figure of Jesus the Messiah, while the former pagans emphasize the Resurrection of Christ. We, who are accustomed to view Christ against the background of our

own day, may find it difficult to realize that through the
ages the figure of Jesus, as seen by the faithful, has been
continually placed in a new light. "In the letter to the
Hebrews Jesus was heavenly high priest, while in the writings of the Church fathers and in Byzantium he was *Chris-
tus victor,* the Creator of all, the Sun-God, Light of Light.
Later he became the Savior who ransomed us, still later
the Christ of the Way of the Cross, and in the Middle
Ages the Christ Child of the Christmas manger.[7] The representative of a certain era will never adopt a previous image
of Jesus. He will always express something of himself in
the interpretation he chooses—his own ideals, dreams, and
cultural background.

And so it is with Francis. He unconsciously divests himself of the image of Jesus on which he had been brought
up. In a feudal era, when princes are revered and pope-
kings, according to Byzantine tradition, consider themselves
the representative of the Lord of Lords, it is not surprising
that the figure of the dying Christ, as portrayed on Byzantine crosses, still has something of the serene monarch,
whose suffering in no way diminishes his divine dignity.
Jesus, Son of Man, is overshadowed by the radiant light
of the Son of God. Undoubtedly influenced by the Lateran
Council, Francis' writings show a strongly Trinitarian tendency, in which Jesus stands out clearly as Son of the Father.

Though he never rejects any part of this view, Francis
nevertheless will unconsciously present to his people a Jesus
figure which had long been neglected, but which in
his day was beginning to reemerge into the foreground.
This was vital to true reform. In their devotions and liturgy
the people cannot spontaneously pray and sing to a God
who seems to them to be "on the other side." A poverty
movement will never portray him in the person of an
elegantly clad prelate.

When we consider the Jesus figure which the followers of
Francis favored, we come to the conclusion that it bears
a surprising resemblance to Francis himself. One indication

in this direction can be found in a work which has come in for a certain amount of criticism, *De Conformitate.* One cannot help admiring the ingenuity with which the author, inspired by many of his predecessors, searches for details which show how Francis resembled his master. But it is precisely here that we see the humanity of Jesus, which was always vividly before them in the person of Francis. Then comes the moment of psychical transfer: Francis is no longer modeled on Jesus, but the faithful see Jesus as Francis was. He has become the poor, sensitive human being. The face of the serene, regal figure on the Byzantine cross is now clouded by pain.[8]

This Jesus is to influence art as well. In his famous *L'Art religieux du XII au XVII siècle,* Emile Mâle remarks that religious art of the thirteenth century reflects all the luminous facets of Christianity. It is significant, though we must take care not to exaggerate, that after Francis' death, in the French cathedrals of the thirteenth century (in Bourges, Amiens, Le Mans), the figure of Christ alters as the figure of Francis makes its appearance. The pediment atop the cathedral of Bourges shows Christ as judge, but he is no longer adorned with crown and gold brocade. The upper part of the torso is bare, showing open wounds.

In general, toward the end of the thirteenth century religious art begins to take leave of heavenly realms. It becomes more human and gradually shows a deep, earthly tenderness. Mary is no longer removed from all joy and sorrow; Christ is no longer the majestic infant with the admonishing finger (as in the St. Anne entrance of Notre Dame in Paris). Mary now nurses and kisses and rocks her baby, like any other mother, and holds him up for onlookers to see.

The influence of Francis here is not unlikely. In the beginning of that century (winter of 1223) he had assembled the farmers and shepherds of Greccio to spend Christmas Eve in the little church,[9] around a manger and in the company of an ox and a donkey (he had no previous ex-

ample for this). And shortly after Francis' death, Jacopone
da Todi was born, the man whose hymns to Mary would
celebrate the joys and sorrows of the Blessed Virgin.[10]

"When we investigate the origins of these new sentiments,"
Mâle tells us, "we again meet up with Francis and his companions. In the twelfth century the gospel appeared as an
idea; in the thirteenth century the friars bring to this idea
new vitality and warmth."[11] Here we see clearly how the
spectrum which colors the figure of Christ is constantly
changing in hue and nuance. The throne and scepter are
fading away, the cradle and cross are advancing.

Development in the view of the figure of Christ has con-
tinued throughout the history of Christianity. After the
Middle Ages came the mystical view of the Word Made
Flesh in the French spirituality of the seventeenth century,
then the veneration of the Child Jesus and his Sacred
Heart, and in the twentieth century Christ the King.

Our era, too, with all its global problems and conflicts,
its search for new "interpersonal relationships," has found
its own figure of Jesus. It is no coincidence that this figure,
sprouting from our hectic "consumer society," bears a
resemblance to that of Francis. Schillebeeckx says "the fact
that our generation yearns for peace and justice, for liberty
and *shalom,* must necessarily impart a very special character
to our Jesus image," and this is to a certain extent true of
every historical period; but our Jesus image is strongly
reminiscent of what feudal man desired in Francis' day.
Both images are a challenge to their society: Jesus, the
avenger of injustice, fighting for the little man, the underdog. It is a representation eminently suited to a democratic
society. One has only to think of a movie like Potter's
The Man Jesus, in which we see Jesus as comrade and
companion, who slaps the apostles on their shoulders and
is capable of a hearty chuckle. Or, in a different perspective,
the Jesus figure as seen by Schillebeeckx: "In the New
Testament I see distinctly the solidarity of Jesus with the
people, and the parallel of the mutual solidarity of the

people in Jesus' name. . . . He truly comes to identify himself with the poor, the most insignificant beings on God's earth, an identification which consists in solidarity, true caring and love, experienced with one's whole being. He demands this of his followers as well."[12]

This is Francis' Jesus figure pure and simple! There is only one difference. It cannot be denied that this ideal humanity of Jesus is sometimes so strongly stressed today that he threatens to overshadow the Father. Because our world sees this new religiosity as going hand in hand with a trend toward secularization, many people are seeking a secularized Jesus, a man of the world, *our* world, who does not shift our problems onto supernatural terrain. They expect him to forget his Father, up there in heaven, and to devote his attention to his brothers and sisters on earth.

In this they are beginning to break away from the "memory of Jesus," that is, from the details recorded about him and passed to following generations. It is impossible to delete any vital part from this memory of Jesus without lapsing into a pseudo Jesus. Thus we entertain certain doubts about the tendency toward displacing the relationship between Jesus and his Father. As one young person put it, in answer to a Flemish questionnaire: "We consider the challenge of brotherly love so great that we do not concern ourselves with the relationship between Christ and the Father." In his conclusion at the end of this questionnaire, the author says, "They [the young people interviewed] have rejected all legal interpretations. Such old expressions as 'The Father willed the expiatory death of his Son' or 'as ransom for our sins' are wholly absent here."[13] An urgent and compelling question confronts Church and theology at the moment: How can this *memoria Jesu* be couched in modern, attractive, and comprehensible terms?

The evangelical Jesus figure has an inner dynamism of its own which, outside the domain of theologists, discovers new ways of reaching the people. A year after John Lennon declared that Jesus had lost the popularity race to the Beatles

(1967), a Jesus revival began in the United States which surpassed all previous revivals, if not in depth at least in originality. It is a young movement, with all the characteristics of lively, carefree youth. The first thing that strikes one is the outspokenness with which the revival is proclaimed. It is quite possible that a young girl will come up to you on the street and confide that she loves you for Jesus' sake. You may pick up the phone and hear that "Jesus loves you."[14] In a bar, or on the podium of a concert hall, the public is informed that Jesus wants to make them happy. These are young people who have turned their backs on society and its bourgeois ideals and conventions. And in the same country in which God was declared dead, thousands of young people are prepared to declare that Jesus lives.

But the most surprising element is that this Jesus is again the living Lord, Son of God, the Redeemer who is capable of bringing true redemption, where prosperity and science have failed. At least this is the view of the more serious groups which have reintroduced Bible reading and contemplation into the heart of their religious experience. Many of them are also striving for a charismatic movement within the Church.

As in Francis' day, there are several interpretations of Jesus, some more socially orientated, others more religious, which could together form the right synthesis. The strength of Francis' reform lies in the fact that, in a Church of pope-kings, he preached the Jesus which all poverty movements of his day had been longing for: the Man "who had renounced all in order to take up the life of a servant."[15]

Footnotes

1. Gal 2:20.

2. *II Celano* 105; *Omnibus*, p. 448.

3. *J'ai choise l'opium,* in a Dutch translation by Liesbeth van Waele,

Ik verkoos opium (Bruges, 1961).

4. K. Rahner, *Ons Geestelijk Leven,* vol. 42, 4, p. 232.

5. *De Conformitate Vitae Beati Francisci ad Vitam Domini Jesu,* solemnly approved by the general chapter in 1309.

6. Rahner, op. cit., p. 232.

7. E. Schillebeeckx, *Tÿdschrift voor Theologie* (1972), 1. This article is of special importance to the figure of Jesus in our time.

8. The first crucifix on which the triumphant Christ is replaced by the Savior in the throes of a death struggle was painted about 1235 by Giunta of Pisa for the church of Porziuncola. A similar crucifix from about 1260 hangs today over the main altar of the Church of S. Chiara in Assisi. One is struck by the thought that this figure on the cross is about to undergo a fundamental change under the influence of Francis. The triumph reflected in this face is to change, in little more than a generation, into pain and desolation. See A. Ventura, *Storia dell' arte italiana,* part V. Greccio is the true source, and not a copy of others in Italy. See also H. Thode, *Franzi von Assisi* (Leipzig, 1935), pp. 447ff., in which he speaks of the Franciscan influence on the biblical images of Tuscan art.

9. According to Bonaventure, Francis had first asked Rome for a leave of absence. This would indicate that he was about to do something completely new. In any case, A. d'Ancona (*Origine del teatro italiano,* 1:106 [see Muratori, Ant. St., II, 29]) has proved that the Christmas manger in Greccio is the true source, and not a copy of others in Italy. See also H. Thode, *Franzi von Assisi* (Leipzig, 1935), pp. 447ff., in which he speaks of the Franciscan influence on the biblical images of Tuscan art.

10. For details of the "Stabat Mater Dolorosa" see H. Nolthenius, *Duecento,* pp. 246, 269, and 502n. She has strong doubts whether Jacopone is the author of this work.

11. E. Mâle, *De religieuze kunst van de XIIe tot de XVIIIe eeuw* (Utrecht, 1949), p. 107. "It is remarkable what a great influence this expert on medieval art attributes to the Franciscans. Did the artists [of the fourteenth century] read the writings of the Franciscans? Or hear their sermons? It is possible, but from the fourteenth century onward Franciscan Christianity was evident to them in a manner even more calculated to move them. It was, first of all, in the Italian art forms, permeated with the spirit of Francis' followers, and in the spiritual dramas that we see this inspirational force, which set before the eyes of painters and sculptors the most tragic scenes of suffering,

pain and death. A new imaginative world was being formed" (p. 107).

12. Schillebeeckx, op. cit., p. 53.

13. *De man Jesus, voor en door jongeren* (Antwerp, 1969), p. 124.

14. See, for example, J. van Capelleven and W. Kroll, *Jesusrevolutie* (Wageningen); Edward E. Plowman, *The Jesus Movement in America* (Pyramid, 1971); Duane Pederson, *Jesus People* (Regal, 1971).

15. See Phil 2:7.

10

The Beggar's Gift

On his return from the meeting with Innocent (1209), Francis passed through Rivo Torto, a hamlet near Assisi. He was intrigued by a dilapidated barn which had been set in a field as a shelter for oxen and donkeys at night. And with the blithe freedom of those who possess nothing and yet consider themselves rich, he and his brothers moved into the barn. This simple structure has come to occupy a special place in the annals of the Franciscan Order. It is looked upon within a special kind of tenderness, as the Bethlehem of the order, where the brothers bedded down on straw like overgrown Christ children. The floorboards supported men who, a few years before, had been noblemen or lawyers and who were now allotted their few square feet of space as bed and sole retreat.[1]

Today, when men are prepared—and rightly so—to fight for equality, it is almost unimaginable that anyone should deliberately choose to be inferior; but the tumbledown barn at Rivo Torto was the symbol of just such a striving. Even the name of the order will later bear witness to this ideal: *frati minori.* These brothers were predestined for "inferior" work, inferior comfort, inferior station. They were—forgive the term—inferior human beings. They threw in their lot with the humble and the poor, and they did so unhesitatingly, openly. They identified themselves with these people by sharing their life and by choosing to be, even among them, *frati minori*.

It is striking how many spiritual leaders who have exercised a deep and lasting influence on mankind display this blend of poverty, authority, and freedom. (Jesus himself is the greatest example of this phenomenon.) But their poverty was the very antithesis of pauperism. Poverty for poverty's sake may never become an ideal if one desires to preserve the spirit of the gospel, because poverty is only one element of the ideal way of life. Jesus himself does not view wealth as an inferior state. "He does not condemn wealth in itself. . . . There are wealthy men among His own friends and acquaintances, and he never refused to accept the help and hospitality of the rich. His well-to-do friends were not barred from the kingdom of God."[2] Zacheus gave half his fortune to the poor—and Jesus did not ask him what he did with the other half, but entered his house without hesitation.

Francis' view of poverty has remarkable depth and refinement. This stands out clearly in the oldest document on the subject, which bears the title *Meeting between St. Francis and Lady Poverty* and was probably written the year after Francis' death.[3] Today the title would never rate a place on best-seller lists, and the allegorical Lady Poverty has about as much appeal as the musty, yellowed pages of *The Lives of the Saints*. But the author of this refreshing work is a poetic soul with deep knowledge of Holy Scripture and a high sense of literary composition. His story resembles a mystery play in which real people play a role. Francis and his brothers are searching for Poverty and finally find her at the top of a mountain, where she introduces herself. Her words are revealing: "I am not uneducated, as many believe. . . . I know the moods of the human heart."[4]

Here Poverty plays the part of the princess who finds the glass slipper and is transformed from slave into mistress. And it is as mistress, as *Domina,* that Poverty appears in this work. Thus one is forced to lay aside the theory that Francis saw Poverty as his bride.[5] But the very heart of Francis' view of Poverty is his conviction that he has made a pact with this lady, who is much more to him than the personification of material renunciation.[6] She is the freedom into which man enters through a treaty with God.

In the Old Testament, after the exile, when riches are no longer considered a blessing from Yahweh for faithful service but a status symbol leading unavoidably to pride, there grew up certain groups, the so-called *anawini,* who wanted to practice voluntary poverty and await in all humility the coming of the kingdom of God. Francis feels a close affinity with these *anawini.* The words of Zephaniah, "Seek Yahweh, ye humble of this earth,"[7] are like a theme that runs through the Lady Poverty book. Those who practice poverty are already in the kingdom of heaven. The great freedom which such a conviction offers is shown by one of the brothers when Poverty asks where the convent of the brothers lies. He spreads out his arms in a gesture that encompasses the whole world and says: "This, Lady, is our cloister."[8]

If the author is describing the situation at Rivo Torto— and we assume that he is—this little book gives us a vivid picture of life there. For example, the meal at the end of the long conversation consisted of "three or four loaves of bread laid on the grass."[9] Even Lady Poverty considered this a bit too frugal, and at her request a brother went into the woods and plucked a few sweet-smelling herbs among the wild grasses. And after the meal, when she asked to wash her hands—she was, after all, a woman—"they quickly fetched a broken bowl, since they had no other." While she poured water over her hands, she looked in vain for a towel, and one of the brothers gallantly offered his habit, which she used to wipe her hands, "giving thanks to God in her heart that he had given her such people as companions."[10] Perhaps the author had a premonition of the conflict which was to erupt around the poverty ideal after Francis' death, symbolized by the broken bowl and the whole one, the habit and the towel.

The strangest thing about this story is its authenticity. On this peaceful mountaintop these men led their simple yet magnificent lives. They looked beyond the visible world and discovered religious depth in everything, the depth offered by the freedom of the gospel. The soberness of the meals is not exaggerated; Francis will go even further. He has convents torn down which are said to be the property of the order. He refuses to inhabit a cell because one of the brothers had called it Francis' cell. The use of books is reduced to a minimum. Where there is only one Bible in a house, he has it torn apart and gives each brother a piece. But he never lost his sense of humor. When a novice who had received permission from his superior to possess a psalter (that part of a breviary containing the psalms) wanted to hear Francis' views on the subject, he called the novice to sit with him next to the fire. "My brother," he said, "once you possess a psalter, you will want a whole breviary. And once you have a whole breviary, you will long to sit upon a bishop's throne like an important prelate and say to your fellow friar, 'Bring me my breviary.'"[11] He himself spent two weeks fasting on Isola Maggiore in Trasimene Lake, with only two loaves of bread, and brought one of them back because he did not want to be exactly like his Master, who had eaten nothing in the desert. And as far as wine goes, says Celano, there is nothing to tell, for Francis barely drank enough water to slake his thirst.

There is a quality of mystery about Francis' poverty ideal. J. Lörz calls it an enigma, a secret—unfathomable, inscrutable—which cannot be unraveled hastily. We must stand motionless before it, and perhaps then it will reveal to us some portion of its being.[12]

Poverty is not a matter of form but of being, of utter freedom from everyone and everything. Poverty is a thing of the spirit. But the spirit can move freely only when it is unencumbered by its environment. Francis was very conscious of this truth, and this led him to the ultimate renunciation: he gave up all he possessed, and ever could have possessed, in order to experience creation in perfect freedom.

Everything belonged to him the moment he gave up everything. The Umbrian hills became his home, the fish and the birds his friends, the woods and trees and flowers in bloom were a gift of God. And there was no living soul whose class or status placed him beneath Francis. His was the lowest caste; he was on the lowest rung of the ladder; and the only people he could see were those above him. No one ever hit out so powerfully, so radically, at the hard core of the passion for possessions. At the misery caused by usury, exploitation, corruption, and all other forms of injustice. A man like this, at the crossroads of political, social, and economic history, is capable of changing the world.

An incisive reform, deeper than that of the Lateran Council, began when Francis left Rivo Torto and set out on his travels throughou t Italy and abroad. He did not shrink from following in the difficult footsteps of his Master. Accessible to all, he gave status to the poor and was beginning to trouble the consciences of the rich.

Francis' attitude toward the rich was remarkable in that he never upbraided or admonished them. He knew that Jesus himself had sat at the table with the rich. He could be sharp in his comments on wealth itself, but rich and prominent people were always treated with the same respect (though no more) with which he approached everyone else. Typical of the manner in which he sees (or rather does not see) the various class distinctions is the following quotation: "All penitent and humble persons, poor and needy, kings and princes, workmen and farmers, servants and masters—all common people and all prominent people, we be-

seech you humbly, as friars and worthless servants, that we
may all persevere in the true faith and in penitence."[13] An
original enumeration, to say the least. The only detectable
preference is perhaps that the poor come before the kings
and the servants before the masters. A forgivable inconse-
quence on the part of a man who says in his rule: "[the
brothers] should be happy to associate with ordinary people,
those whom others despise, the poor and the weak, the sick,
the lepers and the beggars by the side of the road."[14]

"I am not without eduction," Lady Poverty says in the
little book mentioned above. She might also have said: I
am not without charm, without poetry. In his *Pilgrimage
through Franciscan Italy* Jorgensen paints a vivid picture
of life in the famous convents of Greccio and Alverna at
the turn of the century.[15] When he sketches the conversation
of the brothers who, seated before a blazing fire, reminisce
with him over the countless legends about Francis, we see
the dimly lit room and the shadowy figures, and the past
becomes almost tangible. A shabby, centuries-old convent
atop a lonely mountain is a piece of poetry come to life.

But today we ask ourselves whether this way of life is
of any use to us. Though modern man has a genuine respect for Francis, it is tinged with aversion. Though fascinated by a convent such as San Damiano, we are repelled
by the caves of Alverna and Carceri, where Francis spent
long, lonely nights in prayer and laid his head on bare
stone. We cannot help wondering if this man did not af-
flict himself with senseless agonies. It is unthinkable that
anyone could spend a single night in those caves without
risking chronic authorities.

Moreover, one might maintain, if it is senseless to preach
poverty when hunger runs rampant, is it not equally senseless when prosperity reigns? Put in this way, I must object
to the question. Francis did not preach hunger, but rather
inner freedom from the desire for possessions, which makes
it possible to give oneself to God and to one's fellow
man. In this he does no more than follow his Master, who

says to the rich young man: "If you will be perfect, go
sell what you have." He adds: "and give to the poor."[16]
It is not Jesus' fault that others have since put all the emphasis on parting with one's wealth, rather than on giving
to the poor. Jesus recognizes not only the bestowing but
also the beseeching hand. One may reject the ideal of radical
biblical poverty, which Francis preaches, and still embrace
that of radical *un*biblical need. If Frances, in the depths
of his stone caves, should have no message for us, surely
he must speak to us once he emerges from those caves to
give himself to whomever he shall meet.

And here we touch upon the very special relationship
between Francis and the poor. His poverty ideal gave the
poor man the status of a human being. Up to then, the
poor of this earth had been kept in their place. Everywhere
they looked, they saw the familir signs: No Trespassing,
Off Limits, Private Property. It was always a question of
"look but don't touch."

Francis the beggar understood the poor man, though perhaps Francis never experienced such depths of desperation
and shame. When he urged the timid brothers not to be
ashamed to go begging, he was trying to tell them that they
still did not understand the deeper meaning behind the act,
that they were still bound by the inbred prejudices of a
culture in which a poor man had to summon up courage
to humble himself still further. This was intolerable to
Francis, who saw all men as children of one Father and
Jesus Christ as their destitute Master.

Gradually there grew up around Francis a group of "poor
men" who in education and culture rivaled the wealthy merchants, knights, and prelates. Once such men, in disheveled
habits and without a penny to their name, arouse the admiration of the people, write poetry and books, and teach
at the universities, it is clear that no one can ever again
equate "poor" with "inferior" or "uneducated."[17]

There is another, deeper sense in which Francis speaks to
the poor of his day and ours. When he attacked the view

of humanity that was nourished by the feudal caste system, in a strange way he raised the level of begging. F. de Beer speaks of a parallel spiritual revolution: "Up to then prayer had always been directed toward God. Francis prays to man as well. For he too possesses the divine privilege of hearing prayers."[18]

The beggar's outstretched hand enables us to give something of ourselves. We need not be rich or powerful. When one person gives of himself, he always gives something of value, and the giver becomes more human by giving of himself. To give is blessed, but it is the suppliant who provides the opportunity for us to be blessed. Embracing the leper, it was Francis who received. The leper gave him the opportunity to rise above his aversion, to become more human through him.

Gone is the old picture of the condescending benefactor and the imploring suppliant. They are now on the same footing, for giving and receiving represent an exchange of courtesies between two people who know that God bestowed his abundant creation upon all mankind. He gave the brothers this formula: "There exists a king of agreement between the world and the brothers: the latter offer the world their good example and in return the world feeds them."[19] One wonders what kind of reception this "social contract" would receive today, or what the world would think of his view that "alms are an inheritance and a rightful share owed to the poor."[20] Accepted or not, nothing prevents each of us from contemplating the significance of these views.

At a certain point in his life Francis became aware that somewhere things had gone awry with the division of this world's goods. He returned to those primitive days when the good earth was here for everyone. This meant that he was forced to beg in times of need. But everything he touched turned to gold, even the beggar's cup. Begging became a truly human act; the suppliant hand, too, had something to offer. When Francis arrived with his usual "May the Lord grant you his peace,"[21] this simple greeting was his way of saying: Let us level the differences between us and celebrate the brotherhood of man in our own simple way. Francis, the beggar, always felt like a guest.

Whatever our world may think of the poverty ideal of the *Poverello*, here is his answer to a pressing current problem for which our world desperately needs a solution: giver and receiver, rich and poor, should see each other as equals, as brothers and sisters before God. The receiver is no longer the object of the other's charity. And the giver no longer clings unconsciously to the gift, which he somehow still feels to be his. Acquired possessions regain their original luster as "gifts of God to mankind."

Our Western world is beginning to win the "battle against poverty" on the home front.[22] Today, at least in many Western countries, "charity" organizations disappear for want of material need. At the risk of sounding facetious, we might say that it is no longer people who beg, but nations. But they are not received in that atmosphere of refined courtesy which Francis advocated. The rich countries of the world do not offer something of their riches in a symbolic celebration of the brotherhood of man. The poor countries do not request a friendly exchange, they stake a claim; they cry out for conscience money.

It would be incredibly naive to maintain that Francis' approach to his fellow man has any reasonable chance of success in the world of today, where "humanitarianism" is proudly worn as a badge of honor. It cannot be denied that much is done for people in need, but more is accomplished by private initiative than by international cooperation. True humanitarianism is being shattered by the grinding structures of world power and the individual is helpless in the face of this mighty robot. At the root of the structures is no truly human view of mankind. Thus we see how it is possible to use the battle against global poverty to further one's own status and career. The path of the convention speaker toward self-sacrifice, of the manager toward love of one's fellow man, of the public relations man toward unselfish honesty is often blocked by ambition, greed, and egotism. It is not difficult to make a moving plea for famine victims in some far-off land one minute and, the next minute, turn a blind eye to the needs of the man across the street. This very situation is tellingly described by Dostoevsky in *The Brothers Karamazov*. The doctor confides to the *starets* (wise man): "In my thoughts I have a passionate desire to serve mankind . . . but in reality I find it impossible to spend two days in the same room with any man. . . . But still in general I love humanity."[23]

Francis never concerned himself with philanthropy. "Mankind in general" did not interest him greatly, but to the poor creature standing before him he gave all he possessed. As many as five times, Celano tells how, in the dead of winter, Francis gave his cloak to a beggar, with a few words which were touching in their sincerity. "Brother," he once replied, when Celano remarked on Francis' sickly appearance, "I would be stealing if I did not give to one poorer than myself."[24] This is indeed radical equality!

At the end of this chapter, one problem remains. Why did Francis go further than Jesus himself? The gospel contains a few such absolute admonitions as "Give what you have to the poor," but in general it shows a moderate attitude toward poverty. The apostles had some kind of petty-cash reserve and did not feel called upon to sell their nets and boats. The first Christians owned everything in common, but the first friars possessed nothing. Perhaps Francis preferred to do things his own way. Probably, he did not even consider the issue. As ever, his actions were dictated by his character, in which radicalism was inherent. He went to extremes in almost everything, even in his love. It was only this which kept him from falling into the pit of fanaticism.

In our culture, Francis' conception of poverty would be unworkable for a community. Even among the brothers, there was latent criticism during his lifetime, which led to a tragic conflict between radical and applied poverty, between the habit and the cloth, the cracked bowl and the whole bowl.

The fact remains that heroic radicalism has intrinsic value. Francis stands as a lonely challenge to a world where greed and thirst for possessions bring hunger and exploitation. He may have gone further than his Master, but both were traveling the same road.

Footnotes

1. Others, among them Terzi, believe that they took up their abode here in 1208.

2. See Demytennaere, *Bijbelse Leergang* (The Hague, Una Sancta), 3d cycle, lessons 8/9, p. 133.

3. *Sacrum Commercium S. Francisci cum domina Paupertate*. K. Esser and E. Grau published the German text, with an excellent commentary: *Der Bund des Franciskus mit der Herr in Armut* (Werl./ Westf., 1966).

4. *Sacrum Commercium* 24; *Omnibus*, p. 1566.

5. This was the traditional view since *II Celano* and Bonaventure. But nothing in Francis' writings that is not in the *Commercium* supports this view.

6. See Esser and Grau, op. cit., p. 41. Father van Corstanje has made an especially thorough study of this question in *The Covenant with God's Poor* (Chicago: Franciscan Herald Press, 1966). Father Esser had previously published a similar interpretation in *Mysterium Paupertatis* (p. 136).

7. Zep 2:3.

8. *Sacrum Commercium* 63; *Omnibus*, p. 1593.

9. *Sacrum Commercium* 61; *Omnibus*, p. 1592.

10. *Sacrum Commercium* 60; *Omnibus*, pp. 1591–1592.

11. *Leg. Perugia* 73; *Omnibus,* p. 1049.

12. J. Lörz, *Der unvergleichliche Heilige.* Voltaire was one who never understood what this whole question was all about, as witnessed in the following doggerel:

> I am not very pleased with Francis the simpleton.
> He thought that a true Christian must beg in the street,
> And wanted his sons—sturdy lazybones—
> To take a vow to live at our expense.

Ed. Moland, X, 360. Quoted by Omer Englebert, *St. Francis of Assisi* (Chicago: Franciscan Herald Press, 1965).

13. Rule of 1221, 23; *Omnibus,* p. 51.

14. Rule of 1221, 9; *Omnibus,* p. 39.

15. *Het pelgrimsboek in franciscaans Italië,* trans. S. v. d. Velde (Louvain, 1911), vol. I, chap. vi.

16. Mt 19:21.

17. J. M. G. Thuerlings, *De wankele zuil* (Nijmegen, 1971).

18. F. de Beer, *Tÿdschrift Franciscus van Assisi* (1972), vol. 9.

19. See *Omnibus,* pp. 39, 1143-1148, 1531-1596.

20. See *II Celano* 73-74; *Omnibus,* pp. 424-426.

21. Testament; *Omnibus,* p. 68.

22. It would, however, be self-deception to maintain that the world's slum problem is on the point of being solved.

23. Dostoevsky, *The Brothers Karamozov,* trans. A. Kosloff, 11th ed. (Amsterdam), p. 56.

24. *II Celano* 87; *Omnibus,* p. 434.

11

The Prophet
and His People

The prophet who fails to understand his own time is doomed to failure. No matter how authoritative his words, how impressively embellished with biblical and papal texts, if the messenger is not one with the people to whom he speaks, his message will fall in a vacuum.

Francis was the representative of a younger generation which intuitively felt what the people felt, and understood what they expected from their religion. He never consciously analyzed their desires; he simply fulfilled them. To understand how he accomplished this, we must take a closer look at the religious background of Francis' day.

It is difficult for anyone living in our secularized world to imagine the religious atmosphere which surrounded medieval man. Everything was "sacred" in the sense of the French word *sacre,* that is, consecrated either to God or to the devil. Even today, in isolated parts of Italy, one can encounter that awe of mysterious beings, as in the novel *Canne al Vento* by Grazia Deledda. The author was born on Sardinia, "where at night old Efiz saw the mountain spirit'with the seven horns, watched the evil spirits join with the souls of children who had died without baptism, and saw the dragon who had lived there since the time of Christ, plodding through the mud of the swamps."[1]

This is a remnant of a culture in which Christian faith was permeated with heathen fantasies borrowed from the Etruscans and their Roman conquerers. Anyone who has read the chronicles of the thirteenth century, especially Salimbene, may wonder whether that Christianity which lived among the illiterate masses was indeed purified of pagan influences. Wholehearted devotion to Jesus and boundless confidence in the Madonna and the saints existed side by side with black magic, witchcraft, and primitive fetishism. Magical potions rivaled the sacraments, and the magician who had been educated in Siena, the city of black magic, commanded the same respect and admiration as the magnetic street preacher, who was capable of converting whole audiences at one session.

But thirteenth-century Christianity was not exclusively a mixture of magic and superstition, which, after all, appear in every culture in some form or other. A *Summa Theologica,* a *Commedia Divina,* were no more the product of a heathen wilderness than were the Berlinghieris, the Giottos, and the cathedrals. One has only to look at the expression on the face of a medieval crucified Christ or a Madonna at prayer to know that these works of art were inspired by genuine devotion.

Thus Francis was not the lonely hero of the medieval Church, a Moses striking water from a dry rock. Since the end of the twelfth century there was a religious awareness among the people so powerful that its like had not been seen since the early days of Christianity. Holy Scripture had passed into the hands of lay people, who read it without benefit of guide or commentary. A vague desire for personal spirituality led men to take to the roads and the marketplaces, declaring to all who would listen that God could also be found outside the realm of pulpit and clergy. Texts which exposed the establishment's extravagance and love of pleasure struck the people like spiritual thunderbolts.

They suddenly realized that they were not Christians by the grace of their prince or bishop, but that each of them had a personal vocation to live according to the gospel. The individual sought refuge in a group, a brotherhood, which sprang up everywhere—movements that took the form of underground church communities, that fled from a world of cruelty and slavery with the gospel clutched to their hearts, that yearned for personal virtue and personal salvation. And yet the medieval piety cultivated in these groups was not egotistical. They labored with almost unbelievable ardor at works of charity in the old sense of the word: helping poor families, visiting hospitals and prisons, burying plague victims. We may reproach them for having accepted the status quo, for not having penetrated to the root of the evil, but their example of heroic charity would be welcome in today's streamlined world of organized welfare.

These movements are an expression of true biblical metanoia: inner conversion of the old egocentric self, radical surrender to God, desire to give oneself, unthinkingly, to God. Life lay in the shadow of death and eternity. The shudder that passes through one when the *Dies Irae* is sung—this is what the people felt when they thought about the divine Judge seated among the clouds, and the shrill trumpet call which would raise the dead from their graves. Above all, they feared the personal reckoning which would one day come, the angel who would call each one in turn to the foot of God's throne and open the book of life at *his* page. The architectural form of the cathedrals, like sculptured Bibles, suggests that the people actually pictured themselves sitting at the heavenly table, or writhing in a flaming cauldron, tormented by the sharp point of Satan's spear.

The religious revival begins inside the city walls. During

the Crusades the fascinating game of coin and draft begins to flourish, and the feudal lord is obliged to extend the walls of his domain. A new kind of city is born, and with it the merchant and industrial class, the third estate. Without these energetic, freedom-loving, pioneering merchants the religious revival would have been unthinkable. It is no accident that the great herald of the movement sprang from the prosperous merchant class, which imported not only cloth and spices but new ideas, critical ideas, freely exchanged in tavern and marketplace, where no one was overly concerned with the fine line between orthodoxy and heresy.

It is strange to think that urbanization, which in our day breeds unbelief, contributed to the most significant religious revival since the early days of Christianity. The laity discovered new worlds and new cultures, learned to read and write Latin, and at the same introduced the vernacular into law and the courts. Charlemagne was an old man when he first put pen to parchment, and many a knight was better with the sword than the pen. But children at school began to discover books and history, and within a few decades the genius of Dante and Thomas Aquinas would inaugurate the medieval golden age. The new culture of the city, in which this religious enthusiasm originated, made way for their coming.

But as lay people awakened and began to take part in the life of Church and state, conflicts arose. The bishops had to fight the new powers for privilege and leadership. The clergy took up arms against a long-forgotten enemy: heresy.

The merchant ships brought the exotic ideas of the Cathars. Beguins, Bogomils, Humiliati, and Penitents[2] were fascinated by what they found in Holy Scripture. In some ways it was an impromptu, disorderly sort of movement, but it bore the authentic mark of deep faith and great idealism. Skirting the borderline of orthodoxy, it submitted to the pope one day and rebelled the next, risking prison and excommunication. Throughout Europe a new wind of change was blowing, a religious awakening in search of form and leadership.

And then Francis appears. Revolutionary ideas exercise their greatest influence on the masses when they are embodied in one person. Mass communication has provided us a surfeit of leading figures, but the true leader, the personality who dominates his age, is becoming rare. He had his heydey in the Middle Ages. A single orator could spark a war between two cities, arouse the people to join a crusade or burn a heretic at the stake. "We have no inkling of the emotional pitch of the medieval masses," writes Gillet in his study of mendicant orders—"their ability to drop everything and march off, to mobilize behind an idea, a ghost, a mirage."[3] But the idea must have a face, a voice, hands and feet. It must have roots in the deepest yearnings of the people. Only then can the idea, in human form, lead a movement.

Francis met all these requirements. This young man, emaciated and disheveled, is the prophet who fulfills the ideal of medieval revival. What the people had read in Holy Scripture of prayer and penance stood before them in human form. His magnetism draws the whole movement to him and fills it with his spirit. He saves it from disintegration, confusion, and heresy and gives form to what will go down in history as the Third Order of St. Francis.[4]

In those days of religious revival, the thing that above all gave Francis' movement its vitality and power of reform was its lay character. Francis and his companions may have received the tonsure and been drawn into the circle of the clergy (Sabatier), but the people were not aware of this. What they saw were destitute preachers whose words had nothing of the legal, streamlined theology of the day. Their status was ensured because they were defenseless and materially dependent on those who were willing to help them. They did not earn their living by leasing land, as did the feudal bishops and monks, but by working the fields and holding out their hands for a little bread or a few vegetables, with the words "God's blessing be upon you."

As street preachers, they were closer to the people emotionally than were the pulpit orators. Their word was heard
by the people where they felt at home—in the fields, in
hospitals, or in the marketplace, among the stalls and
frolicking children. It was not heard in foreign, just-for-
Sunday places, where stately preachers looked down upon
them from above. Though perhaps not official, their authority
was very real.

Francis' biographers tell us that his preaching had a remarkable effect on his audience, and yet eyewitnesses say
that he was not an impressive speaker. He was not the
type to retire mentally from the world to enter holy spheres,
to climb the pulpit steps with a professional religious expression on his face. His sermon, more often than not,
was the continuation of a conversation.

An extraordinary sense of symbolism characterized Francis' preaching. He saw the reflection of the divine in the
most minuscule element of creation. In this he was a
faithful follower of the Master. Both wanted to show that
all creation is imbued with a deeper meaning. If one reads
the gospel carefully, one realizes that Jesus is a poet who
makes masterful use of the symbol, conjuring up an invisible
reality before the eyes of his listeners. There is a strange
kind of poetry in all his parables and images. It is a kind
of homesickness, a yearning for that supernatural quality
which lies deep within all creation. His images are simple
and gripping, drawn from country rather than city life.
They betray the man who as a boy was close to the land.
In his preaching he calls up the world of the Father through
images from nature: dusk and light, rain and mountain
streams, the wind that blows where it will, the sun that
rises over the sinner and the just man alike. The whole
culture of farmer and shepherd emerges from the gospel
against a symbolic background: the sower who sows on
rock, the lost sheep and the fleeing hireling. Jesus had no
need of profound reflections. He summoned up the mysteries
of the kingdom of God by the use of symbols. Flowing

water became eternal life and the pearls of the merchant gifts of God. And Francis preached the same way.

Great prophets do not owe their influence to the rhetorical form in which they bear witness to God but to the conviction with which they do so, and never more than when they confront their listeners with the necessity of a choice. This is why so many people were moved by Francis, not superficially, as by an impressive speech, but fundamentally, deeply, so that they experienced true metanoia, an inner conversion. And not only simple, impressionable people but men like Pacifico, crowned by the emperor and proclaimed "prince of poetry." While visiting a nuns' convent in Ancona, he happens to hear Francis speak "a few words" to the sisters. Suddenly he sees everything in a new light. He will spend the rest of his life with Francis.

The influence Francis had on the people is illustrated by this quotation from Celano: "When he entered a city the clergy were happy, bells pealed, people were in a festive mood and the women joined in the celebrations. The children cheered and often branches were torn from the trees to wave in welcome, while psalms were sung."[5] This pronouncement may be too neat for our liking, but the general content is verified by other sources: the prophet Francis had become a legend in his own lifetime. To his listeners he *was* the gospel he preached.

This is the kind of preaching that made the farmer desert his ploughshare, the lawyer prefer a friar's cell to a study, and the merchant take to distributing money among the poor. Francis' foremost aim was to win followers; but the religious revival could no more be turned or halted than could the amazingly rapid rise of his order. In only six years the brothers were traveling all over central and northern Italy.

A religious revival often receives tremendous stimulus when, directly or indirectly, it is confronted with the failings of Church leaders. It was inevitable that the people should see the figure of Francis against the background of a luxury-loving and imperious hierarchy. Jacques de Vitry, later cardinal, who had met Francis personally, is quite outspoken about the abuses. In a letter written in 1216 he says:

> During my stay at the Papal Court I saw many things which did not please me. Everyone there was so concerned with temporal and wordly affairs, so busy attending to governments and princes, and had so many trivialities on their minds that they scarcely had time to concern themselves with spiritual matters.
>
> I did, however, find one consolation here: many people of both sexes have renounced all and turned their backs on the world. They are called Friars Minor. Pope and cardinals have great respect for them. . . . By God's grace they have already done much good. . . . They lead the life of the early Church.

Then follows his most cutting criticism: "I believe that the Lord allows this to happen in order to shame the prelates who are like stupid dogs, incapable of barking. He is using these poor simple people to save many souls before the end of the world."[6]

The movement continues to grow. Fifty years later there were an estimated 30,000 to 35,000 brothers in 1,130 convents all over Europe. For seven centuries this organization has found the strength to conquer its own frailty, heal its wounds, and rise again, kept alive by that same everlasting inspiration.

Footnotes

1. *Canne al vento,* first published by Mondadori in 1913.

2. The best-known poverty movements were those of the Bogomils and the Beguins, men and women who did not live in convents but

in so-called almshouses. The Humiliati (whose name is derived from *panni humiliari,* the gray woolen material they wore) to a certain extent crossed the boundary of orthodoxy and were condemned, together with the Waldensians, in 1184. Innocent was able to retain one section of the group by receiving it into a third order (1201). See P. Alphandery, *Les idésmorales chez les héterdoxes latins du XIIIe siècle* (Paris, 1903); J. B. Pierron, *Die katholischen Armen* (Freiburg, 1911); H. Grundmann, *Neue Beiträge zur Geschichte der religiösen Bewegungen im Mittelalter* (1955) and *Religiöse Bewegungen des Mittelalters* (1955).

3. L. Gillet, *Histoire artistique des Ordes mendiants* (Paris, 1939), p. 30.

4. See Gillet, op. cit., chapter XII, on the Third Order.

5. See I *Celano* 31, 36–37; *Omnibus,* pp. 253–254, 258–260. Also *Leg. 3 Comp.* 54; Omnibus, p. 937.

6. This letter is dated October 1216 and appeared in *Speculum Perfectionis,* published by Sabatier. See *Omnibus,* p. 1608.

12

Growth of the Movement

If it is true that sexuality often assumes the air of a triumphant Cinderella parading through the ballroom, it is equally true that celibacy no longer revolves around sexual abstinence as it once did. Modern celibacy concerns itself more with the manner in which one gives oneself to one's fellow man. As A. Durand puts it: "The person closest to the married person has to be the marriage partner. The person closest to the religious may be of continually changing identity."[1]

Francis understood this perfectly. Once the voice of the Most High had made clear to him the way he was to follow, celibacy ceased to be a problem for him. His mission within God's kingdom was no longer directed toward a wife and family. The whole world lay open to him. All humanity awaited him. He was free to go to the poor, to lepers, to Christians and Islamites, free to serve anywhere. The only frontier for this citizen of the world was the horizon and the only family he knew was the family of man.

That does not mean he was emotionally stifled. Francis certainly had other adventures than those recounted by pious biographers, and he never made any effort to bridle his natural charm. Guardini and Mario von Galli say that one of Francis' most notable characterisitics was what the Italians call *cortesia*.[2] Originally, this was the prime characteristic of the courtier, combining grace, elegance, and courteous respect. Through his metanoia, Francis was able to give this *cortesia* deeper significance. Outwardly he remained the man of the world, as Celano tells us on several occasions.

Wherever he went he made friends, and they were friends for life. Among them was Giocopa del Settesoli, the young widow of the noble and wealthy Frangipani, whom he met in Rome and with whom he remained on friendly terms until his death.[3] This frank association with a woman was consistent with Francis' character, his ability to direct his capacity for love toward all mankind. Without benefit of psychology, Francis understood that a man can develop emotionally without a sexual relationship with a woman, but that without integration of the feminine element into his life, he will grow into a frustrated human being.

His association with women was definitely not a favored theme among his biographers. The legends which inevitably grew up among the people were less restrained in this respect, and probably closer to the truth. In any case, the biographers make it clear that the loving devotion of a woman, her care and inspiring admiration, were not lacking to Francis throughout his life.

Clare Favarone was a very special example of this kind of relationship. Celano was the first to describe Clare's life, and the historical events can be verified in a little work rediscovered in 1920 and published under the title *J'ai connu Madame Sainte Claire*. For the most part, I have kept to this source.[4]

Several months after Clare's death in 1251, the convent of San Damiano outside Assisi, where she died, received a visit from Monsignor Barthelemy, bishop of Spoleto, who had been commissioned to interrogate the sisters in connection with Clare's canonization. This convent still stands and is one of the most impressive relics of Clare (as well as Francis). Wandering through the bare refectory, the dormitory where Clare died, the sloping benches used by the sisters at prayer, and looking over the plains from the little flower garden which Clare tended, the visitor might almost think that he was viewing a convent deserted only minutes before, in which the atmosphere of mystic calm has been left behind. It was here, in 1253, that the sisters were called, one by one, to appear before Monsignor Barthelemy to answer under oath the questions he would put to them.

It is difficult to imagine a more reliable witness than a nun under oath, though it is true that facts are often colored by feelings, but we get the impression that the interrogator admonished his witnesses in the same way as a modern colleague might: "We are not interested in the feelings of the witness. Please confine yourself to the facts." The testimony of the nuns is true to life, due in part to the little details which no one would bother to make up—like the remark that one of the sisters began to scream when a heavy door fell on Sister Clare and that it took three men to put it back in place. Reconstructing the testimony of the various witnesses, we see the following story unfold.

Clare's father, Favarone, and her mother, Ortelana, belonged to the high nobility of Assisi and lived in a *palazzo* bordering San Rufino.[5] Clara was born in 1193 and from the age of 10 to 12 lived in Perugia, where her parents settled after fleeing during a rebellion.

Francis was certainly known to Clare. The son of the wealthy Bernardone, who had broken with his father and now roamed the streets as a begger, he must have been a topic of conversation in the Favarone household. When he began to preach in Assisi, Clare came into personal contact with him. We know this from Madonna Bona, who lived in the same house as Clare. Another witness tells us that on the eve of Palm Sunday, after the close of Francis' Lenten meditations in San Rufino, Clare left home for good. In order to leave the house, she was obliged to remove the

heavy beams which barred the back door, a feat which
seems to have caused no little astonishment. After tramping
several kilometers in total darkness, Clare arrived at the
convent of Porziuncola with Pacifica at her side. She was
18 years of age. It is still possible to visit the little chapel
where she knelt before Francis (this fact is mentioned re-
peatedly), who cut off her long hair and laid the penitential
garment upon her shoulders.

It took courage to support this noble young lady in her
flight from home and family, but the young man who had
thrown his garments at his father's feet for the sake of his
evangelical ideal was not overly concerned by a possible
loss of honor on the part of the Offreduccis and the Fava-
rones. Nor did the scandal that might be caused by a late-
night encounter between the lovely Clare[6] and a man of
30 appear to disturb him. The same night, Francis and his
brothers set off through the woods, carrying burning torches,
to entrust Clare to the Benedictine nuns in Bastia. Afterward, Francis decided she might be safer in a convent at
the top of Subasio, and three months later Bishop Guido
granted him the use of San Damiano, along with several
rooms which had been built onto the church.[7] The feminine
branch of his community was a reality.

According to contemporaries, Clare was a woman who
knew what she wanted. But far from dominating those
weaker than herself, she had a rare quality of self-efface-
ment, allowing others to think that she was inferior. As
a leader, she used the same tactics as Francis: she banned
every show of power. Her most characteristic trait was her
calm, a calm born of courage. When the Saracens were
scaling the convent walls and everyone else panicked, Clare
remained calm. She reassured the sisters and went to pray
before the tabernacle. Four eyewitnesses testify to the fact
that the Saracens then retreated.

Her strength of spirit is equally evident in the manner in
which she resisted the Church authorities who attacked her
deepest convictions. One of the witnesses recounts the story

of a remarkable meeting, which must have been extremely humiliating for the prelate in question. Clare was so devoted to the ideals of poverty that, during his visit to the convent, Pope Gregory IX (the former Cardinal Ugolino) was not able to persuade her to acknowledge ownership of worldly goods.[8] "When asked how she could know this, Sister Benvenuta replied that she had been present herself and had heard with her own ears the words of the pope, who beseeched Mother Clare to accept the goods which he himself had brought into the house."

What is recounted here in a few words is proof that Clare did not fit the stereotyped view of the "little nun" who can easily be manipulated by the clerical powers-that-be. It is far more likely that the tyrant Gregory was manipulated. He gathered his things and took leave of the convent.

Clare's master had once written her that he had never been deterred from complete poverty "on the advice of anyone."[9] Clare, who washed the feet of her nuns and sometimes knelt to ask their forgiveness, remained standing before a pope, who himself refused to bow to an emperor. It must have been a very surprised Gregory who left San Damiano. All his clever arguments were of no avail against Clare's sole argument: Francis. Gregory, in any case, is to be admired for his decision not to force his will on her. Later, she was always able to rely on his support.

It is not surprising that so many poets and movie directors have seen the relationship between Clare and Francis in an erotic light, but it is a mystery how Kazantzakis, in his "Pillow of Stone," could have Francis fall in love with the 12-year-old Clare. And there is no evidence that Clare and Francis ever strolled through a field of flowers, as Franco Zeffirelli portrayed them in *Brother Sun, Sister Moon*. Both men, however, understood that when the love of a man and woman is exalted, an exalted form of eros is not impossible. Max Scheler, who also described the friendship between Francis and Clare, sees it as a meeting between senses and spirit (Eros and Agape), unusual in its intimacy.

Life comes under the spell of the spirit, but the spirit too is raised to a higher level.[10]

But we must not let our imagination run away with us, when so little historical information is available, and even that has been colored by pious biographers. However, we may at least assume that this friendship enabled Clare and Francis to bring a lifelong ideal to fuller and richer development.

The feminine branch of the order developed as rapidly as the friars'. For one thing, the time was exceptionally ripe. Francis' work had brought to light a strong desire for contemplative life. Clare's flight from her father's house led to a wave of vocations—her sister Agnes, her childhood friends Pacifica and Benvenuta, her cousins Belvina and Amata, and later her youngest sister Beatrice, and finally even her mother, Ortolana. Three years later, Jacques de Vitry mentions the growing numbers of "minor brothers and minor sisters."[11] The Franciscan revival, however, was not confined to the elite. The middle classes came into it as well, and according to sociologists this is a *conditio sine qua non* for true reform.

With Francis at its heart, the movement, which would later be called the Third Order of St. Francis, was beginning to take shape. Historians do not tell us whether Francis officially founded a third order. It is not mentioned in his writings and even Celano is vague on this point, more so than the Three Companions.[12] But no one disputes that fact that the religious revival developed into a third order in which the spirit of Francis lived on. (This is evident from the rule for this order which was laid down by Pope Nicholas IV in 1289.) The astonishing growth of the order bears witness to the fact that a great idea, though barely structured, can live on for centuries, capturing such great minds as Dante, Rafael, Michelangelo, and Palestrina.[13] Its members were not always saints, but they wished their lives to bear the mark of Franciscan spirituality.

Strangely enough, the movement lacked that very element

which appeals most to modern man—social criticism. If a movement does not revolt against social abuse, it has little chance of success today. One must admit, however, that there was little evidence of open revolt in the medieval Third Order. For one thing, the medieval view of life and worldly values was totally different. The existence of the masses was dominated by the *Dies Irae* and the Last Judgment. Priest and prophet, painter and sculptor awaited the coming of the "Son of Man among the clouds with great power and majesty." Michael and Satan struggled to tilt the balance of the scales in his favor. This world was as transitory as wild flowers, and it is not surprising that those who had nothing to lose drifted into an indifference to the world, an "alienation" which later was vehemently condemned by philosophers.

And yet it would be unfair to say that the Third Order passively accepted such evils as poverty, injustice, and city wars. The movement's will to strike at the heart of these evils was hampered, however, by medieval man's tendency to see the pronouncements of Church and state as the indisputable will of God. Popes took their cue from the theocratic view of government prolaimed in the Old Testament, with its priest-rulers. It was not until the Second Vatican Council that the goods of this world were cleansed of their stigma and people began to be critical of the mentality so succinctly expressed by an old *oratio: Terrena despicere, amare celestia* (Despise the things of earth and love the things of heaven).

But the Third Order, perhaps unconsciously, went to the very heart of several abuses. First of all, in forbidding the oath by which a man blindly bound himself to lord or prince. This threatened not only the feudal system but also the system of military conscription, and it was a blow to those who cast a covetous glance over high castle walls into another man's territory. The fines and prison sentences that were meted out did nothing to break the people's passive resistance, especially when the popes began to realize the significance of their refusal to take the oath.

The influence of the Third Order emanated from another part of the rule as well: "The brothers may carry no offensive weapons."[14] But when we read "except in the defense of the Church of Rome, the Christian faith, or their own land," we can be certain that Francis had no hand in writing this latter passage.[15]

Through its sudden rise, the Third Order was capable of sabotaging the plans of the princes. In Faenze, for instance, the pope released the sovereign's subjects from their oath and the citizens entered the Third Order *en masse*![16]

Today the Third Order does not enjoy the same esteem, though several years ago it boasted about a million members. Once hailed by scholars and artists as an inspiration to true spiritual life, it now shares with similar organizations a kind of benign sympathy, calling to mind old ladies and gentlemen seeking refuge in some antique devotion. With wry humor, Folliet tells us: "Some people see the Third Order as an old, extremely respectable gentleman who is intent on dying a good death; to be absolutely certain of salvation, he piles indulgence upon indulgence out of the spiritual treasure trove of the Order. They are probably confusing the Order with a brotherhood which has all but died out but which was known as the archbrotherhood of a good death. The members patiently awaited the blessings of a holy death, all the while singing pious hymns in sepulchral voices."[17]

This is a caricature, to be sure, but there is a germ of truth in it. Father Roggen, in quoting the above, remarks: "It is a well-known fact that the First Order (that of the mendicant brothers) takes very little interest in its lay movement." And in a way he finds this understandable, in the face of so many other, less languishing groups and movements. But I wonder if the basic idea behind the Third Order is not precisely what spiritually starved twentieth-century man needs and wants, lay groups centered around prophetic figures or convents, whose spirituality, while rooted in the gospel, is not foreign to the age in which we live. The name Third Order is of no consequence. "A rose by any other name will smell as sweet."

Footnotes

1. A. Durand, "Recherches sur le sens de la vie religieuse," *Lumière et vie* (January 1970), no. 96. This excellent article appears in a Dutch translation in *Tijdschrift van Theologie* (1970), no. 3.

2. In his *Living Our Future: St. Francis of Assisi and the Church Tomorrow* (Chicago: Franciscan Herald Press, 1976), Mario von Galli examines the manner in which the word *cortesía* is translated by various biographers of Francis. This serves to show how many-sided this characteristic was; a simple "courtesy" will not do here. Guardini says: "*Cortesía* is in Francis the noble gentility of the knight, his loving friendship for his fellow man." See O. Karrer, *Franz von Assisi, Legenden und Laude* (Zurich, 1945), p. 280.

3. Her name appears in a transaction dated May 13, 1217. Francis was more than once a guest in her palace in Rome (probably in the grain mill, the ruins of which are still to be found on the Circo Massimo). This Palazzo del Settizoni had been built by Septimius Severus on the Via Appia. Its sumptuousness was intended to impress upon all who entered the city the greatness of Rome. The name is probably connected with the seven colonnades, one above the other.
Strangely enough, the Frangipani were passionate supporters of the emperor in the thirteenth century, and two years after Francis' death they ran Gregory IX out of town. But to Francis this support of the emperor was no reason to refuse Giacopa his friendship. She is buried in the crypt under the basilica of Assisi; her epitaph reads: "Here lies the holy and noble Jacoba." A faded fresco shows Giacopa bringing the penitential sackcloth to Francis on his deathbed.

4. It is not certain whether the life of Clare, written in 1255 at the request of Pope Alexander IV, is the work of Celano. P. Hoonhout, in his dissertation *Het Latijn van Celano,* came to the conclusion that there are numerous stylistic similarities to the other works of Celano but just as many differences (p. 234). The text of *J'ai connu Madame*

Claire, originally written in Latin, was the property of the sisters of Florence and was later lost. It was rediscovered in the archives of the municipal library in an Umbro-Italian translation which may be considered reliable. The man who discovered this work, Fr. Lazzeri, published the text in 1920. We have quoted from an edition of the Poor Clare Convent in Toulouse, dating from 1961 and titled *J'ai connu Madame Claire.*

5. While studying the archives of San Rufino in Assisi, Fortini uncovered several documents which show that Clare's grandfather was called Offreduccio di Bernardone. One of his five sons was Favarone, Clare's father (Fortini, op. cit., vol. II, 8, p. 316). Clare is therefore not a member of the so-called Scifi family, who inhabited a castle in Sasso Rosso. Due to corruption of the name Cipi (Scipio), an uncle of Clare, this name appears from the sixteenth century onward.

6. Clare's great beauty was mentioned by witnesses.

7. In the previous chapter, Jacques de Vitry in 1216 speaks of the "lesser sisters" (see *Omnibus,* p. 1608). During the first three years the term convent was not in use, but rather *hospitium* (hospice). Clare became abbess in 1215, at the age of 23. The cloister was introduced in 1219. Clare's biographer (Celano?) recounts that Innocent laughed heartily when Clare requested permission to renounce the possession of property. Such a request had never yet been submitted to the apostolic chair, but he signed the privilege. We can conclude from this that, on the occasion of his first visit to Innocent (in 1206), Francis had not made this request.

8. This probably occurred in 1228, when Pope Gregory was in Assisi for Francis' canonization.

9. See Francis' Testament addressed to Clare's sisters, written in the year of his death, 1226, in *Omnibus* (p. 76).

10. M. Scheler, *Wegen u. Formen de Sympathie* (1922), p. 144. Eng. equivalent: *Nature of Sympathy,* trans. Peter Heath (Archon).

11. See *Omnibus,* pp. 1608-1613.

12. *Leg. 3 Comp.* 14; *Omnibus,* p. 904. See also *I Celano* 36-27, where he speaks of a threefold army of chosen people; *Omnibus,* pp. 258-260.

13. More famous names: Columbus, Murillo, Galvano, Volta, Liszt. See A. Bier, *La pensée économique et sociale de Calvin* (Geneva, 1950), and J. Rupp, *L'Idée de Chrétienté dans la pensée pontificale des*

origines à Innocent III (1939).

14. See chap. V of Third Order Rule; *Omnibus,* p. 171.

15. This clause was absent from the first rule of the old penitential movement, but appeared in the revised rule (chap. 7) of Nicholas IV in 1289. See Theodore Zaremba O.F.M., *Franciscan Social Reform* (Pulaski, Wis.: Franciscan Printery, 1947), p. 127.

16. Dec. 16, 1221. See Sbaralea, *Bullarium Franciscanum,* I, 8.

17. J. Folliet, *Pour un laicat évangelique,* p. 98.

13

Invincible Peace

A dynamic movement such as Francis' could not be confined within national boundaries. Basically, it recognized no frontiers. When Lady Poverty asks where the brothers live and one of them gestures widely with his arms and says, "This is our convent,"[1] his words have missionary significance.

This is the beginning of a new era. These men embody the missionary zeal which had been absent from Church life for centuries. During the assembly of the brothers in 1217, a resolution was passed which contained (for that age) a novel idea: to send its members over all Europe, unarmed, with nothing more in their knapsack than the bread for which they have begged.[2] At a time when people scarcely dared travel over the mountains without the protection of a caravan, this bore witness to an overwhelming religious idealism. We are astonished to see the success of an adventure which, on all accounts, should have failed miserably. In Germany, France, England, and Holland, vocations blossomed and provinces sprang up which have endured and proved their worth right up to the present.

Francis himself was bent on going to his beloved France, where he could speak the language (at least the *langue d'oc*), but he changed his plans on the advice of Cardinal Ugolino, who thought it better for him not to leave Italy. Francis took this advice, at least temporarily, but this did not put an end to his travels. We are not obliged to credit every convent which claims that its church was founded by Francis, but it is certain that for the better part of twenty years he traveled the length of the peninsula, from Romagna in the north to the heel of the boot. A lonely citizen of the world, he traveled through a country marred by boundaries. And boundaries meant war. They were an ever-present challenge to Guelfs and Ghibellines, a constant worry to the pope, and a strategic weapon in the hands of the emperor. The man who had always displayed disregard for frontiers and knew only peace did not stay long inside these confines. When he saw thousands setting off on their "holy" mission of war, he set off with them. But on a mission of peace.

At a present-day peace conference, Francis would probably not be allowed to speak, even if he should ask to do so. He was not a man of ideas, if by "ideas" we mean a structure of tenets on which to base a workable peace plan. But he becomes a formidable man of peace when one begins to search for the fundamental basis on which world peace must be built. The man who marched across the plains of Perugia in helmet and chain mail to join the hotheaded Walter of Brienne, later put these youthful ideals into the service of a lifelong fight for peace—a term that in our society has steadily narrowed, until it is now almost exclusively a political term.

Whoever thinks of peace thinks of war and disarmament, with the greatest possible advantage to oneself. But peace is first and foremost an inner quality. When Francis fights for peace, he does not stop to inquire about the cause of the argument. He does not care who is right and who is wrong. He doesn't ask for arguments, only brotherhood. He doesn't discuss charity, he practices it. Francis may be naive in this, but it is a disarming naiveté, and strangely effective.

The following incident is recounted by an outsider, an archdeacon and theology student. His account is doubly reliable as it was only by chance that he was present when Francis, whom he didn't know, began to speak in the middle of a city square. It happened in Bologna, where the patricians of the city were again divided by petty squabbles. "I studied in this city," he writes, "and had the occasion to hear one of Francis' sermons in the Square of the Little Palaces. Almost the whole population of the city was present. The sermon lacked the tenor and the presentation of an orator. It was no more than a simple call to expel the feelings of hate and malice, and to restore peace. The speaker was poorly clad, slight and unassuming. And yet, with his simple words, he succeeded in reconciling the nobility, men who had been at each other's throats for years. The enthusiasm was so overwhelming that men and women rushed up to him, tore off pieces of his clothing and carried them away."[3]

This type of anecdote conceals more than it reveals. This was a risky adventure, talking to medieval antagonists of peace and reconciliation. Many a preacher has had to face the consequences of trying to interest people in the gospel, when the honor of a gentleman was at stake. Knowing the passionate city life of the Middle Ages, the religious respect which suddenly reverses into demonic rage, we cannot but admire Francis' courage in daring to cast himself into this maelstrom.

The fact that a simple man, a nobody, without the hypnotic force of an orator, with a down-to-earth talk settles a centuries-old conflict can only be explained by some other force. Somehow, his words must have opened a world of such unspeakable love that every shred of hate melted away. Here was a man who saw true peace everywhere in God's creation and bore witness to that peace with touching simplicity. A man to whom self-interest was totally foreign. Even our society would consider him disinterested, of such high integrity that he would be acceptable to all parties.

Francis laid down his peace program in a single sentence. "They bring true peace who in all that they suffer keep the peace in body and soul out of love for our Lord Jesus Christ."[4] These words would sound trite if they were spoken by someone who did not live by them. But Francis' biographers bear witness to the manner in which he keeps the peace "in everything." One of the most famous anecdotes is a story from the Fioretti which, though somewhat embellished, is based on a true incident, which is also mentioned by Celano.

One bitterly cold day Francis and Brother Leo are on their way from Perugia to Maria degl' Angeli (the Poziuncola). Leo went on ahead, but Francis called him back. "Brother Leo," he said, "even if our brothers could make the blind see, the lame walk, the dumb speak, and drive out devils—yes, even if they were able to raise a dead man after four days in the tomb—write this down, Brother Leo— this is not the secret of true happiness." Then he mentions other forms of power and greatness: knowledge of all sciences and books, the secrets of the future and the treasures of the earth, all qualities of man and beast—none of these bring true happiness. The story goes on: "Brother Leo, even if a brother were able to preach so well that he could convert any unbeliever, even this does not represent true happiness." Francis went on like this, walking and talking, for more than two miles. Finally Brother Leo, who had listened with growing amazement, cried out: "Father, in the name of God, tell me what *does* bring true happiness!" Francis answered: "When in a little while we arrive in Santa Maria Degl' Angeli, cold and wet, dirty and hungry, and the porter asks, 'Who are You?' And when we say, 'We are two of your brothers,' the man answers, 'What?! You're tramps, the two of you, who cheat the people and steal alms from the poor.' And when he leaves us standing there in the snow and we patiently accept these insults and vile talk, and humbly say to ourselves, 'The porter has seen through us. God has placed such words in his mouth'—write this down, Brother Leo—*that* is true happiness."[5]

A man who accepts insult in this way is invincible. Although he abhorred war, the pacifism which Francis preached was not inspired by the political situation in his own day. It was part of his way of life. "Christian pacifists do not draw their conviction from some utopian dream, but from the existence and significance of Jesus Christ," writes Canon Raven.[6] This is the responsibility which Christianity bears for world peace.

Footnotes

1. *Sacrum Commercium* 63; *Omnibus*, p. 1593.

2. In that day and age it was downright irresponsible to send men into regions where they did not understand the language. The memoirs of Giordano, who was sent to Germany, are full of tales of brothers who answered "yes" to every question because this word initially had seemed to work wonders—until they were asked if they belonged to a heretical sect!

3. The text by Thomas of ·Spoleto can be found in H. Boehmer, *Analekten zur Geschichte des H. Franziskus von Assisi*, 2d ed. (Tübingen, 1930), p. 16. Thomas says that the sermon was given in the year of the earthquake in Brescia (Christmas, 1222). This story is also recounted in Fioretti 27; *Omnibus*, pp. 1367-1370.

4. *Admon.* 15; *Omnibus*, p. 83.

5. Fioretti 8; *Omnibus*, p. 1318. A remarkable parallel is found in Vladimir Lindbery, *Zo bidt de mensheid* (Utrecht, 1962), pp. 25-26. It is taken from the *Satipatthana*, the eighth path, and concerns freedom from fear. The story is a conversation between Buddha and his

pupil Roerna. We see the same "escalation" as in the story from the Fioretti, which is recounted by Celano in a much simpler form (see *Omnibus,* pp. 1501-1502.) There is, however, a definite difference in the views on freedom in the two works.

6. C. E. Raven, *The Theological Basis of Christian Pacifism* (London, 1952), p. 19.

14

A Prophet on Crusade

A world that has risen from the ashes of two world wars and is threatened by a third has no time for military glory and patriotic heroics. World peace is slowly becoming the ideal uppermost in everyone's mind, the main preoccupation of the media. Western politicians are increasingly hard pressed to find a plausible reason for armed conflict.

But back in the thirteenth century there was hardly a pope who could have issued an encyclical titled *Pacem in Terris* without a sizable twinge of conscience. Every "holy" war was initiated with a *Te Deum,* and the same hymn of praise celebrated every "holy" victory. It is difficult for us to imagine how they justified certain decisions to their consciences, and it is evident that Francis had his doubts on this subject. In the whole body of literature surrounding the figure of Francis, not a single trace of political interest can be found. When Otto IV passed by Rivo Torto at a distance of several hundred meters, shortly after his crowning as emperor, Francis did not consider it necessary to interrupt his work in order to see him. Instead he sent one of the brothers to the highway to announce to the emperor that his glory would be short lived, a prophecy which was to be fulfilled by Innocent some months later.[1]

Since the abandonment of his youthful desire to join the soldier-knights, Francis never considered supporting the pope in his political ambitions. Nor could he be persuaded to strive for a better relationship between pope and emperor, as did Elias, one of his successors. But neither did he urge the people to storm the basilica. In the modesty of his ambitions he is destined to disappoint the religious revolutionary, just as he continually disappointed the champions of the establishment. The latter undoubtedly include Innocent and his successors—in any case, where the Crusades are concerned. Nowhere is Francis' courage more in evidence than when his path crosses this "holy" undertaking.

All his life, Innocent was possessed by the idea of the Crusades.[2] Several months after becoming pope, before he had captured a single royal vassal, he wrote to the count of Tripoli: "Though every day new needs of Church and people should present themselves to us, yet it is the liberation of the Holy Sepulchre which enjoys our most particular care and attention." He was convinced that the Church would never attain world sovereignty until the Saracens had been defeated. Throughout his pontificate he never ceased to exhort, bribe, threaten, and command foot soldiers, knights, and kings alike to recapture the Holy Sepulchre. He did so in a manner which would never have been preached by the Man who rose from that grave.

But this fact is not easily impressed upon one brought up on Old Testament holy war, especially when he is supported in his conviction by someone of the stature of Bernard de Clairvaux, the most influential figure of his century. This advocate of the Crusades removed St. Paul's *miles Christi* (soldier of Christ) from the religious sphere and enrolled him in a political army; besides the cross, he put into the knight's hand a lance and a sword. We can scarcely conceive the enormous influence attached to the promise which this prophet of the Crusades made to his soldiers: whoever should fall in battle is assured of eternal salvation. He need not fear on that *dies irae,* that day of wrath.

> When the judge his seat attains,
> And each hidden deed arraigns
> Nothing unavenged remains.[3]

It is a sad and shameful truth that the Crusades themselves were often a *dies irae.* When the first trumpets sounded (1095), the Crusaders were filled with an idealism for which much had been sacrificed. Their incentives were purely spiritual, devoid of any ulterior motive, political or otherwise. It was not primarily a question of conquering the Moslem but of regaining the Holy Land. But to quote Pirenne, "What the eleventh century conceived and realized as an ideal became, under the force of totally different circumstances, a compulsive principle."[4] Medieval man cannot be blamed for not possessing more vision than his prophets.

From a political point of view, the Crusades were a failure. Islam, formerly torn by inner strife, grew into an invincible power under the challenge of the European invaders. Schisms disappeared, Sytian culture flourished, Cairo became once more a center of world commerce. And when in 1187 Saladin recaptured Jerusalem, it became for Islam, too, a holy city. Entering the city, he ordered the Dome of the Rock mosque to be rebuilt, and had heralds announce to Moslem and Christian alike that the Holy City (*al Quda*) was purged of infidels.[5]

It was probably at this point that the young Count Segni, later Innocent III, first entertained the obsessive thought of destroying the Saracen, religiously and politically. He became not only pope but also a diplomat. In the beginning he respects political rights and attempts to achieve his aims by the mailed fist in the velvet glove. As medieval believer, he took refuge in the Bible, where he found the beast of the Apocalypse,[6] ever willing to assume any form which was required to represent an enemy of Christianity. "The day of liberation now appears close at hand," he writes in 1213. "The power of Islam, whose reign is prophesied in the Apocalypse, has now come to an end."[7] The prophecy has never been fulfilled, however, and the beast of many faces lives on.

Francis' view of the Mohammedan was diametrically opposed to that of his contemporaries, even the most enlightened. When he read in the gospel that he must love all mankind, he found that impossible to reconcile with aggression and killing. Perhaps he was too stubborn to follow a Bernard de Clairvaux or an Innocent blindly, but in any case he felt that the Mohammedan, enemy or not, was his brother and that one didn't kill one's brother to attain a holy objective. He wanted to bring to them his most precious possession: the gospel. He was filled with the conviction, extraordinary for his day, that God loved the Mohammedan more than he loved his tomb. And that possession of the Holy Land was not worth the death of a single Mohammedan.

This was one of the cornerstones of the gospel. Francis knew of Innocent's desire to restore the gospel among his people, but it had to be the whole gospel and nothing but that gospel. For Francis, it was not enough to discourse on the imperial power of Christ, his representatives, and his realm; rhetorical pronouncements, such as "The Holy Land which our Lord purchased for us with his precious blood" and "Each day brings increased sorrow until we know that it has been restored to its former freedom,"[8] were not sufficient to convince Francis.

In the rule which he had put into writing in 1221, he gives a few regulations concerning the work among the Saracens which would have doomed any political crusade to failure even before it got started: "The brothers whose work takes them to the Saracens have two ways of living spiritually among the people: one is to cause no conflict

or dissension but 'for love of God to be obedient and sub-
missive to all men',[9] and to make known that they are
Christians. The second manner consists in preaching God's
word in order to bring them to believe in the Almighty
God, Father, Son, and Holy Spirit."[10]

These are simple words, so simple that in the revised
rule of 1223 legal advisors had reduced the thirty lines to
six. But no one can deny that these words bear witness to
a missionary insight centuries ahead of its time, in which
paternalism and intolerance have no part. Here one finds
nothing of the severity with which even Ignatius of Loyola
and Francis Xavier looked down upon Islam.[11]

It was experience in the missions which led the Second
Vatican Council to proclaim: "As in the course of centuries
no little dissension and strife have arisen between Christians
and Moslems, the Holy Synod urges all men to forget the
past and to labor zealously for mutual understanding."[12]

Francis was the personification for his age of that "mutual
understanding." In June 1219, he and several brothers
boarded ship in Ancona on the Adriatic coast for the bat-
tlefields abroad. They land a month later in Acre, a Crusaders' fort in northern Egypt, and Francis goes ashore
with Illuminato and Pietro di Cattaneo. In all probability,
Cardinal Ugolino was able to mollify the Curia, in the hope
that Francis' presence among the soldiers would arouse
their fighting spirit. For all his perspicacity, he was much
mistaken. Francis had other plans.

There is a great deal of reliable information on Francis'
sojourn among the Crusaders—in fact, more than on any
other period of his life.[13] Jacques de Vitry is significant,
for he met Francis there and in his letters speaks of him
and his companions with the greatest respect.

The realm of Saladin, which comprised Syria as well as
Egypt, was invulnerable in Asia. For this reason John of
Brienne, king of Jerusalem and head of the army of Crusa-
ders, directed his attack on the coast of Egypt and Damietta.
The army landed there in May of 1218 and captured the

city. His opponent was the brilliant sultan Melek-el-Kamil, Saladin's nephew, a devout Mohammedan who, like Frederick II, was the very epitome of the culture of his day. He had informed the fanatic papal legate, the Spaniard Pelago Galvao, that he would be willing to withdraw his troops from Jerusalem on condition that the Crusaders left the Egyptian zone. But Galvao haughtily refused.

It was in September 1219, during this extraordinarily tense period, that Francis and a few brothers landed on the Egyptian coast and set off to visit the papal legate. One can imagine the astonishment and irritation of Galvao when this inexperienced newcomer relates a completely novel plan: he does not want to win the war but to win over the sultan. Galvao, with his dream of destroying Moham-medan power, must have been scarcely able to contain his annoyance at this nobody, who had no interest in his lofty aims and was bent on sabotaging his plans by a peaceable meeting with the enemy. At a time when, for a variety of motives, all Christianity was intoxicated with this one ideal, it appears that at least one Christian was left unmoved. Politics and conquest did not interest him. In his naive simplicity, he saw through strategy and tactics. Whoever wins the sultan has won peace. But Galvao had never be-fore been confronted with such tactics, and he forbade Francis to set off.

It was at this time that Jacques de Vitry met Francis and came under the spell of his personality. In a letter written shortly afterward he recounts how a certain Master Raymier, prior of St. Michael, had entered the order of mendicant brothers, "an order which is expanding steadily everywhere. The brothers live according to the rules of the primitive Church and imitate in all things the life of the apostles. The leader of these brothers is called Francis. He is of such an amiable character that he is respected by all. He has joined our army, but in his religious zeal he does not shrink from visiting the enemy."[14]

Galvao had finally given Francis permission to go to the

Sultan. He only asked him not to endanger the cause of Christianity and to act only on his own behalf. Together with Brother Illuminato, a valuable witness to the meeting, he set off. It was not difficult for a Christian to enter the Mohammedan court, for there was a price on his head of one gold Byzantine, and we will never know how Francis managed to arrive unscathed, unless his cry of *Soudan, soudan* was taken as a sign that he was on a secret mission.[15] He was well received by Melek. This shrewd politician understood the little man with his broken French better than he did the papal legate. There stood before him a man of charity, who was trying to persuade him to place the gospel above the Koran. He probably won more sympathy for the Christians than a whole army of Roman politicians. This was no charming ambassador, armed with tempting proposals. Nor a deserter, trying to win the sympathy of the sultan by a bitter condemnation of pope and Curia. His greatness was evident in his attitude—neither hate for one side nor fawning sympathy for the other. Melek, a deeply religious Mohammedan, was fascinated by his transparent simplicity. He also impressed the sultan because, in contrast with other Christians, he did not show contempt for the holy book and the religious convictions of the Mohammedans.

Francis' mission did not succeed. Melek accepted neither peace nor Christianity. But historical sources bear witness to the sympathy Melek felt for Francis. For the first time, the gospel and the Koran did not meet as adversaries. If we are to believe Vitry, who met Francis personally, the sultan secretly asked him, as they were parting, to pray that God might inspire him to choose the religion most pleasing to Him. In any case, he provided Francis with a pass which would ensure his safety to the border, and even extended it to include freedom to enter the holy places without paying tribute.[16]

Francis and Illuminato leave this exotic world of luxury as poor as they came—leaving behind the palace with the

Moorish colonnades, lakes and fountains, pavilions and scented gardens, such as could only be found in the culture of medieval Islam. He took nothing with him, but left behind a lasting impression. This is evident from a fifteenth-century biography discovered in Cairo, which describes the life of a certain Eskrel—Din, advisor to Melek in the "affair of the monk."

After his return, Francis witnessed the conquest of Damietta on November 5, 1219. Of a population of 80,000, only a few thousand survived the Crusaders and the plague. The situation was so serious that the triumphal entry into the city had to be postponed several months. Cardinal Galvae, at the head of the cheering procession, reached the mosque, which had been rechristened the Basilica of Our Lady, early in the year 1220. Then began the division of the booty.[17]

No war is more repugnant than a holy war. Religious idealism cannot survive blood and plundering. In this city of death, what remained of that spirit of "God wills it"? The mind boggles at the thought of a Christian people striking up a *Te Deum* and, barely an hour later, rushing out of the basilica like a crowd of thugs to pillage and rape. The Crusades may have been a sign of faith, but they did not go down in history as a symbol of brotherly love. There had been pure idealism and sacrifices, but all had been lost, strangled by inane violence.

After an intense struggle with his conscience, Francis had tried to prevent all this misery. "If I try to persuade them to stop the attack," he had said to Brother Illuminato, "they will think me mad. And if I don't try I will regret it the rest of my life." Illuminato, true to his name, answered, "Well, it will not be the first time. Follow your conscience and fear God more than man."[18]

Francis *did* warn against the attack and people probably *did* think him out of his mind. He shared the fate of so many who were centuries ahead of their time.[19]

Footnotes

1. *I Celano* 43; *Omnibus*, pp. 264—265. This took place in December 1209. Fortini is of the opinion that Otto was not on his way to Rome but was returning from there.

2. Innocent had always intended that the Crusades should be the high point of his pontificate. "We solemnly promise," he writes in a letter, "to devote ourselves to the liberation of the province of Jerusalem."

Immediately after his coronation this energetic and resolute figure set about fulfilling this plan. The departure for the East was set for March 1199, but between 1199 and 1201 he was beset with problems. Having lost the support of the nobility, he was forced to appeal to the faithful. Finally, in 1202, with the aid of the prelates, convent orders, and orators, all was in readiness for the crusade. Innocent's conception of the Crusades is closely associated with a reconciliation between the Eastern and the Western Church. Though with the coronation of Baldwin of Flanders on May 16, 1204, the empire went from Greek into Latin hands, several Eastern bishops showed interest in a rapprochement, but most of them remained extremely wary of Rome. This suspicion was strengthened by the misconduct of the Crusaders who plundered churches and convents, dressed their wives in costly liturgical robes, and even went so far as to place a woman of the streets on the throne of the patriarch.

This deeply shocked Innocent. He laments these events in a letter dated July 12, 1205, and addressed to the legate of Pierre de Saint Marcel (Ep. VIII, 126): "How can we hope to achieve unity with the Greek church," he says, "after they [sic] have been plundered and persecuted? They have seen in the representatives of the Latin Church only examples of perversity and the works of darkness, so that they have every right to despise them as dogs. . . . The crusaders have openly practiced incest, adultery and prostitution, and have delivered mothers of families and even virgins dedicated to God into the hands of the soldiers for their pleasure." From 1208 onward, Innocent returned to his original plan of recruiting troops not in the East but in the West. At the time, the situation was extremely favorable for such a plan.

3. *Dies Irae* (probably not by Celano, as some believe).

4. H. Pirenne, *Geschiedenis van Europa,* 4th ed. (Amsterdam), p. 141.

5. See Bassetti-Sani, *Concilium* (September 1968), no. 7.

6. Rv 13:8.

7. Innocent III, Ep. 28.

8. Ibid., Ep. 1, 11.

9. Rule of 1221, 16; *Omnibus,* p. 43.

10. Rule of 1221, 16; *Omnibus,* p. 43.

11. J. Broderick, *Franciscus Xaverius* (London), pp. 95, 108.

12. Explanation of the Church's attitude toward non-Christian religions.

13. See *Bibliothèque bio-bibliographique de la Terre Sainte et de L'-Orient franciscain,* ed. Golubowich. Also notable here is the work of B. Bassetti-Sani, *Mahomed et S. François* (Ottawa, 1959), although we do not consider all the historical claims to be of unquestioned validity.

14. Jacques de Vitry was later appointed bishop of Acri. In 1220 he wrote a letter to a friend in Lotharingen in which he says that he has become acquainted with the *"fratres minores."* He speaks of Francis as the "founder of the Order, who is obeyed by all as the highest prior *(summo Prior),* a man who is simple and unlettered, loved by God and by men." Such a letter is of enormous historical value, because the author mentions the order only in passing. See *Omnibus,* p. 1609.

15. Brother Giordano. See *Sur les routes de l'Europe,* p. 30.

16. He is said to have made Francis a present of a so-called elephant, an ivory reed pipe, which Francis accepted and which is now in the sacristy of the Convento in Assisi (see *Acts of Clareno*). It is doubtful whether Francis withstood the crucial test. The pass should have been given by Melek's brother Moadlem, who ruled the holy places.

17. We must not think too lightly of such a conquest. Damietta was defended by a double wall on the sea coast, a triple wall on the land side, 22 gates, 110 towers, and 42 fortresses, and by a mighty Saracen military force with provisions to last them two years.

This is recorded in the *Gesta obsidionis Damiatae* by A. Milioni, who was born in 1220 and was a friend of the famous chronicler Salimbene. He based his description on the diary of an unknown Crusader who, from May 1218 into 1219, recorded his day-by-day experiences (published by Muratori). Francis remained in the camp of the besiegers from August 1219 until the siege was lifted. According to de Vitry, he marched into the town itself, where enormous quantities of gold and treasure were piled up.

18. *II Celano* 30; *Omnibus*, p. 388.

19. It was surely no accident that the king of Jerusalem, Jean de Brienne, was present at the canonization of Francis (1228). He died in the habit of Francis (Third Order) and expressed a wish to be buried beside the man who had such a different view of the Crusades. See *Monumenta Germaniae Historiae,* part XXXI.

15

Growth Crisis

Renan once called Palestine "a fifth gospel, shattered but still visible."[1] Never was it more shattered than when Francis arrived there after the clashes between Moors and Crusaders. And much was "still visible" to him as he followed almost literally in his Master's footsteps. We may assume that he prayed in the Garden of Olives and climbed to the top of Golgotha. We know, in any case, that after his stay in the Holy Land, Golgotha and the Garden of Olives never left him.

There is more tragedy in Francis' life than romantic biographers and movie producers suggest. And more uncertainty. He is not the prophet of the ecstatic vision, striding confidently toward his objective. From that moment in the square when he stood naked before his bishop until, near death, he asked to be laid on the ground, he knows not only spiritual illumination but spiritual darkness as well. "At night he often went into the chapel alone. It was there that, with God's grace, he succeeded in conquering the fears and terrors which threatened to overpower his soul," says Celano.[2]

Even the very first biographers, with their unshakable
faith in Francis, were not blind to his shortcomings. As
Brother Masseo told him, "You're not handsome, nor wise,
nor learned."[3] He might have added: You are not an orator, nor a lawyer, nor an organizer. Francis is simply not
the type to be cast in bronze and placed on a pedestal.
When Celano tells us, "If he had judged someone unfavor-
ably or an angry word had escaped him,"[4] we must see
this against the spirited background of Umbria, where an
angry word falls more loudly and more harshly on the ear
than in the north. The biographer goes on to tell us that
Francis would immediately go to the person to ask for
forgiveness. Francis was a noble man, but a man all the
same. And as a man he often acted unwisely, made mistakes
in appointing brothers and, above all, overestimated the
spiritual qualities of others. We cannot blame Jacques de
Vitry for his criticism of the order, expressed in a letter
dating from this period. After extensively praising the mendicant brothers, he writes: "And yet I cannot help feeling
that this religious movement is extremely dangerous, for the
following reasons. Not only adults, but also very young men
who have not yet reached maturity live for a short time
under the discipline of the convent and are then sent out,
two by two, into the world."[5] One of Francis' endearing
faults was his indestructible faith in his fellow man. But
sooner or later, such errors of judgment will take their toll.

There is a kind of demarcation line which runs through
the life of Francis the prophet. Before he left Italy he was
still the undisputed leader of the order, who authoritatively
quelled any incipient unrest. But eight months later, when
a runaway brother fled to his master over the seas, he bore
ill tidings. What this brother had to tell was not earth-shattering news, but it symbolized a change of spirit which was
beginning to undermine Francis' work. It was clear to him
that many in Italy had lost their absolute faith in him, and
that his most precious ideals were being assailed. He had
always been a violent opponent of Curia privileges; never-

theless, Brother Philip, surnamed the Long, had taken advantage of his absence to procure a papal bull of excommunication. Sanctions were taken against brothers who tried to live according to the spirit of their master. The housing of the brothers had taken a form which was in sharp contrast to the ideal of poverty. These were signs that a slumbering discontent with Francis' leadership was coming into the open.

Before his departure for Egypt, Francis had appointed two vicars. Matthew of Narni was to remain in Porziuncola to receive new members while Gregory of Naples traveled, visiting the brothers to guide and advise them. They probably panicked in the face of the growing abuses; in any case, they did not react in the spirit of their master. They lacked his intuition and expected laws to work miracles. They "took steps," which is the easiest way for an insecure authority to assert itself. It can be done without vision, without insight into the deeper origins of a problem. A piece of parchment and a quill pen were in this case sufficient, and the result was a so-called constitution.

In it, freedom and inspiration were shackled. Stricter rules were laid down, which strayed far from the spirit of the order. The number of fast days was increased and certain foods were forbidden. When this news reached Francis, abroad, he was at table with several brothers. Turning in surprise to Pietro di Cattaneo, he said, "What should we do now?" And the faithful Pietro replied, "Master Francis, do whatever you think best, for you are in authority." "Very well," said Francis, "let us eat what has been put before us, according to the gospel."[6]

We see here the eternal struggle between the pioneer and his followers, between the original idea and its practical application. It is a crisis of growth, and it is inevitable whenever a movement attempts to absorb a great diversity of minds and spirits.

In many biographies, even modern ones, this crisis in Francis' movement is viewed as a dangerous phenomenon.[7]

They maintain that he should have had the opportunity to carry through his original idea. Apart from the historical fact that no movement ever leaves the original ideas of its founder intact, we may ask ourselves if, alone, Francis would have been capable of placing this magnificent vision of his in his own time, and for all time. He must not forget that dozens of intelligent men had joined the order. They were not always as willing to give up the study of theology as Bernardo and Pietro di Cattaneo. How was Francis to lead in a world which was not his? It is true that he had certain remarkable qualities, in the sense of a richness of thought and feeling. And he had more than his share of that quality known as "social intelligence," a rather vague term combining creativity, power of improvisation, and the ability to get along with people at every level. With his religious intuition, he saw through the coldly legal spirit of the theology of those days. He penetrated the secrets of scripture more with the love of the heart than the logic of the mind. But he lacked the erudition to go any further. When he says, "The true philosopher considers eternal life the highest possible achievement and the man who humbly and without vanity studies Holy Scripture will easily come to a knowledge of himself,"[8] this is a profound thought. But it does not help him convince the theologians and lawyers, who sought not only eternal life and knowledge of self but a deeper insight into revelation.

We find some reassurance in Francis' letter to the professor of theology, Anthony of Padua, who had joined his order: "Brother Anthony, my bishop! I, Francis, wish you well. It is my desire that you give the brothers lessons in holy theology, as long as this study does not extinguish in them the spirit of holy prayer and devotion as laid down in the rule. God be with you."[9] This note proves that Francis was not opposed to theological study as such. It was written late in life (1224) and is probably a mature conviction, similar to that in his Testament: "The brothers must reverence and respect all theologians and all those who serve

God's word, as men who grant us spirit and life.'' Perhaps the growth crisis itself played a role in the development of his thinking.

This crisis centered on two questions: Was poverty to be practiced in the radical sense advocated by Francis himself, and were the brothers to be allowed to devote themselves exclusively to study? These problems bear the germ of a struggle which is to last for centuries. Francis' poverty ideal is undeniably heroic, but it does not solve the problem of whether all the brothers, in their diversity of talents, can find a place at Rivo Torto. It is a touching symbol of relinquishment, to tear apart a Bible in order to give everyone a page, but does it mean that one is less convinced of the value of books?

Nothing can detract from the nobility of Francis' ideas. They put an indelible mark on everything they touched. But although Francis was convinced that the Almighty had revealed to him how he was to live the gospel, there were many brothers who could not accept that God had laid down each and every detail of this revelation exclusively to Francis.

A growth crisis is always painful. It is not a question of death and rebirth, but rather of a kind of evolution. If the central idea does not emerge from the crisis strengthened and purged, then it has failed. The strength of Francis' personality can be seen in the manner in which he realized his central idea in the face of every opposition. Later it will be left to others, wise and far-seeing or narrow-minded and insular, to carry on the idea.

It is not uncommon to find among men of stature—popes, political leaders, founders of world concerns—men who are capable of coping with the most overwhelming opposition from outside, but who appear lost as soon as they encounter the slightest resistance from their close associates. Francis belonged to this category. He had opposed the powerful authority of his father, had borne the ridicule of his fellow citizens, and had refused to allow cardinals, and even the

pope, to change any part of his original ideas. He acted,
though on a lower level than his Master, as having full power
as though invested with authority. With deep humility and
in the face of death, he did not hesitate to write in the
same unequivocal terms, "The Lord has dictated to me that
I should do penance in the following manner. . . . The
Almighty himself has revealed to me that I must live according to the standards of the gospel."[10] But he was un-
sure in the face of the resistance and suspicion of his
brothers. He may have been guileless, but he was not blind:
"Francis knew full well that some people pretended to agree
with him while deep in their hearts they were of quite another opinion. They praised him when they were with him,
but mocked him behind his back."

One cannot help wondering if Celano himself had such
a high opinion of Francis during his life as would appear
from his biography. De Beer points to a passage from his
first work. After praising the deep humility of his master,
he cries out with true contrition: "What a misfortune for
us that we have lost you. . . . Your absence is our just
punishment for not having done everything we could to
know you while you lived among us."

Gone were those years when Francis as absolute leader,
with Bernardo and Pietro di Cattaneo, Egidio, and others
at his side, traveled the length and breadth of Europe. Most
of the brothers had never met Francis, and they demanded
solutions to new situations and expected to be consulted
in their application. They were true to the central idea:
the gospel was a precious home to them, but a home with
many rooms.

In his search for a way out of this crisis, Francis took
a course he had never taken before: he went to Pope
Honorius and asked for counsel and protection. From the
account of his visit and other early sources, we do not
get the impression that the papal residence was a holy
of holies to which only princes and cardinals were admitted.
If Giodano de Giano is to be believed, there was a free

and easy relationship which today strikes us as most remarkable. He claims to have gone with several other brothers to see Pope Gregory IX for the purpose of deposing
Elias, the later minister-general. The pope was having his
siesta and could not be disturbed. Just the same, they took
the evangelical freedom of entering the bedroom, waking
His Holiness, and holding onto his legs until he was prepared to listen to them. (If it's not true, it should be!) This
proves, in any case, that the brothers did not view the pope
as a supernatural phenomenon.[11]

At least as reliable a source is the visit of Francis to
Honorius, as described by his biographers. Honorius was
in Orvieto at the time, and when Francis arrived he was in
conference. Francis lay down in front of the door and waited
until the pope came out. Then he stood up and said: "My
Lord, as you occupy a high position and are often involved
in very important matters, the poor cannot always come to
you. . . . You have given me many popes [titles used in
those days for important officials]. Now give me one who
will always be close at hand when I need him and who,
in your name, will listen to me and help me straighten out
my affairs and those of my brothers."[12]

As protector, Honorius gave him the cardinal for whom
he had asked, Ugolino, bishop of Ostia. This giant of a
man, influential and progressive, was related to Pope Innocent, with whom he shared not only the same view of
the papacy but such qualities as asceticism and legal perspicacity. He is one of those medieval figures who combine
secular allure and ascetic piety, intertwining things heavenly
and things earthly.[13]

Ugolino has gone down in history as the symbol of the
official Church confronted with a movement which had
sprung up spontaneously. It is above all Sabatier, expert
on things Franciscan, who viewed this interference as a
catastrophe. "The Church in the person of Ugolino was
commissioned, if not to dispose of the movement, at least
to contain it so drastically that several years later it had

almost completely lost its original character."

Around the turn of the century this hypothesis was viewed as a brilliant discovery. The Franciscan Order was seen in a new light. Everyone's sympathy went out to the underdog. Francis was said to have watched helplessly while his movement was pruned and cut back until nothing was left but a poor, miserable excuse for an order.

Sabatier is not without arguments for his theory. Nevertheless, this view of the affair appears to me unrealistic. For one thing, it does not jibe with the character of Ugolino. It may be true that this powerful figure, who had a lawyer's keen sense of order, emphasized—perhaps even overemphasized—the regulating side of his role of patron. But he did so more because of his very real sympathy for Francis' original ideas than because of any desire to please the Curia, where he himself had many opponents.

He was a kind of spiritual Robin Hood, whose knightly ideals culminated in a passionate desire to protect the weak and to bring down the strong. Later, when he had become Pope Gregory IX, Emperor Frederick II understood that he was no longer dealing with the weak Honorius. And even before his protectorship, the Curia understood that Ugolino placed Francis' ideal far above the luxury and intrigues that were all too common among the prelates. This rough and ready character thoroughly enjoyed introducing his friend, Francis, into places where he was least welcome. He once took a whole procession of elegantly attired prelates and knights to an annual meeting of the brothers. He led them past the hastily erected huts where the hundreds of delegates were housed. "Look carefully and see how these brothers sleep: upon straw, like cattle. What will become of us, who enjoy such comfort and even then abuse it?"[14]

When in 1219 Francis was preparing to leave for France and happened to meet Ugolino in Florence, the latter strongly urged him to remain in Italy. "There are many prelates in the Curia who want to make things difficult for you. But other cardinals—and I am among them—love your order. A cautious tactician would probably have sought a that you do not leave the country."[15]

Sabatier's theory also fails to take into account the character of Francis himself, which expresses itself so clearly under the protectorship of Ugolino: he knows how to obey without giving up his independence. When he asked for protection, it was clearly not his intention to submit his most cherished ideals to the judgment of Ugolino. He remained in command. This is evident from the manner in which he stands up to Ugolino, humble but unshakable, whenever a fundamental aspect of his mission is involved.

Ugolino's admiration and friendship for Francis were unflagging. Francis was gifted with the kind of charm which, in spite of human failings, made him unassailable, no matter how exalted the position of his critics. He moved among them with ease, and without the commonly displayed obsequiousness. When Ugolino was about to visit the pope with Francis, he trembled at the thought of the unexpected turn an interview could take when Francis was present. His carefree spirit was never more in evidence than when matters of protocol were to be reckoned with. Celano, who never shows much sense of humor, nevertheless causes a smile when he describes how the cardinal implores all the saints of heaven to prevent his protegé from making a fool of himself. His prayer was heard. "He surrendered," Celano tells us drily, "to the goodness of Almighty God, who never forsakes the faithful in their hour of need."

Celano then describes how Ugolino was rescued from his distress. (We must not forget that Celano was commissioned to write this account by Ugolino, who surely recounted this incident to him, though in a somewhat different style.) "He [Ugolino] brought Francis before the pope and the venerable cardinals. In the presence of all the princes of the Church, Francis received from the pope his blessing and permission to speak. He began without the slightest sign of fear or awe. The exaltation of the spirit came over him and he could no longer control his joy.

As he spoke he was almost dancing, not like a tight-rope walker [!] but as a man consumed by the fire of divine love. . . . Not only did he cause no laughter, he moved them to tears. All were greatly touched, and they admired the power of grace as well as the conviction of the speaker."[16]

It is well-nigh certain that Celano, with his Byzantine respect for everything concerned with the prelacy, did not really understand Francis' carefree spirit. Celano epitomized the feudal spirit of his day, which only accentuated the originality with which his spiritual father approached Church authority.

It is not easy for a cardinal-patron to collaborate with a figure like Francis, but they finally agreed on the following arrangement. Francis provided the inspiration and Ugolino put that inspiration into concrete form; Francis knew what the Lord had revealed to him, but Ugolino knew how best to handle such revelations within the Church. With his influence and insight, Ugolino could have molded the order into an impressive organization, or, to borrow from Sabatier, he could have contained it so completely that every shred of Franciscan originality would have disappeared. He did neither.

Although it would be unfair to view Ugolino as the Vatican charmer with winning ways, who after listening patiently does whatever he thinks best, he still has flaws. We are safe in assuming that he did not always respect Francis' ideal of radical poverty, and that several times he hurt Francis deeply.

A particular sad example of this had to do with a house in Bologna. When Francis arrived in the city after his return from Syria, he heard people talking about the "house of the brothers"—a house of study, of which there were many in Bologna, which had been furnished by the provincial of the area. A simple fact, and yet it represented a real challenge to a man who saw one of his most cherished ideals disregarded. The brothers had accepted property. The heroic simplicity of the gospel had been compromised. (We must keep this in mind if we are to understand Francis' reaction.) He was suddenly confronted with a mentality which ran counter to that of Rivo Torto and Porziuncola, and he felt called upon to set an example for the whole order. A cautious tactician would probably have sought a compromise, but this impulsive figure, threatened with the failure of his ideal, was capable of taking a whip to the temple-goers. He reacted with the sternness of an Old Testament prophet. "When he heard about 'the house of the brothers' Francis left the city and sent word that the brothers were to leave the house immediately. They did so, to the last man. Not even the sick dared to stay, and left together with their brothers."[17]

Probably no one suffered more under this harshness than Francis himself. But the man who forbade the brothers to speak of "Francis' cell" could not sanction the term "the brothers' house." He did not begrudge the foxes their holes, nor the birds their nests, but his brothers were not allowed to possess the stones upon which they laid their heads.

In making this decision Francis had the support of the majority of his brothers; and this incident shows that he was able to oppose the new trend. But a single interdiction cannot halt a changing mentality. With the irresistible force of a natural law, the movement was becoming an institution, with a need for security and a desire to adapt to the surroundings.

It is significant that the house in Bologna was a house of study. Francis' order began as a classless community of lawyers and farmers, theologians and poets, rich merchants and confessed sinners. Eating from the same bowl, wearing the same habit, making merry around the same poor table —all this is within the reach of an idealistic community. But later, when a deeper vision and a more refined and intellectual culture come to play a role, differences become apparent and controversies arise, not in spite of but precisely because of the brothers' love for that original idea.[18]

The house in Bologna was a symbol of the conflict between the strict "Leo group" and the "Elias group," which wanted to adapt to new circumstances. Ugolino sought a solution for this conflict. Being a lawyer, he arrived at a formula: he would buy the house, retain possession, and the brothers would be allowed to use it. Ugolino knew Francis well enough to know that, deep in his heart, he saw through this plan. But the Cardinal was a practical man, and hadn't studied law in Paris and Bologna for nothing. He rejected the spirit and retained the letter—a remarkable interpretation of Paul's words: "We have nothing, but possess everything."[19]

This was not the only area in which the growth crisis gave the order a more practical dimension at the cost of Francis' vision. In 1220 Pope Honorius decreed that from then on the brothers were to spend a year in the novitiate before being accepted into the order and, furthermore, that they were no longer free to travel at will. It cannot be denied that these measures were dictated by common sense. And yet this meant that Francis was forced to give up one of his dearest ideals, dating from the early years, when a penitent vagabond, a usurer, a libertine, or a bandit could arrive on the doorstep and, that same day, be received into the classless community of mendicant brothers. This was only one of Francis' sublime follies, which had to make way for hard reality.

This cost Francis many an anguished hour, when nightmares about the imminent failure of his ideals tortured him. His weakness lay in lack of organizational ability and excessive trust in improvisation. He made mistakes—but it is certain that, with more organizational talent, he would never have become the lovable figure who is so dear to so many. When Francis fails, we cannot help wondering if he would have had a greater influence on his day if he had succeeded. Francis lived alongside brilliant popes and emperors, who held the Church and the world in their sway. But who remembers their names today?

We truly need Francis' original and unbusinesslike ideal-ism. We cannot resist the comparison with Pope John XXIII, who opened a holy door without knowing where it led. But John understood that, no matter what, that door could not remain closed. And Francis realized that the gospel has to be lived radically if it is to be lived at all. When his impulsive actions had disastrous results, this was regrettable. But if he had had the normal dose of ordinary common sense, his name would long ago have disappeared among the multitude of efficient leaders who chose to walk the middle of the road. When he refuses to own anything, or kisses the hand of the leper, we may wonder if he has acted wisely. Whichever path he took, Francis never walked the middle of the road.

Footnotes

1. *Vie de Jésu* (Paris, 1861), p. xcix.

2. *I Celano* 71; *Omnibus*, pp. 288–289.

3. Fioretti 10; *Omnibus*, pp. 1322–1323.

4. *I Celano* 54; *Omnibus*, p. 272.

5. Huygens, op. cit., p. 76. This passage is considered by many to be a marginal note which somehow became part of the text. However, on the basis of the manuscripts, Huygens believes that the text is indeed authentic.

6. Giordano di Giano, *Sur les routes*, pp. 71, 72.

7. H. J. Berger, *Kijk op het leven van alledag* (Amsterdam, 1972).

8. *II Celano* 102; *Omnibus*, p. 446.

9. This note is now generally accepted as genuine. It was written at the beginning of 1224, before Anthony left for southern France. It is an extremely important document as, in a way, it decided the question whether Francis was for or against study. Under certain cir-

cumstances, he had no objections.

Anthony was born in Lisbon in 1195 and was a canon regular of St. Augustine. More or less by chance, he attended the chapter of the Friars Minor in Porziuncola in 1221. This made such a deep impression on him that he joined the order. Anthony was not a bishop, but Francis uses this title to show his respect for a professor of theology.

10. Testament; *Omnibus*, pp. 67–68.

11. See H. Th. Laureilhé, *Sur les routes*, p. 58.

12. *II Celano* 25; *Omnibus*, p. 383.

13. See Huizinga, *Merkwaardige voorbeelden*, chap. 12. Eng. equivalent: *Waning of the Middle Ages* (New York, Doubleday).

14. *II Celano* 63; *Omnibus*, p. 415.

15. *Spec. Perf.* 65; *Omnibus*, p. 1192. This must have been in 1216, some years before he was appointed Francis' patron and protector. Celano could not deny that Francis had enemies: "Were there not many people, especially in the beginning, who conspired to bring about the downfall of the fledgling order?" And later: "To Francis, many of them seemed like a pack of angry wolves."

16. *I Celano* 73; *Omnibus*, pp. 289-290.

17. *II Celano* 58; *Omnibus*, pp. 412-413. Also *Spec. Perf.* 6; *Omnibus*, p. 1132. The two texts are the same and the source is almost certainly Brother Leo, Francis' confessor and probably an eyewitness.

18. From 1223 on, schools suddenly spring up throughout the order. Many theologians followed Anthony of Padua, the best known of whom are Bonaventure, Roger Bacon, Occam, and Duns Scotus.

19. 2 Cor 6:10.

16

Movement and Structure

"**F**rancis himself is not important," a young Capuchin writes today. "But then he did not want to be important. He only wanted to make the gospel his life and assemble around him a group of men who desired to follow that same way of life. In this he succeeded sublimely. He showed us that it could be done, and we are grateful to him for this. But that is really all he means to us. As far as the life he lived is concerned, and the way that he lived it—we can learn nothing from him."[1]

The writer takes us back to the little church of San Nicolà, where Francis goes to the altar, opens the missal, and finds—his Lord. What he then says and does has retreated far into the past for that young Capuchin. "I do not often think of Francis. He himself referred us to the gospel."

If I agreed completely with these words I would never have written this book. And yet they give pause for thought, for this young man speaks for a large portion of his generation. And the words of Paul Valéry are still valid: "Youth foretells by its very existence." The older generation can only guess what the future will bring, but youth is closing in on it.

The trend that is evident in the quote about Francis is not new. It is the age-old longing to see beyond the superficial and transitory, to search for the true nature of things. The novel element is the total rejection of the personal cachet which Francis gave his order. It is a mystery to me why the writer became a Capuchin and not, for instance, a Jesuit. His view is that of many young people and he unconsciously betrays the fact that the Franciscan Order, like almost every other order, is going through an identity crisis.

It is of little use to ask how Francis would have reformed his order had he lived today. His greatness lies in the fact that in *his* day and *his* situation he found the words and actions which appealed to religious men *then*. He was a man of the Middle Ages and a man of Umbria, and it is as such that we must see him. Francis as he was is gone forever. Whoever wants to exercise the same influence today must discover and shape the religious stirrings of our day.

But this does not mean that Francis can no longer inspire. The Capuchin's judgment of Francis is vague—"make the gospel his life . . . assemble a group . . . that same way of life." *How* did Francis live by the gospel? And *how* did he shape the group around him? Francis' answer—the answer of Francis the mystic and prophet—cannot be ignored by anyone who believes that great men have a message for all ages.

It is strange to think that Francis' movement really started out just as the Capuchin writer says. During its initial stages, he did not intend to formalize the movement by structures. Those pieces of parchment which he and his brothers presented to Pope Innocent III, though we refer to them as a rule, were scarcely worthy of the name. The original text has been lost, but apparently Francis was partial to this rule, even after he had composed others, for he writes later in his Testament: "The Almighty himself revealed to me that I should live according to the holy gospel. And I had this written down in a few simple words, and my lord the pope confirmed it for me."[2]

In the course of time, certain provisions were added under the force of circumstances, though as a whole it remained somewhat haphazard. The tragedy of such a movement is that sooner or later its free and natural rhythm must be contained. Movement becomes organization, and an organization needs the discipline of a constitution.

So when, in the midst of a crisis in his order, Francis realizes that the movement must be given a more definite form, he sets himself down, as the penitent idealist he is, to fulfill a task for which he feels not the slightest inclination: to produce a new and better rule for his order. He retreats to the quiet of nature, spends long hours in prayer, and then dictates (he was already partially blind) what would come to be known as the Rule of 1221.

Francis took no great pains to make this work a masterpiece. He called it *"forma vitae,"* which is generally translated as "way of life." But the word *forma* tells us that he means this evangelical rule of life to be the all-inspiring source and foundation of religious life within the order.

No wonder, then, that in the midst of the regulations and clauses the inspiration of Francis is tangibly present. On the last page he breaks into passionate prayer, as if, suddenly freed from legal chains, he could forget about regulations and say what was in his heart. "Let us all, everywhere and always, daily and without interruption, sincerely and humbly, believe in Him, guard Him in our hearts and love Him, honor Him, adore, serve, praise and bless Him the Almighty, exalted and eternal God."[3]

If Francis had been allowed to write his own, personal *forma vitae,* it would have been a religious masterpiece, as heartwarming and passionate as the above prayer, but he did not have the opportunity to do so, since others had convinced him that the order had to have a legally sound rule.

But this rule, too, had its failings. It was accepted by the chapter of the order in 1221,[4] but was not considered worthy of papal approval. No legal Church document could end with a prayer like that! Also, there were certain disjointed passages which needed a bit of polishing, and probably the more practical minds in the order, with Cardinal Ugolino their spokesman, urged Francis to write a new piece, shorter, more orderly, and better suited to be submitted to Rome for approval.

Francis was a failure as a writer of rules. He would have to do his work over. Armed with the necessary instructions and good advice, he again retreats into loneliness, with Brother Leo and a Bologna-educated legal man, Brother Bonizzo. He retires to the quiet of Fonte Colombo in the Rieti Valley, where the little church still stands, and where one can still see on the wall the probably authentic signature of Francis, the Greek letter *tau*.[5] One can visit the stone cave, with the magnificent view over the plains, where in prayer and meditation Francis penned his thoughts and submitted them to the judgment of his brothers.

This so-called Second Rule, which was approved[6] by Pope Honorius, is much shorter, and one cannot escape the impression that here is a man who is no longer allowed to be himself. Original impulses alternate with legally polished phrases, and one feels intuitively what this attempt to make the best of a bad thing must have cost the author. To a certain extent, he succeeded in his task, but something of Francis was lost in the process.

Comparison between the Rule of 1223 and that of 1221 indirectly illuminates the situation in which Francis found himself with respect to his legal advisors and, through them, the Lateran. In the Rule of 1223 much has been omitted which was not suitable for an official Church document. Besides the closing prayer, one misses the heartwarming cry, "And whoever comes to the brothers, friend or foe, thief or bandit, he must be received in a friendly manner."[7]

This is truly Francis. Nowhere in his writings do we find

a more original view of the social breakthrough and the realization of world brotherhood. This passage from the rule is indeed surprising; but all his life Francis startled popes, cardinals, exegists, and theologians with the originality of his follies. As he does here with the refreshing remark about thieves and bandits. No wonder that this passage was omitted from the later rule. An order cannot forever attend to the needs of guests who have even less notion of the rights of property owners than the followers of *il Poverello!*

The fact remains that even the Rule of 1223 is truly inspired by Francis. The author has so remained himself that the style of the piece bears no resemblance to the manner in which the Curia was accustomed to express itself. Alongside the legal formulas of Bonizzo and Ugolino,[8] one is struck by the carefree colloquialism of Francis. One might be excused for thinking that Francis is not quite used to having legal advisors, but is too modest—or no longer free—to reject any of their suggestions. But this is not true. The Rule of 1223, too, is his work. *Le style, c'est l'homme,* and this document, with its constant deviations where concentration is of the essence, betrays the mobile, inventive mind of the author. One must respect the tact of the legal expert, Ugolino, for supporting Francis in this. Following a passage on clothing, Francis felt compelled to add: "And they may with the blessing of God patch their clothes with remnants or anything at hand."[9] (We can see Ugolino nodding patiently.) This gives Francis yet another idea: "And I admonish and warn them not to judge or look down upon those who are attired in rich and colorful garments and dine on fine foods; but rather let everyone judge and look down upon himself." Having mildly admonished his brothers to speak humbly, politely, and gently to others, as is expected of them, he suddenly says "and they may not ride horseback." The consoling remark that "those who cannot read need not trouble themselves to learn" was not the work of a judicial advisor. Nor those sections in which the brothers are allowed the freedom, within the legal framework, to express something of a personal inspiration.

In view of the above, I cannot credit the theory of Sabatier and others that Francis' flame was extinguished by a papal candle-snuffer. The official Church did not publicize his rule. It did not even take the trouble to provide it with an original foreword, but considered the standard form sufficient.

I would almost support the apparently paradoxical claim that it was not the Curia or Ugolino who undermined the inner force of the rule, but Francis' own brothers when they undertook to comment on it! Some of them viewed the rule as an ascetic document which was to be interpreted as strictly as possible. They succumbed to the pull of monastic life and saw poverty more as ascetic constraint than evangelical liberation.

They did not understand Francis' evolution in his view of poverty. He had an aversion to commentators, which is understandable when we consider that he lived in the golden age of legalistic thinking. During the first thousand years of Church history the dioceses enjoyed a great measure of freedom. Later, Rome sought, not always without reason, a certain centralization, and slowly its influence began to grow. But, as Führmann says, "there was still a long stretch of canon road to be traveled before all rights were sealed within the papal cross."[10] After Gregory VII[11] and especially after Innocent III, the authority and influence of the lawyer-popes and their Curia was on the increase. Even in matters of law, the parallel pope-emperor was evident. From now on, popes would establish the laws without consulting the local synods. The universities of Bologna and Paris raised canon law to one of the most influential branches of the Church. The gospel was revised according to canon law.

This legal *nouvelle vague* did not spare the convents. While Francis was aiming for a sublime simplicity, the true meaning of the rule sank steadily deeper under the spade of the excavating commentators. They discovered in the rule a wealth of opportunities for falling into mortal sin. Anyone who can summon the courage to read the complete explanation of the rule in the *Speculum Minorum* will discover no fewer than sixty-one occasions.[12] Rome later reduced this number to twenty-five—still quite a respectable number for brothers who had fled the world with all its temptations. This process, which led from inspiration to casuistics, from casuistics to unimaginative docility, and then to a suffocating asceticism, was not limited to Francis' followers. The idols of religious youth in those days were often young men who preached a rigorous cult of rule, with no opportunity for free interpretation. The law, whether of Church or state, must be upheld. But things have come to a sorry pass when the book of law is placed on the altar between two lighted candles.

The commentators had little understanding of the freedom Francis left to his brothers. It was never his intention to deprive his followers of the inspiration which God granted them. Father Esser remarks that on ten separate occasions Francis makes use of a formula which relieves the rule of its coercive character.[13] His favorite expression was "as God inspires you," which withdraws the barrier the rule placed between God and the brothers. With his knowledge of human nature, Francis wished to guard his brothers against "holy" indolence and the temptation to barter one's responsibility for the slavish observance of a set of rules. Moreover, he realized that at times God might even consider rules and regulations an obstacle to his inspiration.

The rule may have brought to a close the period in which the brothers were free to travel as they wished, but it was of a frankness and openness unknown in the old abbeys. The brothers are not bound for life to one convent, but are allowed to go from place to place in small groups. A missionary bishop writes in his diary: "Two priests and a brother worker. A few months ago they moved into an apartment in a modest working-class district. The little group lives simply and to the other apartment-dwellers, and indeed to the whole neighborhood, they belong here. I spent an evening there and shared a meal with them. They were stimulating hours. This way of life, this communal form, the twofold development of a charisma so beautifully keyed to the tradition of St. Francis of Assisi, this evening prayer around the table at which the Eucharist is often celebrated . . . this is the true poverty for which the Church of today is searching.''[14]

In spite of his liberal views on freedom, Francis never considered authority as something to be reserved for emergencies. He found in the gospel not only love but a form of obedience. It is not easy to penetrate the consciousness of a man who believed that he had been entrusted by the Almighty with a special mission, a man who addressed his letters ''to all the clergy'' and ''to all Christian believers,'' and who nevertheless bowed to Church authority.

More than once this caused him serious inner conflict, particularly when the official Church obstructed his inspiration. He was not one of those faithful who humbly lay their enterprise at the foot of the papal throne and then await the verdict. His very first meeting with Innocent shows an independent attitude.

But he seems never to have known the crisis of one who continually asks himself if he should *allow* himself to follow the Church. He knew its weaknesses and those of its leaders, as few others. But he saw through them as through a clouded window: ''I want to take refuge in them [the priests] though they may persecute me. . . . I do not choose to see what is sinful in them, because I see in them the Son of God, and they are my masters.''[15]

Perhaps there are readers who wonder impatiently why Francis did not protest more vehemently. Was it not the duty of a man who had such influence over the people to turn his gaze to other gospel texts than those on poverty and docility? These are perfectly natural questions today, when demolishing structures is something of a daily pastime. Putting aside the question whether Francis possessed the necessary qualifications for a religious revolutionary, we know that he proposed an evangelical change of heart. Not the protest of the prophet is of primary importance but his inspiring example. Knowing Francis' impulsive and sometimes fiery temperament, we can assume that at some point in his life he was confronted with the choice between rebellion and resignation. But he felt instinctively that for *him,* in *his* situation, the best, indeed the only way was eloquent silence. In the midst of the hierarchical class society of Church and state in which he lived, he does not go around distributing pamphlets, but he writes in the Rule of 1221: "Thus the brothers may hold no position of power, and certainly not among themselves."[16] This may make him seem defenseless, but it is a glorious example of true "fraternity and equality."

The history of the rule shows how Francis undertook the same task with which kindred spirits in today's religious movements are confronted. He placed the veil of his rule around a "few parts of the gospel." And although, or perhaps because, his was not a legal mind, the veil rests as lightly as the *peplos* on the shoulders of the women of Greece. It is clear that this veil could not be meant for all ages. But Francis created, for his own age, a harmony between movement and structure which has endured for centuries.

Until this period, the power and influence of the founder were almost absolute—he *was* authority. Only when he had become a stranger to many did this influence wane. He was obliged to transfer that power to an authorized rule, and this was, for him, the sign that his day was over, especially in light of his failing health. He resigned as minister-general, though he never lost his inner authority.[17] His resignation had far-reaching consequences. His movement had lost its wild offshoots, and with them its amazing spontaneity. As so often happens, authority came to rest in the hands of the middle-of-the-roaders.

Footnotes

1. *Franciscaans Leven* (1967), 50:239.

2. Testament; *Omnibus*, p. 68.

3. Rule of 1221, 23; *Omnibus*, p. 52.

4. Giordano reports that at the chapter of 1221 (at which he was present) no fewer than 3,000 brothers were in attendance. According to Eccleston, who was not present, 5,000 brothers from all parts of the world were assembled there. Because there were not enough beds and the brothers had to sleep on mats, this chapter has been called the "Chapter of Mats."

Giordano remarks: "I have never experienced such a chapter, as regards the number of brothers as well as the solemn atmosphere engendered by the presence of so many important personages [among them Ugolino and Anthony of Padua]. And although there were a very great many brothers, the people living in the neighborhood were so friendly and helpful, that after seven days they were forced to close the door and refuse all further gifts. They remained two extra days in order to finish all the food which had been donated." Giordano could never quite forget the luxury of that chapter. (See *Sur les routes*, p. 30.) Francis was seriously ill during this chapter; he was suffering from malaria and an eye affliction, and had Elias present to the brothers what he wanted to say. "He sat at Elias' feet and tugged at a corner of his habit when he wanted to say something; Elias leaned forward to listen to him," says Giordano, who is extremely reliable when it comes to matters of detail.

5. In all probability, Francis was inspired to adopt this remarkable signature by a passage from Innocent's opening speech at the Fourth Lateran Council. "Tau," the Pope had said in connection with Ez 9:4-6, "is the last letter of the Jewish alphabet. He who bears this sign upon the forehead has submitted all his deeds to the power of the cross; in the words of the Apostle: 'They have crucified their flesh with all its vices and greed' (Gal 5:24)." The *tau* signature is on Francis' letter to Brother Leo and on the earliest manuscript of his Letter to the Clergy.

6. By the papal bull *Solet annuere* of Nov. 29, 1223. This has been preserved in the sacristy of the convent next to the basilica in Assisi.

7. Rule of 1221, 17. *Omnibus*, p. 38.

8. In his bull *Quo elongati*, Ugolino, then Pope Gregory IX, writes: "And we assisted him in composing the abovementioned rule (1223)

as well as in acquiring papal approval, when we occupied a lower office"—that of cardinal!

9. Rule of 1223, 2; *Omnibus*, p. 59.

10. H. F. Führmann, "Pseudo-Isodor in Rom," *Zeitschrift für kirchliche Geschichte* (1967), vol. 68.

11. Gregory VII stresses the amicable nature of his contact with the bishops. See L. Meulenbery, *Tijdschrift van Theologie* (1970), 1:48ff.

12. *Speculum Fratrum Minorum* (Venice, 1530), compiled by several brothers.

13. *Sint Franciscus* (1965).

14. See *Katholieke Informatie* (Nov. 20, 1971), 28:28.

15. Testament; *Omnibus*, p. 67.

16. Rule of 1221, 5; *Omnibus*, p. 35.

17. His successor was Pietro di Cattaneo, who died within a year. He was succeeded by Brother Elias Bonbarone, who was not a priest.

17

Alverna

It might be considered a strange gesture for a noble-man to grant a monk the uses of a mountain. Only a man of the Middle Ages could conceive such a preposterous plan, a man like Orlando del Cattani, count of Chiusi. One evening, during a party, he was so impressed by Francis' words that he offered him the use of 4,000-feet-high Alverna. He added: "By Mount Alverna we, and the witnesses here present, mean the whole area with the trees, rocks, and meadows which form this mountain, from the summit to the area which surrounds the foot on all sides."[1]

Orlando believed that anyone who could preach so compellingly needed space and solitude in which to prepare himself. "The mountain," he maintained, though not from personal experience, "is most suitable for someone wishing to do penance."[2] And from then on Francis and his brothers had their hermitages there.

Today, many people take quite a different view of the hermit's life. They do not object to Francis' visiting hospitals, cutting off the sleeve of his habit to give to some creature even poorer tha himself, or going about preaching

his message of peace. But when he retires to pray in solitude—well, they shake their head at the mere suggestion of
such an unproductive enterprise. Why hide somewhere on
the top of a mountain when there are so many wrongs to
be righted down in the valley? Anyone who has ever scoured
the countryside in search of someone to fill a position of
responsibility must view with irritation the monasteries of
Carmelites and Trappists, where so many useful lives are
"wasted" in prayer and contemplation. Every hour in which
no ships are unloaded, no motors hum, and no plows fur-
row the earth is lost to prosperity.

By such standards, Francis could indeed look back on a
completely wasted life. This man, who was capable of heal-
ing so much of the misery around him, spent many years of
his short life in one of mankind's most unproductive activities. He even had to resist the temptation to do nothing
but that. Even after he understood that the Lord meant him
to offer the Church of his day the radical example of the
gospel, he regularly interrupted his work to pray in solitude, sometimes for months at a time.

Perhaps "interrupt" is not the right word. He knew from
experience—and in a deeper sense than Count Orlando meant
—that a prophet who devotes himself exclusively to work
will find himself saying things which are no longer based
on personal conviction. Whoever sees the retreat of the
monk into the mountains as egocentric escape understands
nothing of the inner strength with which that monk descends
the mountain and enters the world again.

In August 1224 Francis climbed Alverna. The tourist who
today ascends the mountain by car will find it difficult to
imagine what it cost the poor, exhausted body of Francis,
mounted on a donkey, to follow those winding paths to the
top, where steep rocks suddenly open to a view of the
valleys below. Worry, deprivation, and sickness had taken
their toll of this 42-year-old man. But what happens now is
typical of the truly religious man: while the body steadily
weakens, almost to the breaking point, the spiritual ascent

continues. Biographers tell us little of Francis' spiritual development, but enough to know that the man who makes his way laboriously to the top of Alverna passed through many phases as he came closer and closer to secret union with God. And closer to the moment at which that unity will be symbolized by a tangible sign.

Francis always felt at home high in the mountains, and now he sought release from the latest cares and problems of his order, the disappointment and misunderstanding. He allows himself to be brought to a cave in the rock face. Today a grating covers the place where Francis slept, and the damp slabs of stone have changed very little. A mysterious happening took place in his life, around age 24; it suddenly made him a man with an all-pervading vision, so overwhelming that the rest of his life was devoted to its realization. We can never understand this experience. It is Francis' deeply personal secret. But to put it very simply, in an instant he was captured forever by Jesus Christ and his gospel. Year by year he penetrated ever more deeply into the existence of God, until he reached the highest form attainable on earth, the mystical vision of God. He is to experience it for forty days in the loneliness of Alverna (from the 15th of August to the 29th of September, the feast of St. Michael). He shuts himself off from his brothers, and only Brother Leo is allowed to bring him a little bread and water, as sustenance on his spiritual journey toward the invisible and unknowable.

Released from care and worry, he surrenders himself to prayer. But with Francis, the words of prayer continually flow into wordless ecstacy. Sources which quote Brother Leo, an eyewitness, tell of Francis' emotional outbursts. In his many hours of seclusion, Francis would call out to his Lord; then all would fall still again. The body lay helpless in the grip of the mind; consciousness of the world outside disappeared; time ceased to flow. Everything faded away before the unspeakable, which the mind was experiencing. If a brother happened to intrude, he discovered a figure which showed no sign of life, save for the expression of the eyes, which stared into an invisible world. The bishop of Assisi, who once entered Francis' cell without knocking and found him in ecstacy, "was suddenly seized by a paralysis of fear and was unable to utter a word.[3]

Celano also tells us how Francis took a few brothers and retreated into the loneliness of the mountains in order to speak with God about the problems of his order. "And slowly an unspeakable joy and happiness penetrated the depths of his soul. The exaltation began, fear and doubt disappeared, and he went into ecstacy."[4]

In the normal development of a contemplative life, mystical experiences are seldom lacking. Many mystics have tried to describe these experiences, and although they are the first to admit that their words are a mere stammering approximation of an indescribable happening, there is a fundamental similarity in their descriptions. At such moments the presence of God is experienced as the nearness of a person, a presence felt without benefit of senses. It approaches a kind of all-transforming union between God and man. "In true contemplative life," says Ruusbroeck, "we feel that we are being swallowed into a bottomless chasm of endless happiness where we experience no distinction between God and ourselves."

Francis never discussed his mystical experiences, and though we may wish that we could enter the depths of his consciousness, we must remain outside. Only those may enter who (like his biographer Bonaventure) have experienced this vision of God. What Francis felt and saw during those nights of prayer in the caves of Umbria and Sabina remains a secret, but something of the atmosphere, something tangible, is still commemorated on Alverna.

Every night for more than seven centuries the bells on Alverna have summoned the brothers from the Chiesa Maggiore, the convent church, to a small chapel. There, two of them point to a stone before the altar while the others sing: *Signast hic, Domine, servum tuum signis redemptionis nostrae* (Here, Lord, is your servant [Francis], signed with the signs of our redemption). The chapel stands on the spot which, shortly after his death, the brothers indicated as authentic, and it almost seems as if in all those 750 years nothing has changed.[5]

Anyone who, having the day before toured the busy Italian cities, joins the procession through the dark night and listens to the centuries-old Gregorian hymn might be excused for thinking he had been returned to a medieval world, filled with a medieval faith. He no longer finds it strange that Francis and his brothers lived here in their hermitages. Indeed, it seems somehow fitting that here, at the pinnacle of his mystical development, Francis experienced a miracle.

It is important to realize that this is no legend from the Fioretti. For one thing, Celano, who describes the incident, is an educated man and it is certain that he knew the act of canonization. His account is corroborated almost literally by the Three Companions, one of whom at least (Leo) was with Francis on Alverna. Here, first of all, is Celano's account.

[During his stay on Alverna Francis received from God the following vision: a man in the form of a seraph with six wings appeared above him in the air. He was nailed to a cross with outstretched arms, one foot over the other. Two wings were raised above his head, two others were stretched out as for flight, and the other two covered his body. This vision greatly amazed the servant of God, and he could not understand its meaning. . . .

His mind had not yet fathomed it and his feelings were totally involved with this vision, when the traces of four nails began to appear in his hands and feet, as he had just seen them on the crucified seraph.[6]

This is the phenomenon that has since become known as stigmata. (It will not be difficult for the reader to accept it "as a phenomenon.") As early as the last century, Dr. Imbert-Gourbeyre compiled a catalogue of persons who possessed the stigmata, in which, after more or less critical examination, 321 cases were noted.[7] It cannot be denied that there are cases of wounds in hands and feet which are psychopathological in origin; however, some deeply religious persons have had the stigmata, and science, at least to the present, has been able to find no satisfactory explanation. A critical physician and psychologist, Dr. Biot, concludes his extensive study of stigmata with the confession that he faces a mystery. A Catholic who cannot be accused of extreme liberalism, he writes at the end of his study: "We believe that there is no proof that the stigmata are supernatural in origin and represent a sign from God. We can summarize our conclusion as follows: the mystery of the stigmata remains a mystery."[8] Even more significant is his statement: "Let us not forget [with respect to the form of the stigmata] that one single fact is absolutely unique: Francis' hands and feet show the marks of nails. What the followers of the *Poverello* saw distinguishes itself completely from that which witnesses [of other stigmata] have since recorded."[9]

When we examine the phenomenon more closely, we see that other stigmatized persons, in contrast with Francis, show no more than wounds. The Three Companions report that at Francis' death they saw nails which had been formed by his own flesh. And Celano, who almost certainly was present at Francis' funeral, says: "His hands and feet seemed to be pierced in the middle by nails, the heads of which were visible in the palm of the hand and on the instep of the foot, while the point of the nail emerged on the other side."[10]

Few facts in Francis' life were observed by such a multitude of witnesses as his stigmata. Besides the Three Companions and Celano, we have Brother Benizzo, who cried out in tears: "My sinful eyes have seen them (the stigmata) and my sinful hands have touched them." Francis' successor mentions the stigmata in his funeral oration and

Bonaventure based his statements on the testimony of eye-witnesses.[11]

If one believes that on Alverna Francis underwent the most exalted mystical experience imaginable, he will readily accept that what happened there was more than a clinical phenomenon. In this atmosphere of ecstatic love, the total synthesis of mind and body, the phenomenon of the stigmata has become a symbol of Francis' likeness to his Master. For his followers, it was tangible proof that God, on Alverna, had accepted this man and with him his order. The Church has given this event a special place in the liturgy. It has inspired countless artists, and Dante says of it:

> Nel crudo sasso, intra Severe ed Arno
> da Christo prese l'ultime sigillo
> che le sue membre du'anni portarno.[12]

In our secular world, not only the miraculous sign but the Christian mystique as a whole have lost much of their credibility and influence. "It's too late for your kind of mysticism," a man says to his pious wife. "We don't have time for all that. All these years so little has been done with all that mysticism that now we have almost everything left to do. That's why we need level-headed organization men. History shows, Nelly, that mysticism is extremely dangerous for the development of humanity. Instead of making the blind see, it has closed many eyes. It has made people immune to the suffering of others."[13]

The figure of Francis, as he experiences the presence of God, represents a problem to the nonbeliever. Francis cannot be anything but the victim of an illusion: He speaks to nothingness, he labors for a hallucination. If he finds here the strength for a life of service—and no one will deny that he does—it is in a nonexistent dimension, eternal perhaps and founded in charity, but no more substantial than air. Thus the nonbeliever does not shrink from explaining the experience of Francis on Alverna. An emaciated ascetic, product of a cultural background full of mystical symbols, spends weeks in isolation high on a mountain. Such a man cannot but live in a fantastic dream world. And if his dream hero is a god, then this god will speak to him, as he spoke to Moses on Mount Sinai.

This explains much—but not why so many people gaze in admiration at that figure kneeling in prayer, why they are not satisfied by the explanation psychiatry offers. It seems to me that a psychiatrist who interprets religion as a delusion may be right if he is talking about neurotic forms of religious experience, but here the theory of illusion is tried to the utmost. Is it not possible that Francis, in an area in which his mastery was supreme, has looked one dimension deeper than the psychiatrist—into a dimension which remains forever closed to purely scientific minds?

Perhaps it was this dimension which Hamlet meant when he said "there are more things in heaven and on earth, Horatio, than are dreamt of in your philosophy."

Footnotes

1. Act dated July 9, 1274. This act was drawn up by the heirs of Count del Cattani and confirms the story from the Fioretti concerning the offer he made on May 8, 1213. See Fioretti, "Consideration on the Holy Stigmata"; *Omnibus*, p. 1431.

2. Ibid.

3. *II Celano* 100; *Omnibus*, p. 444. See also *Leg. Major* X, 5; *Omnibus*, pp. 708–709.

4. *I Celano* 26; *Omnibus*, p. 250.

5. The chapel was built in 1263, when several brothers who had known Francis personally were still alive. This placing of the altar may be considered historically authentic.

6. *I Celano* 94; *Omnibus*, p. 309.

7. *La stigmatisation* . . . (Bellet, Clermont, 1894). The first, in chronological order, is that of Francis. Then there is a kind of outbreak of stigmatizations. Dr. Imbert-Gourbeyre noted thirty-one in the first seventy years after Francis' death.

8. Dr. Biot is chairman of the Institute for Endocrinology and Psychology in Lyons. His work is titled *L'Enigme des stigmatisés* (A. Fayard).

9. Loc. cit., p. 111. He adds: "Objectively considered, this is an essential difference, comparable to the distinction which physicians would make between a fracture and cancer."

10. See *I Celano* 95; *Omnibus*, p. 309.

11. Eccleston, 13. See *Sur les routes*, p. 125. In 1914 F. Pennacchi published in *Miscellanea Franciscana* (XV, 129–137) a document from the archives of Sacro Convento (Str. XIV, 1) containing the names of several witnesses who had seen the stigmata, both before and after Francis' death. The document was written by an unknown brother in 1237. For the most part, the witnesses who are mentioned appear in the documents of the city of Assisi. See Fortini, op. cit., p. 449.

12. We prefer to use the Italian text (*Paradiso*, XI, 36): "On the stony rock between Tiber and Arno he received from Christ the ultimate sign which his members bore for two years."

13. Fem Rutke, *Open brief aan de Rots* (Bruges, 1970), p. 118.

18

Praise to You, My Lord

There is a hymn which Francis is said to have recited on taking leave of Alverna, which begins: *"O monte, monte di Dio* . . . Holy mountain, fertile mountain, on which God has desired to reside." And it ends: *"Monte Alverna . . . non ci vedremo.* We shall not meet again."

It is difficult to say whether this hymn is the work of Francis, but it was indeed prophetic: Francis never saw Alverna again. He spent two more years traveling through Italy, and this leads us to believe that his illness had not yet reached its final stages, though traveling was torture for him due to the stigmata.

The chronological sequence of Francis' travels throughout Italy will probably never be established with complete certainty.[1] We know that from Alverna he returned to Porziuncola, but apostolic wanderlust gave him no peace and he set off again, astride a donkey and accompanied by a few brothers. In 1225 he was in Subiaco, where he had spent two months in the Benedictine convent in 1221. Walking the steep road to the convent gate, one feels the intense loneliness of the spot and understands why Francis was attracted by it. He must have made a deep impression on the Benedictines. There is an authentic picture of him[2] on the wall of the chapel, and in a missal dating from before 1238 his letter "To All the Clergy," which found its way to the convent during Francis' lifetime.

After a short stay, Francis set off over the Abruzzi and arrived in Sarnano. The following incident took place in this region and was recorded by an eyewitness in the middle of the thirteenth century. When, toward evening, Francis was preparing to leave the little town of San Verocondo on his donkey, the farmers called him back and said, "Brother Francis, don't go on. Stay with us. There's a dangerous wolf prowling about that could devour your donkey and might do you serious harm." Francis, who had had more than one encounter with wolves, answered: "What have I ever done to Brother Wolf that he should devour our Brother Donkey? Good-bye, brothers, and fear God."[3]

Several months later he was back in Porziuncola, weakened by an intestinal disease and half blind, with a cloth over his eyes. His condition caused such concern that Elias, then minister-general, appointed four brothers to keep watch over him.

It was becoming clear, even to Francis, that he was suffering from an incurable disease and that his days of travel were past. He asked to be brought to San Damiano to take his leave of Clare and her sisters.[4] He was installed in a dilapidated hovel next to the convent, where he was overcome by a terrible depression. There are situations in life which approach absolute suffering, when fear, pain, and loneliness blur one's whole existence like an impenetrable mist. Francis went through this kind of hell, so that even his strong spirit threatened to succumb. He had to endure a crisis of loneliness from God, torn by doubt whether he would ever win back the love of his Master. It is (to us unimaginable) the emptiness of *le manque de Dieu*.

He spent his days and nights in complete darkness—in physical darkness as well, since his eyes could not bear the light of even one candle. Biographers also mention a plague of mice that year, so that Francis knew not à moment's peace. All the while he felt the terror of one who, in the face of death, believes that his whole life is a failure. But Francis did not curse the day of his birth. In all his despair and desolation he knew one thing: that God exists.

This crisis lasted two months, and then—in a flash—came the answer: the overwhelming certainity that he was in God's love and would remain there. Exultation went through him and irresistible inspiration. He began to sing: *"Altissimu, omnipotente, Bonsignore* . . . Most high omnipotent good Lord. . ."

It is with these words that the Canticle of the Creatures begins.[5] It is one of the most simple and yet most unfathomable creations in literature. Even before the discoveries of the philosopher Bachelard and his school, Chesterton intuitively understood that "from this one poem it is almost possible to reconstruct the whole person of Francis." This is true. No other work, by Francis or by any of his biographers, more clearly, more deeply, reveals his personality than the Canticle of the Creatures. It is rooted in his childhood years, but only later did it burst forth spontaneously, in a moment of tremendous emotion.

The "prologue" to this poem lay in the anguish he had just passed through. Without this anguish, the work is incomplete, inexplicable. Without it, we could never understand that *"Altissimu, omnipotente, Bonsignore"* is not a formal opening but an expression of unutterable gratitude, bursting from a soul that has been released from fear and has found peace. The *Altissimu* is a cry from the heart, as if Francis is trying to fly to the arms of his Lord. A composer who at the close of his symphony finds that his instruments cannot begin to express what he wants to say, has the human voice sing out above the rest. Francis calls on all creation.[6]

The feeling of liberation which enveloped him explains the absence of any quality of menace in the elements. Francis knows that water can cause floods, that fire can destroy, that wind can turn into a hurricane. But the cosmos holds no threat for him, and he feels compelled to give expression to this inner peace.

The poem is simply constructed: first the opening address to the Most High, then six stanzas in which the elements are arranged in pairs, descending from sky to earth. Brother Sun and Sister Moon, Brother Wind and Sister Water, Brother Fire and Sister Earth are called upon as the heralds of this song of praise.[7] We give here the translation of the poem from the Italian, conscious of the loss of the magnificent sound of this language, then still in its primordial form.[8]

The Canticle of the Creatures

Most high omnipotent good Lord, to Thee
Praise, glory, honor, and every benediction.

To Thee alone Most High do they belong.
And no man is worthy to pronounce Thy Name.

Praise be to Thee my Lord with all Thy creatures.
Especially for Master Brother Sun
Who illuminates the day for us,
And Thee Most High he manifests.

Praise be to Thee my Lord for Sister Moon and for the stars,
In heaven Thou hast formed them, shining, precious, fair.

Praise be to Thee my Lord for Brother Wind,
For air and clouds, clear sky and all the weathers
Through which Thou sustainest all Thy creatures.

Praise be to Thee my Lord for Sister Water,
She is useful and humble, precious and pure.

Praise be to Thee my Lord for Brother Fire,
Through him our night Thou dost enlighten,
And he is fair and merry, boisterous and strong.

Praise be to Thee my Lord for our Sister Mother Earth,
Who nourishes and sustains us all,
Bringing forth diverse fruits
and many-colored flowers and herbs.

Praise be to Thee my Lord
for those who pardon grant for love of Thee
And bear infirmity and tribulation,
Blessed be those who live in peace,
For by Thee Most High they shall be crowned.

Praise be to Thee my Lord for our Sister Bodily Death
From whom no living man can flee;
Woe to them who die in mortal sin
But blessed they who shall be found in thy most holy Will;
To them the second death can do no harm.

O bless and praise my Lord all creatures,
And thank and serve Him in deep humility.[9]

Reading the poem for the first time, one might be excused for thinking that the Canticle belongs to that genre of biblical hymns in which man praises God in his creation. Looking more closely, however, we see that the personality and character of the poet is expressed to a greater degree than in such biblical hymns. Celano says of Francis, "He used the universe as a ladder by which he ascended to the foot of God's throne," but such pious rhetoric tells us nothing about Francis the man. Deeper than piety is the inborn character of the man, which gives form and substance to that piety. Why, for instance, did Francis (and only Francis) see "brothers" and "sisters" ' where other religious figures see only symbols?

What is so striking in this poem is the extraordinarily strong affinity Francis had for the world around him. In the great family of creatures he met all beings with trust, sensitivity, and respect. It is more than poetic imagery when he calls sun, wind, and fire his brothers, and moon, water, and earth his sisters. He has extended *fraternité* and *égalité* to the whole universe. On his travels through Umbria he had always felt that he was one with his friends—the hills, clouds, trees, and murmuring streams along the way. Thus *Sor acqua,* Sister Water (which can be found on the water jugs of Assisi), is the expression of a loving union with water, which he fondly calls "humble, precious and pure."

Francis, who all his life fought against the desire for possessions, did not recognize the pride of the "lord of creation." One does not possess one's brothers and sisters. Foreign to him was the mastery over creation, the dream of our technocratic era, but he penetrated the secrets of matter far more deeply than the nuclear scientist. What continues to amaze and fascinate us in Francis' personality is an unimaginably deep sense of God's immanent presence in his creation. The exact manner in which he felt God's nearness in a bird or rock, the sun or a flower, remains his secret; but one can understand how this man, in his spontaneous religious enthusiasm, could talk to the birds and the fish about God's love. The legends in which these creatures listen in fascination are acceptable as heartwarming poetry, but we would not do justice to the true Francis by placing him in some naive fairy-tale world.

There is something here which goes much deeper. Two elements in his character form a unique synthesis. Francis had a natural affinity for the cosmos, but because he was also a mystic, he experienced God and the universe as one. And this is a fundamental aspect of his personality. Celano, too, understands that this is unique, and the examples he gives corroborate and confirm this uniqueness. "Never did a man have such love for all creatures; he spoke to them of the Lord and urged them to praise him. He allowed candles and torches to die out, rather than extinguish these lights, which are the symbol of eternal light. When the brothers went out to chop wood, he forbade them to destroy the trunk of a tree, thus giving it a chance to bring forth new shoots. . . . He picked up worms from the ground lest they should be trodden upon by passersby. To save bees from starvation in the winter, he had good wine and honey brought to them. He called all creatures his brothers, but had a special love for the most gentle of them."[10]

And yet this does not tell us all we want to know about the Canticle of the Creatures and its maker. Two elements form the unique Franciscan character: the mystical surrender to God and an extraordinary sensitivity to nature. This was evident to Scheler, the phenomenologist. "It was reserved for one of the greatest sculptors of soul and mind in the history of European man to synthesize, on the one hand, an un-cosmic Christian mysticism and on the other, a cosmic-vital emotional bond with the being and life of nature." And later: "I believe that in this Francis had no predecessor in the history of Western Christianity."[11]

When we listen only to the words of the Canticle we think we understand it. The poet is glorifying God in his creation. But we forget that in the words of Ricoeur, only the philosopher has truly learned how to read—slowly, deeply, with respect, and with one thought uppermost in his mind: there is more here than the words I am reading.

Why did Francis write the way he did? Why did he call on the elements, and choose precisely these attributes with which to describe them? Why does he call water humble and not rebellious? Why does he see the beauty of fire and not its destructive power? Voltaire may have remarked, with some wit, that the adjective is the enemy of the noun, but it can also reveal its depths, and the depths of one's own soul. A forest at dusk may be romantic to one person, terrifying to another. Why? Psychology has made it possible to penetrate the meaning of words to a point where even the speaker is not aware of their true significance, because it has slipped into his subconscious. If it is possible to bring these background details to the surface—and this is the aim of modern psychology—one gains a truer insight not only into the words but also the speaker. This is an important aspect of the study of the Canticle of the Creatures, which enables us to penetrate more deeply into

the personality of Francis. The excellent study by E. Leclerq has been of enormous help in this respect.[12]

Francis does not only observe the elements; by giving
them names he attributes to each a certain value. Thus, for
example, he calls water humble. But this value originated
in his own personality, and he would probably not be able
to explain why he chose this word.

Let us consider the qualities attributed to the moon and
the stars. "In Heaven Thou has formed them, shining,
precious, fair." At first glance, nothing could be more
straightforward. What could lie behind these simple words?
But it is worth noticing that, with the exception of the
Canticle of Creatures, the word precious is used only when
Francis speaks of the Body and Blood of Christ in the
Eucharist. He means here a sacred, mysterious treasure. He
sees the stars in the same way—not in their reality but as
if in a dream. And in this dream they take the form of
something precious, a necklace of jewels emerging from his
inner cosmos. The "precious" brilliance of the sky is the
reflection of a great inner splendor.[13]

Thus it is possible to study in detail each cosmic element in the Canticle of the Creatures, (as Leclerq did)—the
names and qualities the author has given them. If it were
also possible to understand completely how Francis' inner
"cosmos" was projected into the outside universe, we could
enter the very heart of his life, his love and his poetry.[14]
But it is clear that his cosmic-mystical talents give everything an original color and nuance. The chemist would be
surprised to hear Francis call water humble, but Francis
does not see a chemical compound, or raging sea, or turbulent waterfall. He sees water as he has dreamed of it
in the peace and humility of his soul. "I express myself
by giving expression to the cosmos," says Ricoeur.

The Canticle of the Creatures throws fresh light on what
his biographers tell us. "We who lived beside him constantly witnessed how, inwardly and outwardly, he rejoiced
in all creatures, so that when he touched one of them his

spirit was no longer here on earth, but in heaven." This and many other texts from Leo reveal how, in his subconscious, Francis dreamed the world and, in his imagination, saw it as sacred. Anyone who has difficulty understanding this phenomenon may share Voltaire's view of Francis; he called the poet of the Canticle of the Creatures "a fanatic and crazy man who walks about stark naked and speaks to the animals."[15] I prefer Renan's view: "The most beautiful religious poem since the gospel, the most complete expression of modern religious experience."

Francis exhibited great love for the universe, not only in the Canticle of the Creatures but in all he did. To him the cosmos was an earthly symbol of the divine. "Children have a much more refined sense of the inexpressible than adults," says H. Halbfass.[16] But this gift diminishes as they grow older. In Francis this talent reached extraordinary proportions, combined as it was with his mystical qualities. (Francis contrasts sharply with a man like John of the Cross, who renounced every earthly value.) Duber notes: "A man of heavenly and earthly fire, as Francis was, is rare among those who lead an ascetic life."

When Teilhard de Chardin wrote to his cousin Marghérite, with whom he carried on a long and intimate spiritual correspondence, that she should search for a saint whose "holiness is dynamically sustained by participation in earthly affairs," he recommended, in addition to Catherine of Siena, Francis of Assisi. It is not surprising that a controversial mystic and scholar like Teilhard should feel such an affinity for Francis, whom he admires as "one of the most perfect images and revelations the Church has ever known."[17]

Heavenly and earthly fire. In his "Comment je crois" (1934), Teilhard says that the originality of his faith lies in the fact that it has its roots in two worlds. By his education and intellectual training he is "child of heaven," but through his temperament and professional study "child of earth." Life had placed him at the center of two worlds, but this did not cause any spiritual rupture within Teilhard.

"After 30 years spent in search of inner unity, I have the feeling that a kind of natural synthesis has taken place between these two streams within me."[18]

Francis never took pains to analyze himself so deeply. His nature was too spontaneous. The symbol-sensitive child within him, matured and deepened, could still express fairy-tale wishes. He had the cattle and donkeys given extra hay at Christmas. And he once expressed a wish that the emperor have grain strewn over the highways for the skylarks on feast days.

Francis' contact with the creatures of this earth represents a liberation from the trivial and commonplace of everyday life. Through his sensitivity to the religious symbol in nature he saw in everything the divine depths, not rationally but intuitively. A lighted candle in a dark chapel brought him into the almost tangible presence of the Light. A poppy in a field was a greeting from Beauty itself. Today we see God in our fellow man, while God himself often seems to fade out of consciousness; but to Francis it was in his fellow man that God was closest, especially in the poor and sick. In them the person of the suffering Son of Man was most tangible.

His experiences with animals must have been of a remarkable intimacy, especially in a region where animals were treated as brutes. Thus it is not so strange that a skylark could not be persuaded to leave his shoulder and that a pheasant followed him around. Some of the stories have become almost legendary, but we must remember that they were written down directly after his death, and in such profusion that one cannot deny that there was a very special relationship between Francis and animals. In the Fioretti, a few historical facts have been developed into stories which both touch and amuse us. Here is one of the most famous stories, which, despite its legendary quality, is a true picture of Francis.

In Gubbio a wolf was on the loose, a huge, wild, ravenous beast; and whoever dared to venture outside the city walls took care to be armed. Francis, feeling compassion for the people of the town, disregarded their warnings, and placing his faith in the Lord, he and a companion went out to meet the wolf face to face. "The terrible wolf ran at Francis and his companion with bared teeth. But Francis made the sign of the cross over the animal. It stopped dead and closed its mouth. Francis commanded him: 'Come here, Brother Wolf. In the name of Christ, I forbid you to harm me or anyone else.' The beast came up to him and lay down at his feet. And while the heads of the fearful citizens of Gubbio appeared cautiously over the top of the wall, Francis spoke to the wolf of the evils of devouring people, who are, after all, created in God's image. 'And now, Brother Wolf, I want there to be peace between you and the people. You must cause no more trouble here. Then your crimes will be forgiven you, and neither man nor dog will ever hunt you again.' "[19]

What follows is a product of popular imagination, which always tries to make a good story even better. Nodding its head and wagging its tail, the wolf signified its agreement with the saint's proposal. He was converted on the spot, and from that moment on went from house to house to receive food, humbly and with bowed head. He died in an aura of saintliness, mourned by the citizens of Gubbio.[20]

Many sources mention Francis' habit of talking to animals, in which there is nothing remarkable. When he says, "Praised be our Creator, Brother Pheasant,"[21] this is a kind of pious conversation whose secular form is quite common: a man talking to his dog, for instance. But Francis goes further. Too many sources mention his conversations with birds and fishes for us to consider these stories mere legends. Divested of popular fantasies, they show that this man was so moved by God's love at the sight of beasts that he felt compelled to share his rich religious experience with them.

Our Western world has lost this sense of the cosmos. Many symbols of "the world beyond the stars," which for thousands of years have fascinated man, have been emptied of meaning. As science strides steadily forward, there is less need to use symbols to call up the invisible world, and the poet is being replaced by the scientist. But the latter expresses himself in graphs and statistics while the poet may use but a single word. With one image, the mystic expressed a religious reality for which the theologian has to resort to a whole network of ideas. And in a Church where, in my personal view, these networks of ideas are threatening to destroy religious simplicity, the very next step is a crisis of faith.

On the other hand, theology must keep watchful guard over symbolism. The religious image, literally and figuratively, can present itself as reality. The arts, even the truly great art of the Middle Ages and the Renaissance, provided the people's imagination with concepts in which the mysteries of faith appeared as in a dream. These concepts had enormous power for good, but they often had a destructive influence. The image was reduced to infantile religious faith, and the crisis came when science, secular and religious, begin to show that these concepts did not reflect reality in the scientific sense. And not only the images but often the mysteries they portrayed were thrown overboard.

Today, many churchmen and laymen are striving for sobriety and simplicity, especially in the liturgy. However, seeing the imagery of the Canticle of the Creatures, one wonders if we have not traveled too far in the wrong direction, ending in the cold emptiness of ideas. The religious man cannot do without images in striving to reach God. He cannot breathe in empty space.

When our cult of faith is reduced to sheer words, the mystical atmosphere disappears. Many of us long for ancient cathedrals, abbeys, and liturgical forms; with their aura of hallowed climes. I would go so far as to say that when children are bored by a religious service, some essential of the perceptible, sensual forms which were a part of our liturgy has been lost. Now that in the Western world the symbol is being devalued, it is time to subject not only the symbol but the whole Western world to closer scrutiny.

Francis' life is characterized by symbols, the continual celebration of God in the cosmos. Even when his eyes could bear no ray of light and he lay dying in a miserable hut, he could sing of Brother Sun, shining with great brilliance: *"Di Te, Altissimo, porta signification."* "O you, Most High, he bears the likeness."[22]

Footnotes

1. Terzi has attempted to establish the network of travels undertaken by Francis during the last two years of his life. See Terzi, op. cit., pp. 137ff.

2. This is the earliest known portrait of Francis which bears the letters *FR*(ATER) *FRA*(N)*CISCUS*. The absence of the halo leads experts to conclude that it must have been painted before the canonization (1228).

The picture bears the words *Pax huis domui* (Peace be with this house), which was his customary salutation. It was signed with a *T* (the *tau* was Francis' customary signature, as we have mentioned). A second portrait of Francis has been discovered in this same chapel. On an old fresco in the chapel, portraying Pope Honorius III blessing an altar, two other figures are visible behind him. One is clean-shaven and the other bears a remarkable resemblance to the other portrait of Francis. This could provide additional proof that Francis was a deacon.

Several points are worth mentioning here. The following text appears under the fresco: "In the second year of the Supreme Pontiff [the pope] this cross was painted. Before he received the supreme honor, he lived here a heavenly life during two months, in July and the torrid month of August. He tortured himself with holy practices. He was as a saint who in ecstacy is received into heaven—he did not live, but Christ lived in him. Because of all this, pray here with respect." This text had always been applied to the Supreme Pontiff, but the historian Domenico Federici found this strange. He made a study of his own and came to the conclusion that it refers to Francis. The "supreme honor" is then the canonization, or perhaps the stigmatization.

The earliest portrait dating from before 1228, which is mentioned above, must have been painted by someone who had seen Francis. The next two portraits date from 1228—one in the palace of Giacopa de Settesoli and the other in the Church of St. John and St. Paul in Spoleto. There is a picture in Greccio, dating from 1230, in which Francis' eyes are being wiped with a cloth. Then there is a painting by Berlinghieri (1260) in the San Francesco Museum in Assisi and one by Cimabue (about 1280) in the lower church of the basilica of Assisi (retouched).

3. *Actus Franciscanae Historiae* (AFH), I, 69, 70.

4. There is some disagreement over where Francis spent these months of illness and where he wrote his Canticle of the Creatures. Terzi (op. cit., pp. 146ff.) has strong arguments to support his view that it was not San Damiano but La Foresta in the Rieti Valley (then known as San Fabriano).

5. The earliest -extant manuscript dates from 1279 and is in the library of the city of Assisi (manuscript 388). The bars of music above it indicate that the poem was sung. It is not known whether Francis composed the melody. See the article by H. Nolthenius, "Sarafijnse Muzikanten," *Roeping* (February 1946), and her unpublished doctoral thesis, "De Oudste Melodie van Italië."

6. In his thinking, Teilhard de Chardin is closely related to Francis. On p. 71 of his *Homme de l'Univers* (Paris, 1961; Eng. equivalent: *Hymn of the Universe* [New York: Harper & Row, 1972]), Teilhard cries out, "May you be blessed, oh harsh master and sterile soil! You are hard to touch, you who only yield to violence, and you force us to work if we want to eat."

7. God has to be praised *per* the sun, the moon, etc. But *per* not only means "by mean of" but also "through." Most probably, it seems to me, Francis was not consciously aware of the fine distinction between the meanings of *per*. He used the term with both of its meanings simultaneously.

8. The translation is from Fr. Auspicius van Corstanje O.F.M. See his magazine *St. Francis* (1970), 4/5, p. 256.

9. See *Omnibus*, pp. 130–131.

10. *II Celano* 165; *Omnibus*, pp. 494–496.

11. *Wegen und Formen der Sympathie* (1922), p. 141. We see here a striking resemblance between Francis' devotion and the Jewish piety displayed in the so-called Hassidim. The probable founder received the

name Baäl Sjem Tov, and it is said that when he prayed he used to spring and dance. He taught an itinerant preacher the language of the flowers and the birds, and also spoke to animals. The deepest origins of Hassidism are difficult to trace, but they are imbued with the same spirit we see in the Fioretti. Like Francis, the Hassidim felt the immanent presence of God in all creation. "They knew how the divinity revealed itself in creation; they showed how sparks from God's being shone in all beings and taught the people how to search out their deepest origins" (M. Buber, *Tales of the Hassidim* London, 1958).

12. Eloi Leclerq O.F.M., *The Canticle of Creatures: Symbols of Union* (Chicago: Franciscan Herald Press, 1977). He bases his conclusions on the findings of Bachelard, Eliade, and others on the psychical background of the primeval images which man has used since the most primitive times. Man has the imaginative capacity to create something new, but in addition Bachelard distinguishes "the other forces which plumb the depths in their search for the primitive and eternal." Among these are the primeval images which have always fascinated man: sun, moon, and stars; wind, water, fire, and earth.

13. Ibid., pp. 8-9.

14. "Je m'exprime en exprimany le mond; j'explore ma propre sacralité en déchiffrant celle de mond" (*Finitude et Culpabilité II*); Bachelard, *La Symbolique du mal*, p. 19.

15. See Omer Englebert, *Saint Francis of Assisi* (Chicago: Franciscan Herald Press, 1965), p. 25.

16. *Fundamental-catechetik* (Düsseldorf, 1968), p. 94.

17. In her last work, *Sohn der Erde: der Mensch, Teilhard de Chardin* (Frankfurt A.M., 1970), Ida F. Görres made a study of Teilhard de Chardin's relationship to women. She uses this quote on p. 45.

18. There is affinity here, but there are also marked distinctions between these two figures. J. Maritain, who is no great admirer of Teilhard, nevertheless admits: "I think in the first beginnings of Teilhard's thought there is a poetic intuition—something extraordinarily strong—of the holy and limitless worth to be assigned to creation. I am dreaming of a Lucretius who might have been a Christian" (*Un Paysan de la Garonne* (Paris, 1966), p. 175).

19. Fioretti 21; *Omnibus*, p. 1349.

20. In Gubbio there is a church on the spot where Francis met the wolf and another where, according to the legend, the wolf is buried. Under the walls of this church (St. Francis of Peace) the skull of a

wolf has indeed been discovered. See L. M. Craker, *Gubbio, Past and Present*.

21. *II Celano* 70; *Omnibus*, p. 498.

22. Canticle of Brother Sun; *Omnibus*, p. 130.

19

Brother Fire

Italy has many cities to which popes have fled. At every gate of Rome, Christ might have asked *Quo vadis?*— Where are you going? Honorius, pious but weak, who had been driven from the city by rebellious crowds, chose as his refuge the beautiful Rieti Valley, where so many places were dear to Francis. Fonte Colombo, where he composed a rule; La Foresta, the woods where he held his retreats; Poggio Bustone, which he called "my hermitage;" and Greccio, where he and neighboring farmers spent Christmas Eve around a manger, in the company of an ox and a donkey.

Cardinal Ugolino, concerned about Francis' health, advised him to come to Rieti, where the papal physician could treat his eye disease (1225). This was to be his last journey—a circuitous one, from Assisi through the Rieti Valley and Siena and back to Assisi. It was probably in La Foresta that the papal physician examined Francis and concluded that the only hope lay in cauterizing the infected skin around his eyes with a red-hot iron. It was hoped that this would bring relief from the unbearable headaches he had been suffering. Francis wanted to postpone the attempt until Brother Elias, general of the order, had given his permission. But Ugolino considered it dangerous to wait any longer and it was decided to undertake the treatment.

The sources, based on the experiences of Brother Leo (who was with Francis at the time), mention a remarkable incident. When Francis came face to face with Brother Fire, whom shortly before he had praised as "full of power and strength," he addressed him: "Brother Fire, noble and useful above all creatures, deign to be courteous, knowing the love I bear you and will always bear you for the sake of him who created you. Temper your heat that I may bear it."[1]

The writer goes on: "After these words, he blessed the fire with the sign of the cross. All who were then with him left the room out of compassion for him, and he was alone with the physician. When the latter had finished the treatment and the others had returned to the room, Francis said: 'Faint of heart, why did you flee? I can truly say that I felt not the slightest pain, not even the heat of the fire. And if this treatment is not sufficient, let them prepare again the red-hot iron.' The physician himself was filled with astonishment and said, 'Brothers, believe me, not only a man who is sick and weak, but even the strongest among us would fear that he could not endure such a burning pain. Francis did not move, nor even give the slightest indication that he was in pain.' "[2]

We are not obliged to believe every detail of this account, but is it not possible that Francis, with his cosmic-mystical love, could accomplish more than a fakir? Be that as it may, this "blessing of the fire" is inextricably connected with the Canticle of the Creatures, which Francis composed during the last year of his life, and he came to experience it ever more deeply. In telling of the treatment for his eyes, the brothers mention that Francis loved fire "above all other elements." This is not strange, for there is a certain resemblance between fire and his temperament. Moreover, in fire he felt the immanence of God, a living God—power and beauty, "beautiful and joyous and strong." Not the static, cold God of the philosophers but Jehovah, who consumes burning offerings on the altar and descends upon his people in tongues of fire. When Francis asks Brother Fire to be courteous for the sake of the love he bears him, Francis, unconsciously, is speaking to him who permeates that fire.

Having composed the Canticle of the Creatures, Francis seems to feel more strongly compelled to express himself in poetic form. Twice he will add to his poem, in moments of emotional stress. On the first occasion he was staying in the bishop's palace in Rieti, where he had been taken to convalesce after the cauterization. He had heard that there was a feud between the bishop and the mayor of Rieti, and the conflict had reached such proportions that city and diocese were torn by hostility and the mayor had been excommunicated.[3] The origins of the quarrel did not interest him, any more than the status of the antagonists. He who lives in discord with another is always in the wrong, and the ban of excommunication could not alter that. Francis was sickened by the sight of hatred; he could not simply look on and let matters take their course.

One would have to experience a medieval vendetta to appreciate what it meant to attempt to make peace between the two raging parties. Moreover, considerable risk was involved in trying to come between two influential hotheads, and Francis had the wisdom not to set to work openly. He is Orpheus, who tames the raging beast, and his weapon is the Canticle of the Creatures. Confronted by the hostility of these two men, he realizes that his song of brotherhood among all creatures is not complete. Sun and moon, wind and water, fire and earth can know no peace as long as Brother Man lives in enmity, and he composes the verse:

Praise be to Thee my Lord for those who
grant pardon for love of Thee,
And bear infirmity and tribulation,
Blessed be those who live in peace,
For by Thee, Most High, they shall be crowned.[4]

Francis has faith in the power of his poem. He sends one
of his brothers to the mayor with this message: "Brother
Francis requests you, as a favor to him, to come to the
episcopal palace together with the most prominent citizens
of the town."[5] If he agrees (which he does), two brothers
(one of them Leo) will stand in the courtyard of the palace,
before bishop and mayor, and sing the new verse.

Francis does not follow events from a safe distance; he
accepts the risk of failure and has himself brought to the
square in front of the cathedral, sick and blind, with a
bandage over his eyes. Perhaps it was the presence of this
poor, blindfolded figure that worked the psychological miracle
which was about to occur. The thoughts of the two opponents are not recorded. The *Speculum Perfectionis,* in all
simplicity, merely describes the results:

When the song had ended the mayor spoke, saying,
"Listen, all of you. I must grant forgiveness to the bishop,
whom I wish to see as my lord. Even if he had murdered
my brother, I should still be willing to grant him pardon."
He fell at the feet of the bishop: "I lie before you, O lord!
I will do whatever you shall command me, for love of
our Lord Jesus Christ and his servant Francis." The bishop,
in his turn, took the mayor by the hand and said, "In my
position I should have been humble, but because I have an
irascible nature you must forgive me."[6]

Today it is difficult to imagine such a scene. But in that
world of medieval faith, where heaven and earth were closely
intertwined, such a psychological breakthrough is credible.
It was, as Sartre says, the world of "the devil and the good
God."

On his sickbed in the episcopal palace, Francis prepared
for his departure from this world. Through the decline of
his body and the ascent of his soul toward God, he had
grown away from this earthly existence. In a way, he had
even grown distant from what for so long had fascinated
him above all else: reading the scriptures. When the brother who was nursing him saw his pain, and that he was
scarcely able to breathe, he said: "Father, the scriptures
have always been a source of consolation to you and have
brought some relief from your sufferings. Let me send for
an exegist to explain a few passages from Prophets." Francis' answer was surprising: "It is a wondrous thing to seek
help in the testimony of scripture and to find there our
Lord and God. But for myself, I have delved deeply into
the scriptures and they are ever with me as a source of
meditation. I have need of nothing else, my son. I know
Christ, poor and crucified."[7]

The situation in his order must have caused him great
anxiety. Since Elias had taken over management of the
order, the influence of this powerful figure was felt everywhere. Elias did not consciously oppose Francis, but he
lacked the loving simplicity with which Francis had always
treated the brothers, even when they had done wrong. A
document has been preserved which contains Francis' reply
to a letter from Elias, dated 1223—three years before his
trip to Rieti. Apparently Elias had been too harsh in his
treatment of a wayward brother and he wanted to know
how best to handle the matter. Francis' reply, in a few
sentences, is one of the most touching passages in all his
writings. It deserves to be displayed in all the confessionals
of the world, directly under the crucifix.

> This is how I will discover if you love the Lord and me,
> his servant and yours, if you do this: In all the world there
> may be no brother who has ever seen in your face that he
> must take leave of you without your mercy, when he sought
> mercy. And if he does not seek that mercy, then you must

ask him whether he does not desire mercy. And if you should meet him yet a thousand times, love him more than you love me, and bring him in this way to the Lord. And be always merciful to such people. And if possible make it known to the guardians [local leaders] that you have decided for yourself to act in this way.[8]

It was clear to Francis, even then, that a new spirit had begun to enter the order. Though he was confined to bed, he knew that the unity of the early days was gone. His blind eyes saw keenly, and he was not unaware that, after his death, Brother Elias would take quite a different course than his own confessor and intimate, Brother Leo. Probably, Leo himself confided his anxiety on this subject to Francis. His views on poverty and radical observance of the rule were diametrically opposed to those of the "progressives" under the leadership of Elias.

In Spoleto, I saw one of the notes, in Francis' own hand, written to Brother Leo. The barely legible words are heartwarming, and in the course of centuries many a brother must have read them as if they had been written to him personally. The somewhat fearful conscience of Leo (not a lion, says Francis, but a lamb) is evident, as well as the great measure of freedom which Francis granted his brothers. He writes:

Brother Leo, your brother Francis wishes you salvation and peace. I would like to speak to you, my son, as a mother. All that we have discussed on the way I can summarize in this message. I advise you—even if you should later find it necessary to come to me—I give you this advice: if you find that you can in some other way more closely follow in the footsteps of the Lord God and do his will, and imitate his poverty, do this with the blessing of the Lord God and with my approval. And if you find it necessary for the salvation of your soul or for encouragement, and you want to come to me, then come, Leo, by all means.[9]

The intimate simplicity of this note has gone down in history as an authentic testimony to the relationship between Francis and his brothers. But there is no doubt that these words were later used as a weapon in the so-called poverty controversy. The followers of Leo and Elias stood side by side at the bedside of the man who bound them to each other, but the last few years had convinced Francis that after his death the conflict would flare up. He desired to use his influence one last time, as dying patriarch, to prevent this conflict, and he dictated the document which has come down to us as his "Testament."[10]

As is true of the Canticle of the Creatures, it is important to know what preceded the writing of this Testament. Divorced from the circumstances under which it was written, it might seem to be no more than a few incoherent passages on poverty, obedience, respect for the clergy, the celebration of the Eucharist, and the like. But seen in the light of an approaching farewell, it acquires far deeper meaning. Francis is going to the Father, and they will not see him again. He wants to leave them a testament, the kind of covenant Christ meant when he said "This is the sign of the new covenant."[11]

It was Fr. van Corstanje, more than anyone else, who elaborated on this idea of a covenant and connected it with the "covenant of the poor" in the Bible. At the close of his study he writes, "Not only did Francis understand that God surrounds the poor with a very special love, and wants to draw up a new and eternal covenant with them. He went further. Francis made an alliance with his brothers, a covenant, in order to bind himself as well as them to the path that his poor Master had chosen to follow, and thus to share in the divine riches of God's covenant."[12]

The Testament is written in a halting, Italianized sort of Latin, uncorrected by later stylists (this is what makes it so touching). In the face of death, he shares secrets long kept: "The Lord has imparted to me, Brother Francis, the following manner of doing penance. . . ."[13] (Study of Fran-

cis' writings reveals that "penance" means metanoia, inner
conversion, by which one enters the kingdom of heaven.)
Francis goes on: "For when I lived in sin, a leper was to [14]
me a horrible sight. And the Lord himself brought me into
their midst and I showed mercy to them. . . . Then I
remained for a time with them, and retreated from the
world."

Reading the Testament, one is struck by the tragedy of
a man like Francis, whose being was permeated by trust in
his fellow man, feeling called upon to employ such phrases
as "it is my explicit will" . . . "I strongly forbid" . . .
"demand the obedience of all brothers" . . . "And the
brothers must not now say to themselves, 'This is a new
rule,' for it is only a reminder, an exhortation, an admonition that I, little Brother Francis, give to you, my good
brothers, with the intention that it will help us to better
observe the Rule which we have promised the Lord to
obey."[15]

Francis fears that after his death they will disregard his
words, and he understands that a change of course is
generally justified by a so-called new interpretation. For this
reason he adds, "I sternly forbid anyone to add anything
to the rule or to these words in the sense of 'This is to be
interpreted thus and so.'" When he wrote these words,
Francis knew in his heart that the new interpretation had
for some time been a reality. And not only did the Testament fail to prevent schisms, it was quoted by all parties
as proof of the justness of their interpretation. Thus it
met the same fate as the gospel.

"In the sixth month before his death" (April 1226),
Ugolino has Francis brought to Siena, to an even more
famous specialist,[16] but to no avail. Then Minister-General
Elias arrives in Siena and takes over from Ugolino. He sees
that his master is dying and has him taken to Assisi.

Elias Buonbarone, as we have seen, was one of the most
brilliant men of his day. His love for Francis must have
been similar to Ugolino's but with a certain ambivalence:

he truly loves and admires Francis, but is critical of him, as the pragmatist is always critical of the idealist. The organizer and politician, with his prudent reserve, is faced with a man who is moved purely by the spirit. Elias' awe-inspiring authoritarianism and reckless thrust toward his goal remain within acceptable limits, as long as the respected idealist is beside him, but once freed of this moderating influence, these qualities know no bounds. A man like Elias—brilliant, temperamental, progressive—affects people in different ways. Thus it is almost impossible to form a proper judgment of this man, who was trusted by Francis and Clare, who was admired by Celano in his first biography and condemned in his second (though not mentioned by name), who was sent by Pope Gregory (Ugolino) as emissary to the emperor, later excommunicated by him, elected general in 1232, later deposed, and at last died in the bosom of the Church. Historians still argue the authenticity of the sources and the importance of Elias to the order,[17] but few will disagree that he cared for his master with loving devotion during the last months of Francis' life. With his knowledge of human nature, he knew exactly how to handle Francis, as was evident when his master was taken to a nearby hermitage, where he fell ill and began to spit blood. In spite of the danger, Francis refused to be treated. With commendable psychological insight, Elias pointed out to Francis that medicinal herbs are also God's creatures. Seizing upon just the right text, "God causes medicines to sprout from the earth, and a wise man will not despise them,"[18] he had Francis were he wanted him, and Francis was forced to comply.

But the "earthly medicines" came too late. They were powerless to help that poor body which, like Brother Donkey, had for twenty years borne the burden of a restless spirit. Elias understood that all hope was gone and he had Francis brought back to the city which would forever be joined to his name, Assisi. This last journey passed through Elias' birthplace, Cortona, and Perugia. If Celano is to be believed—and his account has the ring of truth—Francis was overtaken by a group of beggars. With heart-rending gestures, one of them said that he had just lost his wife and was left with four children. The allegation has a familiar ring, but Francis was not the type to stop to verify the facts. He answered: "Here is my cloak. If you sell it, be sure you get a good price for it."[19] Then a skirmish broke out between the man and the brothers, who tried to keep the cloak, and the beggar was persuaded to accept other offerings in place of the garment.

Such stories illuminate several aspects of the situation. While it is true that to most people he met along the way, Francis was a destitute saint, he was seen by these medieval have-nots as an influential monk who associated with popes and cardinals. To still others he was a precious relic, and it was not strange that he was protected on this journey by a group of soldiers. Until the very moment that he was solemnly carried to his last resting place, citizens of Perugia and other cities might try to seize his body; so the people of Assisi were doubly on guard, for they remembered all too well that, several months before, the body of St. Crispolto (whoever he might have been) had been secretly disinterred by citizens of Bettona and carried off to their village. Thus they were intensely grateful that Francis should wish to die among them. The following passage from Celano typifies the character of medieval man: "The whole town was filled with rejoicing and everyone gave thanks to God. They hoped that he would die close by," and this, Celano adds, "was the cause of the general rejoicing,"[20] Assisi would be assured of his relic!

In Assisi, Francis was brought within the security of Bishop Guido's palace, and armed citizens mounted guard on the walls, still fearful that, after his death, the brothers might try to carry the body away. To relieve the boredom of the soldiers, Francis had the brothers sing loud choruses of the *Laudes Deo*.

Francis, however, did not wish to die in an episcopal

palace. After a few weeks, Elias received permission from the city council to transfer his master to the place which Francis had always viewed as the heart of his order—Porziuncola. Again the armed escort appeared, and he was placed on a litter. He left the city for the last time through the Porta Portaccia.

Halfway down the road, he asked his bearers to stop. Today, standing near the Casa Gualdi, one looks upon the same sight which met Francis' eyes that day. He wanted to bless the city he had loved so dearly. His blind eyes sought the familiar silhouette and he prayed, ending with the words: "Lord Jesus Christ . . . may this city always belong to those who know you and glorify your blessed name forever and ever. Amen."[21]

Then they carried him along the road, which one can still travel today, to the church and huts of Porziuncola. His travels had come to an end.

Footnotes

1. *Spec. Perf.* 115; *Omnibus*, p. 1254.

2. *Leg. Perugia* 48; *Omnibus*, pp. 1026–1027.

3. Contrary to the traditional view that this event took place between the bishop and the mayor in Assisi, we have chosen to follow Terzi (op. cit., pp. 154ff.), who believes it took place in Rieti. Before the cathedral stands a statue of Francis by Giordano Nicolette. One of the most important arguments in support of Terzi's view is that the bishop of Assisi could not possibly have been in Assisi at that time. See Fortini, op. cit. (II, 508–532), for arguments supporting the other view.

4. Canticle of Brother Sun; *Omnibus*, p. 131.

5. See *Leg. Perugia* 44; *Omnibus*, pp. 1022–1024. Also *Spec. Perf.* 101; *Omnibus*, pp. 1237–1238.

6. *Spec. Perf.* 101; *Omnibus*, p. 1238.

7. *II Celano* 105; *Omnibus*, p. 448.

8. Letter to a Minister; *Omnibus*, p. 110.

9. Letter to Leo; *Omnibus*, pp. 118–119. Until 1860 this note was preserved in the convent of the Conventuals in Spoleto. Some thirty years ago it came into the possession of a parish priest in Spoleto; he was considering selling it to an American, but Pope Leo XIII was able to retain it and donated it to the city of Spoleto. It is now in the treasure room of the cathedral.

10. Few of Francis' writings have appeared in so many manuscripts and been so extensively commented upon—against the author's will—as his Testament. The earliest mention is in the bull of canonization by Gregory IX (Sept. 28, 1228), two years after Francis' death. Extensive studies have been made of this Testament by K. Esser O.F.M., *Das Testament des H. Franciskus von Assisi* (Münster, 1949 [an English version to be published in 1978 by Franciscan Herald Press]) and by Auspicius van Corstanje O.F.M., *The Covenant with God's Poor* (Chicago: Franciscan Herald Press, 1966).

11. See Lk 22:20, Mt 26:28, Mk 14:24, 1 Cor 11:25.

12. Van Corstanje, op. cit., p. 144.

13. Testament; *Omnibus*, p. 67.

14. Van Corstanje, op. cit., p 144.

15. Testament; *Omnibus*, p. 67.

16. *I Celano* 105; *Omnibus*, p. 369.

17. A study of Elias is to be found in F. v. d. Borne O.F.M., "Antonius en Elias," *Collectanea Franciscana Neerlandica* (1948), vol. VII.

18. Sir 38:4.

19. See *I Celano* 88; *Omnibus*, p. 435. Also *Spec. Perf.* 31; *Omnibus*, p. 1158.

20. *I Celano* 105; *Omnibus*, p. 320.

21. There is some doubt about the authenticity of this prayer.

20

Sister Death

Our Western world has a tendency to dissociate death from its age-old myths and mystery. The symbolism which used to surround death is disappearing from our culture and our art, and this is a milestone in the evolution of man's view of death.

In the late Middle Ages, death was referred to as macabre[1] —merciless, sinister, terrifying, with a sarcastic grin on its ghostly face. In the imagination of the artist, its vision took the form of the *danse macabre,* with a chilling portrayal of the uncertainties of life, its transitory riches and fame, as in the Cimitierè des Innocents in Paris, where kings and cardinals, monks and noblemen gaze in fascination at a cadaver, symbol of their coming fate. We feel the artist's hatred of the class society, which deepens into perverse delight at the ghoulish fate which no one can escape.[2]

This malicious delight in another's suffering disappears in the following century, and what remains is sheer horror. The original of the *Ars Moriende,* the art of dying, shows devils with calves' heads and long teeth—ghastly symbols of the torments to which a dying man is subjected. This art is more religious than the *danse macabre,* but it is a religion of fear: fear of eternal judgment. In his final hour, every man is overcome by doubt: Is God a merciful God? This is the hour of Satan, in mortal combat with the angel.

The further development of the image of death is recounted in the work of Roger de Gaighières, based on the evidence of thousands of French tombstones. During the Renaissance, the religious character of death fades away and the figure of the dead person is endowed with a certain human nobility. In sharp contrast, the seventeenth century again portrays death as in the *danse macabre,* grinning and horrible. The reclining figure on the tombstones makes way for a skull and crossbones, hourglass and scythe, as the symbols of death's terror.

Today, all this has changed. In our Western culture, death is no longer sinister. The image has blurred until death is reduced to the negative, the nonexistent, devoid of spiritual value. Worse yet, death has become absurd. What is more senseless and ridiculous than life's steady ascent, its increase in power, grace and wisdom, which, in the end, leads inevitably to a slow descent into nothingness? "The story of a life . . . is the story of a failure," says Sartre in his *L'Etre et le Néant.* We can delay death but we cannot defeat it. On a wall in the cathedral of Lucca I read these words: "Death is immortal. All the rest will pass away."[3] Nothing can withstand the force of biochemistry. In the end, spirit is no match for matter.

Today, even a theologian who believes in immortality might see death as an "impertinent fact," devoid of intelligible meaning. Schillebeeckx believes that only he who is prepared to accept the purely profane message of absolute death "will ever understand the liberating message of the gospel."[4] *Vita mutatur, non tollitur.* Life changes but does not pass away.

Where faith in a resurrection is lacking, the inevitable occurs: death is banned from polite society. Although it remains an important theme in art, philosophy, and science, it is no longer an object of cynical derision, as in Schopenauer, and literature offers many moving examples of the death theme. But society has done with death. And because the individual cannot escape death, immortality is necessarily transferred to the endlessly evolving culture. Man will die, but mankind will escape this most terrible of all failings. This alone gives a person the strength to devote oneself to the world of one's grandchildren. This is not as mad as it may sound. For the nonbeliever, it is the only way to escape from the absurdity of inescapable destruction. He must accept the consolation that when he is gone, his influence on the affairs of this world, however small it may have been, will live on. After 2,000 years, many a modern man has consoled himself with the words of Horace: *"Non omnis moriar—*Not all of me will die." I shall live on in what I have created and procreated. *"Monumentum egegi aere perennius."*

For the believer, too, death is the end of his earthly existence. But behind its merciless, macabre absurdity, Christianity has always guarded an element of hopeful, expectant surrender. This was never more evident than in Francis' century. The dead are represented on tombstones with open eyes; they are alive. The artist chose to portray them as already part of that imperturbable peace which shines from the stained-glass windows of the cathedrals. No one experienced this intimate relationship to death in a more original manner than Francis. No greater contrast is possible than that between Sartre's *échec* (failing) and Francis' surrender to "our Sister, Bodily Death."[5] Several days before his death, Francis added a new verse to his Canticle of the Creatures:

All praise be yours, my Lord, through Sister Death, From whose embrace no mortal can escape.

Only unshakable faith in God enables a man to thank him for death, with its decay and dissolution. But one might accuse Francis of having contributed to that decay; no brother had served him better than Brother Body, or been so ill treated in return. One suspects that he considered his body something outside his ego-existence, a sort of beast of burden created to serve his spirit. He viewed it with a mixture of humor and anxiety. Only Francis could have been serious when he asked the brother who was nursing him, "Tell me, Brother, what do you think of the reproaches with which my conscience plagues me about my body? Do I give in to it too much because of its sickness?" This brother was apparently a man of great tact. He has Francis admit that his body has always obeyed him, and then asks, "But Father, where is your courtesy? Does one treat an old and faithful friend thus?" "You are right," the sick man answers. "Be content, Brother Body, and forgive me. I am prepared to do whatever you desire."

The medicine comes late. Too late! "How can one save a body that is simply falling apart?" sighs Celano.

The reaction was typical of Francis, and shows the pity he felt for that poor body of his, that had served him faithfully for twenty years. Now he can only say, "It no longer knows what pleasure is, for this long sickness has robbed it of all zest for life."[7]

Not only the spirit but the body longed for death. With perfect calm he inquired of the physician who was treating him, "What do you think of my case, Doctor? Please tell me the truth, for by the grace of my Lord I am not so petty as to be afraid of death." And when the doctor gave him, at the most, three weeks to live, he cried out, "Sister Death, welcome!"[8]

Sister Death is more than a poetic figure or a manner of expression; it is a symbol of Francis' approach to death, in its evangelical interpretation. Ennobled by the resurrection of our Lord, death comes to Francis lovingly, as a sister. Death cannot be cruel to him, for she comes to console. After sun and moon, the elements, and man, she is the last of the creatures, come to carry her brother to the dwelling place of the All High.

They say that the dying person passes through various phases: rebellion, partial acceptance, longing for "just a little more time," depression, and finally acceptance.[9] Francis had entered this last stage, but I doubt if, after his metanoia, he experienced the other four phases. He had long been free from earthly ties, and this gave him an exceptional form of peace in the face of death. He had reached the stage of relinquishment long before the doctor spoke the final verdict.

Leclerq sees in Francis' Canticle of the Creatures this relinquishment of self and a steadily stronger realization of God as being in its fullest sense. "The center of gravity has been shifted; no longer does it lie in the ego and its personal interests, not even its spiritual needs. It now lies in the mystery of being."[10] Francis' surrender of self to God, expressed in loving service to his fellow man, is to be completed and fulfilled by his death. He has the brothers lay him naked on the floor, for he wishes to have nothing for himself. He even reveals the "secret" of his stigmata, which he had kept so long. Sister Death is loving but demanding; it is her will that the dying man should not depart this life unreconciled with being.

Francis had recently added to his canticle the following:

> "Woe to who die in mortal sin the second death can do no harm."

The "second death" is the repudiation of being and the absolute embracing of the ego. More terrible than Sartre's "Hell is other people" is "Hell is myself."

A man who for years has looked forward to this meeting with God cannot but see the moment of his death as the climax of his earthly existence. It is a cause for celebrating, and Francis has his own way of doing so, inspired by his Master's words of farewell.

He is going to die a death that befits him. We see here that same quality of whimsical inventiveness that we have so often encountered during Francis' life. He wants his friends around him—Elias, Leo, Bernardo, Angelo, and many others. Under the circumstances, it is not strange that he should also invite the woman who had been his lifelong friend, Giacopa de Settesoli. He asked her to bring a gray habit and the honey cake she had so often baked for him. His stomach had long been unable to handle the honey cake, but it was a last courtly gesture of friendship for this woman, who would sorely miss him. He sent a letter of farewell to Clare, who was herself seriously ill and fully expected to die before him. "Tell her," he said to the messenger, "that she must no longer be sorrowful. For before she dies she and her sisters will see me again."[12]

To all who had loved him with almost passionate fondness, he had been the symbol of the *forma vitae,* the "way of life according to the gospel of our Lord Jesus Christ," as the rule described it. His inspiration and religious genius had come to them as a gift from God.

He begins the celebration of his death with an *agape.* Loaves of bread are brought, and he blesses, breaks, and distributes them to his friends.[13] Then he has the thirteenth chapter of the gospel according to St. John read aloud. This chapter, indeed the whole farewell address, is full of remarkable and surprising passages when read against the background of Francis' death. He feels himself to be the most unworthy follower of his Lord, but does not shrink from having the most striking parallels between his farewell and death and that of his Master read aloud.

"Children, I can remain with you only a little longer. A new commandment I give you: You must love me as I have loved you, and you must love each other likewise."[14] And there must have been a very special meaning in the words "I pray for those who by Your word believe in me, so that they may all be one as you, Father, in me and I in you."[15]

For several hours he lies with his eyes closed, surrounded by his brothers, each with his own memories of what this man meant to him. Lovingly, Sister Death bends over him and carries him away to the unspeakable mystery.

This occurred around the beginning of October. Outside the hut, twilight fell over the Umbrian plains and night came. Tomorrow a new sun would rise, "beautiful and radiant with great splendor."

Footnotes

1. This word is derived from a proper name, probably Macabré. *"Je fis de Macabré la danse,"* says Jean de Fèvre in 1370. See Huisonga, *Hefsttij der middeleeuwen,* 5th ed. (Haarlem, 1941), p. 201.

2. Male, op. cit., p. 168.

3. *Thanatos athanatos, ta loipa thnété.*

4. *Tijdschrift van Theologie* (1972), 4:428.

5. Here we depart from the translation by Father Auspicius van Corstanje O.F.M., who speaks of "Brother" Death. It seems that death, which Francis experienced as something feminine (*la morte*), would conjure up a rather different emotional world if it were to be seen as masculine.

6. Canticle of Brother Son; *Omnibus,* p. 131.

7. *II Celano* 210–211; *Omnibus,* pp. 530–531.

8. *Leg. Perugia* 65; *Omnibus,* p. 1042. Also *Spec. Perf.* 122; *Omnibus,* pp. 1262–1263.

9. See E. Kübler-Ross, *On Death and Dying* (London, 1969). The author admits that during her research she met very few deeply religious people.

10. Leclerq, op. cit., p. 181.

11. Canticle of Brother Sun; *Omnibus,* p. 131.

12. *Spec. Perf.* 108; *Omnibus,* p. 1246. They would meet again after his death, when his body was carried past San Damiano and the sisters were allowed to see him (and the stigmata) for the last time.

13. It is strange that none of the biographers mentions administration of the sacraments to the dying Francis—reconciliation, viaticum, anointing of the sick. See B. Knipping O.F.M., *Rubens, De laarste communie van S. Franciscus van Assisi* (Leiden, 1949), pp. 16–18.

14. See Jn 13:34.

15. See Jn 17:20–21.

Epilogue

Why You, Francis?

For two years the body of Francis remained in the simple church of San Giorgio, where as a child he had learned to read and where he had first addressed friends and fellow citizens after his return from the desert. But when Francis' patron, Ugolino, was elected pope (Gregory IX), Ugolino felt called upon to confirm the saintliness of his protegé. He initiated the canonization process, which he chose to entrust to those same cardinals whom he had warned Francis against. After the canonization, he ordered that a basilica be built in Francis' honor—the future center of a world cult. The project was supervised by Brother Elias, whose design for this edifice was so brilliant that even today it evokes the amazement and admiration of architects. This monumental building, perched on the edge of a hill, was completed within two years. On May 25, 1230, Francis' body was transferred to the basilica, and now rests in the crypt of the lower church.[1]

Those who cannot help wondering if all this reflects the spirit of the *Poverello* should visit the basilica and then the little church of San Damiano. They will realize that a dead prophet is helpless in the hands of his admirers. This is not to say that Ugolino and Elias consciously betrayed Francis' ideals; they were simply convinced that he ought to take his rightful place in the annals of Church history. The throngs of buses before the basilica and the endless crowds of pilgrims on the stairs to the crypt bear witness to the success of their efforts. Brother Masseo would surely shake his head in amazement and ask again, "Why does the whole world follow you, seek you out, Francis? Why you?"[2]

The question cannot but intrigue us. How is it possible that, in a world filled with prophets, the wisdom of a medieval saint has the power to attract thousands to his birthplace? Seven and a half centuries after his death, he is still capable of capturing the imagination of believers and nonbelievers alike. This cannot be attributed simply to the impressive basilica, with its magnificent frescoed walls. Somehow, this man has the answers to the basic questions of life. He shows us that, without possessions, without power, without particular talent or education, it is possible to impart a new and sublime meaning to our existence.

Many prominent thinkers of our day have failed to discover this meaning. Jean-Paul Sartre recounts in his autobiography (*Les Mots*) how, as a child of seven at play, he once had the feeling that he was a traveler without a ticket. Years later, at the end of a "painful experience of extended duration" (atheism), he recalls the incident: "I am again that traveler without a ticket that I was at the age of seven."

Though Francis also knew the agony of such a "painful experience," he was well aware of his destination. He had his ticket. Everything which he experienced in the cosmos—love or beauty, pain or misery—was spontaneously directed toward that unfathomable mystery in which the cosmos rests. His relationship to the beggar or the leper, beasts or the elements, was endowed with a new and unending dimension, touching upon the fundamental questions of existence: Whence?

Why? Whither? And in his reply Francis still speaks to us: "From God, for God, to God."

Today's Christians will perhaps be most struck by the calm certainty of Francis' faith. When I arrived in Spoleto in the midst of a personal crisis, it was as if at the sight of those plains all human squabbles faded away, and I inhaled the quiet calm which Francis and his brothers experienced as they traveled across those fields and plains. All at once, it was clear to me how deep the chasm is between that medieval faith and the anxious, groping search for faith which characterizes our modern world.

The feverish tempo in which a new world is arising, and also the impact of advances within the Church itself, have eroded the old certainties. Traditions, standards, age-old practices are disappearing or being unrecognizably altered. Many Christians feel lost, left behind, stranded in the midst of doubt. For many, this uncertainty is intensified by enthusiastic exhortations from various groups who maintain that at last they are on the right road. Faith, we are told, is an adventure, a march through a wilderness of doubts. The deepening of one's faith is said to be nothing but a steadily increasing uncertainty about a steadily decreasing credo. A Christian who has reached adulthood no longer feels capable of maintaining anything at all about God. He has, with the philosopher, arrived at a kind of emptiness.

One cannot deny that doubt has a definite function to perform, and, admittedly, ours is not the psychologically static world of Francis. Once the believer has begun to ask questions, he has progressed one step further, disengaging himself from stultifying comfort, from the quiet and stability which preclude advance or change. And we must not forget that one who has never gone through a crisis of faith is even more vulnerable than the "twice borns" (as William James calls them), who have already conquered one crisis.

But doubt can never be an ideal. If faith is nothing more than a waterfall of problems, thundering over the edge of a precipice into the depths, the human element has been

lost. Man cannot live on uncertainty, and if he does not
give up in despair, he becomes a kind of religious nomad,
lost in the world of exegesis, dogma, and such like. Roam-
ing through the theological marketplace, he may easily be
sold the most spectacular items. Or he may seek comfort
in the company of like-minded souls in doubt. The joyful
message of the gospel has become inscrutable, something that
must be carefully studied and examined. Man's meeting with
the figure of Jesus Christ, the celebration of the Eucharist,
prayer, and life after death are no longer experienced, they
are pulled apart, anxiously examined, and interpreted in the
light of a few shreds of theological knowledge. What the
searching Christian-in-doubt has yet to realize is that he
has more need of prophets than of theologians.

In the face of all this doubt stands Francis. Though he
had a humble admiration for true theologians, he did not
theologize. More poet than thinker, he spontaneously followed
his intuition, which guided him safely through the perils
of exegesis and dogma straight into the arms of his Lord.
He was the epitome of evangelical unconcern, who surrendered to the bliss of faith as to the glory of the sumptuous cosmos.

Today he is a prophet with charisma, who in his inimitable fashion tells the whole world that God did not give
us a *Summa Theologica* but an Apocalypse, that God is to
be sought less in the hubbub of discussion than in the quiet
of prayer, that when Christians strive to free the world from
violence, injustice, and material need, they must be more
than politicians or glorified social workers.

No one will deny the value of theological contemplation.
Today we have more need than ever of thinkers who have
the courage to seek new paths, to speak in the language of
today to the Christians of today, to run the risk of error,
or of being branded as heretics. But this new world of re-
newal and revolution can indeed be terrifying, amid the
welter of confusing claims and the excessive pluriformity of
ideas and language. Confronted with publications on political

theology, secular theology, critical theology, *e tutti quanti,*
all in their own jargon, one wonders how the priest in his
pulpit can ever hope to find some kind of clarity and certainty to offer the faithful. Is it not possible that the short-
circuit between theology and what used to be called "care
of souls" is one reason why so many Christians seem to
have lost their way? In Francis' day, the theological jurists
of Bologna and Paris lost themselves in abstract discussion,
thousands of miles from the people. But theology ought to
be the humble servant of the faithful. It is the task of
theology to provide the people with spiritual nourishment,
and above all to see that this nourishment is digestible.

The Christian has a duty, of course, according to his
capacity, to reflect upon his faith. But this may never
interfere with the moments in which, carefree and joyful,
he surrenders to the Lord and his message. When he enters
a place of prayer, he must turn his back on all discussion.

Many of the faithful, exhausted by the arguments and
debates within the Church, long for a Christian such as
Francis. Someone who not only preaches but also illuminates.
Who does not offend for the sake of truth, who does not
pride himself on his orthodoxy or his progessiveness. Who
is not forever calling down God's wrath, or swaying from
side to side in beatific tolerance. In short: a simple believer in whom the grace of the Holy Spirit has become
tangible.

Francis is a prophet—not only through his mystical surrender to God. He loved his fellow man in many wonderful,
original, fascinating, and moving ways. We have only to
leaf through a life of St. Francis to realize that his love
was permeated with what every human heart longs for:
simplicity, warmth, and radiant goodness; and that this love
was given to everyone as a matter of course, so that no
one ever felt unwelcome in Francis' presence. The key to
Francis is his conviction that God permitted him to spend
his life in the service of his fellow man, whose inferior he
always felt himself to be.

This is the kind of love we long for. Francis is the
kind of man you would want to have around you, in your
home, at your sickbed. You could talk to him when no one
else seems to understand. You could tell him things you
have never told a single living soul. He wouldn't be in too
great a hurry to listen, would never be bored or simulate
interest, would never be irritated by your faults nor demand
more than you could give. You could go to a man like
that, with such heartwarming goodness, knowing that he
would always be waiting for you, as he waited for his
brothers. "If you ever need encouragement or want to talk
to me, Leo, then come!"[3]

This, then, is what is meant by being truly man. It is
not bound to the forms of one culture or another. A culture
does not automatically improve with increasing technique or
prosperity, but to the degree that men are truly men.
Neither the philosophers nor the scientists nor the statesmen
prove the worth of a civilization, but rather men like
Francis of Assisi.

This does not mean that we must immediately pack our
bags and leave for the hut at Rivo Torto or the caves of
the Umbrian hills. His form of asceticism, his experience
of poverty, went with him.[4] Many things, unknown to
Francis, await us. Our world *demands* radical social reform, *demands* protest, and even revolution, in the face of
violence and oppression. And, perhaps, todays' prophets
will have to be more like the figures in the Old Testament
than Francis was. But they cannot do without his New
Testament inspiration, which consumed him that he might
bring forth good fruit.

Like the olive tree I saw on the hill one climbs to San
Damiano: a hollow skeleton of bark, as twisted and riddled
as a sculpture by Zadkine, but in its crest a luxuriant
crown of olives.

Footnotes

1. The place where Francis died was made into a chapel in 1230 (the present building dates from 1340). The lower church, where he is now buried, was completed within two years after the cornerstone was laid by Pope Gregory IX. The upper church, convent, and bell tower were completed in 1239. The basilica was consecrated in 1253, after which Guido of Siena, Giotto, Cimabue, and their pupils were able to commence the embellishment of the building.

It was decided to move Francis' body three days ahead of schedule, for fear of disturbances. When the procession had left the little church of San Giorgio and was approaching the basilica, it was attacked by archers at Assisi, in this way expressing their deep interest in the priceless relic. Elias hastened to bring the last remains into the new building and hide him there.

The original tomb was really a room, approximately 6 by 12 feet, carved out of the rock under the main altar of the lower church and covered on four sides with thick travertine glass. Elias had the stone sarcophagus placed in the tomb, which was surrounded by a heavy iron grill. The top was covered by an iron screen, and Elias himself placed three bars on top which reached from wall to wall, so that Francis could be seen from above. This privilege was occasionally granted to high Church personages, up to 1477, when Sixtus IV ordered the entire tomb to be sealed off. He wished to be free of the worries which had plagued one of his predecessors, Eugene IV, who had to protect the relic when Perugians again attacked Assisi and tried to remove the body to their own city. But sealing off the tomb brought new problems. There were rumors that the body had disappeared, and even that Francis had been assumed into heaven. In an attempt to put an end to these rumors, Pius VII ordered that the ground under the church be searched in secret (1818). After fifty nights, the authentic remains of Francis were found and identified. The body still lay in the original position. Through contact with the air, however, it quickly disintegrated, except the bones. The stone upon which Francis' head probably rested has withstood the ravages of time. See *Bibliotheca sanctorum* (Institute Giovanni XXIII), part V: "Francesco d'Assisi," and *Arch. Conv.*, X, 21.

2. Fioretti 10; *Omnibus,* p. 1322.

3. Letter to Leo; *Omnibus,* p. 119.

4. In a speech in 1972, Pope Paul VI said: "The *Poverello* of Assisi was born into a commercial and industrial milieu. His world was similar to ours in that a portion of the human family was permeated

with a mentality which worships property and possession. Adult lay
persons should not copy Francis but learn from him a new style of
life. Rather than retreat from this world, and from their responsibility,
they should together contemplate what they are about." See *Av-
venire d'Italia* (Oct. 2, 1972).

Historical Notes & Sources

Today many people are skeptical—and perhaps rightly so—of the historical reliability of medieval hagiographers, but it would be an exaggeration to see in Francis of Assisi a man who perished in poetic legend. Even a modest study of the sources will serve to refute this view, for even from the cold, bare facts a historically reliable figure emerges.

It is true that the figure of Francis is to an extent shrouded in legend, but historical studies enable us to distinguish truth from poetry, at least on the most important points. And we must not forget that pious legends often give a truer picture of a personality than a construction of mere facts.

Especially since Sabatier opened new perspectives in the study of St. Francis at the end of the last century, fresh publications constantly appear on the life of the *Poverello*. The Bibliotheca Sanctorum of the Lateran Library lists about 1,500 titles of books, studies, articles, etc., which represent only the most important works.[1]

As we remarked in the introduction, these historical notes should properly appear at the beginning of the book.

We have placed them at the end only because they are so extensive (despite the fact that only those sources are listed which are mentioned in the text).

Francis' Writings

Most of Francis' writings date from the last years of his life. Perhaps that is why almost all of them were dictated or written in collaboration with others. The only extant documents in his own handwriting are two brief notes to Brother Leo.

The dictated works generally display quite a good style and a commendable knowledge of Latin, and Francis' care-free spontaneity is often in evidence. In addition to the two rules (of 1221 and 1223), we find among his works spiritual admonitions, letters (to his brothers, "To All the Clergy," "To All Persons in Authority," etc.), and finally his Testament.

It is not certain that the Canticle of the Creatures was written down during his lifetime. In any case, no manuscripts are extant. The oldest manuscript was written shortly after his death and is extremely reliable, as all the brothers probably knew it by heart.

These writings total less than a hundred pages, but they form, indeed they must form, the basis of every biography of Francis. Although they contain few historical facts, their value lies in the authentic witness of Francis' person and convictions, even though they become truly valuable only when seen against the background of the other sources.[2]

Primary Sources

These are the oldest biographies, based to a large extent on eyewitness accounts, and with or without the use of additional sources. We restrict ourselves to the three works which appeared within twenty years after Francis' death. The most important of these is the hagiography by Celano, from which we have quoted extensively.

I Celano

The first work on Francis' life and person was of an official nature. Immediately after his canonization in 1228, Pope Gregory IX (Ugolino) commissioned a work devoted to his friend and protegé. The author he chose was Thomas of Celano, who had been received into the order by Francis himself in 1215. Celano was a highly educated man, a poet and an orator, and just the man to compose a work which would appeal to Pope Gregory. He completed his assignment quickly; less than six months after the canonization, Gregory IX gave his approval to the work (February 1229 in Perugia).

In his foreword, Celano says that he has done all in his power to clarify "the words which I myself heard Francis speak and the facts that I learned from expert and reliable witnesses. This was my task—no more and no less." Gregory undoubtedly read the work carefully and apparently discovered no discrepancies in it. A manuscript of Celano's work (now in Paris) contains a note to the effect that *"papa recepit, confirmavit en censuit fore tenendum*—The pope has accepted and confirmed (the work), and made known his wish that the people should adhere to it."

We must keep in mind that we are not dealing here with a biography which meets today's critical-historical standards. Though Celano never consciously twisted the facts, we cannot expect a medieval hagiographer, who was transferred to Germany only six years after taking his vows, to produce a penetrating historical and psychological analysis. Nevertheless, the Francis who emerges from the pages of Celano's work is the same man whom other eyewitnesses have described to us. Many of the historical data are undeniably authentic, since Celano had not only the opportunity but the explicit intention to verify the facts. Moreover, other independent sources confirm the information he provides. It is worth mentioning that Fortini, uncontested expert on the Umbrian archives, found nothing in Celano's work which failed to pass the test of these sources.

The Three Companions

In 1244, in the face of almost universal criticism, Brother Elias was forced to resign and was succeeded by Crescenzio da Jesi. In that same year the latter issued an appeal to all the brothers to write down everything they knew of Francis, whether based on their own experiences or that of others. The only reply which is still extant is a letter from Brothers Leo, Rufino, and Angelo, who knew Francis intimately and who provide a wealth of information on the person and life of their spiritual father. This letter, which is written in several different hands, is considered to be an authentic document composed by the Three Companions.

Or is it? This is the crucial question, sometimes known as "the Franciscan question." There are many experts who doubt the authenticity of the work and believe that someone else was responsible for its composition, someone who made generous use of texts from II Celano. There is indeed room for doubt, and historians have been debating the point for years.

Now, however, the problem seems to have been resolved, thanks to the intensive research carried out by Fr. S. Clasen O.F.M. As early as 1964 he was convinced of the authenticity of the work, and in 1967 he published a brilliant study on the early Franciscan sources.[3] He worked out the genealogy of some 150 specimens of handwriting and reduced them to a few basic types. Clasen's conclusion is that the so-called Legenda Trium Sociorum (here *legenda* means simply "document") is indeed the work of Leo, Rufino, and Angelo, and a most valuable primary source. Moreover, it has the flavor of true Franciscana, which, even more than the historical facts, contributes to our understanding of the man Francis. The findings of Fr. Clasen are generally considered to be authoritative.

II Celano

In 1244 the general chapter requested Celano to write a

new life of Francis "because many things were missing from his first work." For some time people wondered whether *II Celano* was the background for the Three Companions, or whether he simply made use of this work in writing his second book. The study by Fr. Clasen has established that the latter conclusion is correct. *II Celano* was not received favorably—people said he had not done justice to the miracles!

I and II Celano

The next question has to do with the relationship between these two works. Even a superficial reading shows that the second work not only provides new information but views material from the earlier work in a new and different light. This is particularly striking when Celano is describing Francis. *I Celano* sees Francis as an empty-headed spendthrift who "until his twenty-fifth year wasted his life in a most despicable way." The second work, however, presents us with a young man with a heart of gold "who never allowed himself to do anything which might cause another injury." His mother is first portrayed as one of those parents who "set a truly shameful example for their children," while she later appears as a kind of St. Elizabeth who says to neighbors, "I will tell you how this son of mine will turn out: he will become a son of God."

No one has made a more thorough study of this question than F. de Beer O.F.M.[4] He takes particular pains to compare the conversion of Francis as described in *I Celano* with that in *II Celano*. De Beer concludes that the second work is more than just an addition to the first. The author has again written a life of Francis, but from another angle.

Apart from the fact that the sections on Francis' youth contain a few discrepancies, there are no notable conflicts where facts are concerned. Admittedly, Francis is now portrayed as a kind of super-saint, but the happenings that are based on historical fact can stand the test of modern criticism. Thus if one confines oneself to the facts and leaves the subjective considerations for what they are, it is quite possible to collect extremely reliable and authentic material for a biography from *I* and *II Celano,* as well as from the *Three Companions.*

Other Important Sources

Speculum perfectionis

This work belongs to the group of documents which are attributed to Brother Leo, and which indeed bear the stamp of that pious, somewhat timid, and yet stern character. The *Speculum* was published in 1898 by Sabatier as a true biography, written by Leo and originally published before *I Celano,* in 1227. But then a manuscript was discovered which bore the date 1318 (a possible misspelling: XIIIXVIII for XIIXXVII).

Naturally, this unleashed a storm of controversy among historians. According to Clasen, this work is a double source, containing stories from the Leo documents and from *I Celano.* The *Speculum* is authentically Franciscan in spirit, but, despite its true historical basis, it would be wise to exercise caution where actual facts are concerned.

Legenda major of Bonaventure

The general chapter of 1260 authorized Bonaventure, theologian and mystic, to write a new life of Francis. With this purpose in mind, he set off for Italy (he was a university professor in Paris) to meet brothers who had known Francis personally, Leo and Illuminato among others. The work he subsequently produced is known as the *Legenda major.* It is of deep spirituality, but as a historical source it cannot compare with the abovementioned primary sources. The passing years brought a steadily increasing glorification of the figure of Francis, and Bonaventure's work fell victim to this development.

This work cannot be dissociated from his other publications which contain much important material about Francis. Bonaventure stresses the role Francis played in the history of the Church, but he was not sufficiently critical of the legends which were beginning to emerge and which sometimes reached ridiculous proportions (such as the story that predicted that Francis would return to earth just before the Last Judgment).

In 1266, several years after the appearance of Bonaventure's work, the general chapter made a regrettable and incomprehensible decision: all works devoted to Francis (with emphasis on those of Celano) were to be destroyed! The *Legenda* by Bonaventure was to be handed down as the one and only biography of St. Francis. We are indebted to all who consciously or unconsciously ignored this decree, thus ensuring that the figure of Francis has not been obliterated.[5]

The Fioretti

The Fioretti ("Little Flowers of St. Francis") represents a kind of poetic reflection on Francis, the life he had led and the people and circumstances connected with him. These stories have gradually departed from historical fact and begun to lead a life of their own.

In the second half of the thirteenth century two Franciscan brothers (only the name of Ugolino di Sernano is known) collected a series of stories under the title *Actus B. Francisci et sociorum ejus.* An unknown brother selected fifty anecdotes, translated them into Italian, and edited them to form a poetic whole (at the beginning of the fourteenth century).

This work has to a certain extent suppressed the historical Francis, and there are many people who feel that the true Francis has been buried in legend. It is also regrettable that the figure of Brother Juniper, however touching and lovable in his simplicity, has come to occupy such a central position. Some experts have even chosen to publish the Juniper stories as a sort of appendix to the remainder of the book. Nevertheless, this figure, with his apparent lack of common sense, represents a truly Franciscan humor and spontaneity. (A typical example of these stories is the following: When Juniper's superior had finished giving him such a tongue-lashing for his latest stupidity that his voice gave out, Brother Juniper offered him a dish of porridge and, as it was dark, held a lighted candle aloft. "If this doesn't help," he said, "I'll eat it myself. Then you can hold the candle for me.")

This work should not be read for its historical reliability but for the elements of simplicity, faith, and mystical grace which it exudes, which without a doubt are based on the historical figure of Francis.

Chroniclers and Non-Franciscan Sources[6]

In 1221 Giordano di Giano was sent to Germany by the chapter. In 1262 he dictated his memoirs, which, in spite of a certain loquacity, are a valuable source of information. Di Giano knew Francis and the first brothers personally, and is the only author who describes occurrences from Francis' life after 1219 in detail. Scarcely any inaccuracies have been found in his work.

Around 1260, Thomas d'Eccleston produced a history of the English province.

Salimbene d'Adam, who was received into the order by Elias at a very early age, edited his chronicle from 1282 to 1287. He goes into great detail and his work is rambling and verbose. His criticism of Elias is extremely harsh, though he recognizes the latter's brilliant qualities.

Jacques de Vitry and Thomas of Spoleto also are worthy of mention. Both met Francis briefly, and details of their experiences are given in the footnotes.

Diplomatic Documents

These include, first of all, the papal bulls and letters which have been published. Though such publications represent an enormous amount of time-consuming research, it is essential that such papers become available to the student of Franciscana. Thus Sabatier, for one, was unable to form a proper judgment of Innocent III because, in his day, many letters written by this pope had not been published. Even today, the historian would be wise to be cautious in the defense of his own interpretation.

Archives

These were discussed in the Introduction. The archives of the city of Assisi, the Sacrum Conventum (the convent next to the basilica of St. Francis), the cathedral of San Rufino, the city of Perugia, and others are primary sources. They are of importance not only for the facts concerning Francis' life but also because they provide better insight into the religious, cultural, and sociopolitical background of the times. They are also useful in verifying information provided by biographers and in establishing the chronological order of events.

In General

No matter how reliable the sources one makes use of, *the* biography does not exist. According to his own interpretation, every biographer attempts to combine the personal and factual information in such a way that a psychologically and historically reliable figure emerges from his work. In a way, his work is creative, in that intuition and imagination are indispensable. What we have said of Jesus Christ is equally true of Francis: there are many Francis figures, but only one Francis.

The aim of this book is to view this fascinating human being in the light of what is meaningful for all times, as well as for our own day. The true identity of this simple yet mysterious figure—in other words, who Francis really was—only God knows.

Footnotes

1. It is impossible to mention separately all the works devoted to the Franciscan sources. We would, however, like to mention the *Journal Sint Francisus* and "Gids van evangelisch leven," 3(1966). 1:18-59 in which the well-known Franciscologist Fr. Fidentius van den Borne O.F.M. provides a survey of sources: "Nieuw Licht na 50 jaar bronnenstudie."

2. An especially good edition of Francis' writings, with explanatory comments, is that of Kajetanus, Esser, *Die Schriften des II Franziskus von Assisi, Einführing* (3rd ed.; Werl./Westf., 1963).

3. S. Clasen O.F.M., "Legenda antiqua S. Francisci, *Studia et documenta franciscana* (1967), V, xxxii.

4. *La conversion de S. François, Etude comparative des textes relatifs à la conversion and Vita I et Vita II* (Paris: Editions Franciscaines, 1963).

5. See F. v. d. Borne, in S. *Franciscus* (1963), no. 7 pp. 15ff.

6. For details of the chroniclers see the work of M. Th. Laureillé, from which we have quoted freely: *Sur les routes de l'Europe au 13e siècle* (Paris, 1956). *XIII Century Chronicles*, Franciscan Herald Press, 1956.

Bibliography

This bibliography, prepared by the editor, lists selected English titles on the sources of the life of St. Francis, biographies, works on his message, his spirit, and his Orders. For more complete bibliographies see Masseron-Habig, *The Franciscans,* pp. 479–506; Englebert, *St. Francis of Assisi,* pp. 497–601; and Habig, *St. Francis of Assisi: Omnibus of Sources.*

Sources

Brooke, Rosalind B. *Scripta Leonis, Rufini et Angeli, Sociorum S. Francisci: The Writings of Leo Rufino and Angelo, Companions of St. Francis.* Oxford: Clarendon, 1970.

Brown, Raphael, trans., ed. *Fifty Animal Stories of Saint Francis as Told by His Companions.* Chicago: FHP, 1958.

_____. *The Little Flowers of St. Francis.* Garden City, N.Y.: Hannover, 1958.

_____. *Our Lady and Saint Francis: All the Earliest Texts.* Chicago: FHP, 1954.

Fahy, Benen, trans., and Placid Hermann, ed. *The Writings of St. Francis.* Chicago: FHP, 1964.

Fleming, John V. *Introduction to the Franciscan Literature of the Middle Ages.* Chicago: FHP, 1977.

Hermann, Placid, trans., ed. *St. Francis of Assisi: First and Second Life of St. Francis, with Selections from Treatise on the Miracles of Blessed Francis, by Thomas of Celano.* Chicago: FHP, 1962.

————. *Via Seraphica: Selected Readings from the Early Documents and Writings Pertaining to St. Francis and the Franciscan Order.* Chicago: FHP, 1959.

Karrer, Otto, ed. *St. Francis of Assisi: The Legends and Lauds,* trans. by N. Wydenbruck. London and New York, 1948.

Masseron, Alexandre, ed. *Memorable Words of Saint Francis,* trans. by Margaret Sullivan. Chicago: FHP, 1963.

Meyer, James, trans., ed. *The Words of St. Francis: An Anthology.* Chicago: FHP, 1952, 1966.

Robeck, Nesta de, and Placid Hermann. *St. Francis of Assisi: His Holy Life and Love of Poverty (Legend of the Three Companions,* trans. by N. de Robeck, and *Sacrum Commercium,* trans. by P. Hermann). Chicago: FHP, 1964.

Roggen, Heribert, trans., ed. *Spirit and Life: The Gospel Way of Life in the Writings of St. Francis and St. Clare.* Chicago: FHP, 1970.

Shirley Price, Leo, trans., ed. *St. Francis of Assisi: His Life and Writings as Recorded by His Contemporaries* (the life is *Speculum Perfectionis).* New York: Harcourt, 1959.

Vian Nello, ed. *Golden Words: The Sayings of Brother Giles of Assisi,* trans. by Ivo O'Sullivan. Chicago: FHP, 1966.

Biographies

Ancelet-Hustache, Jeanne. *Once Upon a Time in Assisi:*

The Life of Saint Francis Told to Children, trans. by Sister M. Clarissa. Chicago: FHP, 1955.

Chesterton, Gilbert. *St. Francis of Assisi.* New York: Doubleday Image Books, 1957.

Cuthbert, Father. *Life of St. Francis of Assisi.* Third edition. London and New York: Longmans, 1912–1960.

Englebert, Omer. *St. Francis of Assisi: A Biography,* trans. by Eve Marie Cooper, revised and augmented by Ignatius Brady and Raphael Brown. Chicago: FHP, 1965.

Hegener, Mark. *The Poverello: St. Francis of Assisi.* Chicago: FHP, 1956.

Hermann, Placid. *Seraph of Love* (life of St. Francis in blank verse). Chicago: FHP, 1959.

Jörgensen, Johannes. *St. Francis of Assisi: A Biography,* trans. by T. O'Conor Sloane. London and New York, 1912; Garden City, N.Y., 1955.

Lloyd, Teresa. *The Poor Man of Assisi: Saint Francis.* Chicago: FHP, 1962.

Heritage

Aeby, Gervais, et al. *Call to Commitment: In the School of St. Francis,* trans. by Michael D. Meilach. Chicago: FHP, 1964.

Bettoni, Efrem. *Nothing for Your Journey,* trans. by Bruce Malina. Chicago: FHP, 1959.

Brady, Ignatius, trans., ed. *The Marrow of the Gospel: A Study of the Rule of Saint Francis of Assisi by the Franciscans of Germany.* Chicago: FHP, 1958.

Breton, Valentine-M. *Franciscan Spirituality,* trans. by Flavian Frey. Chicago: FHP, 1957.

––––––. *In Christ's Company,* trans. by Michael D. Meilach. Chicago: FHP, 1961.

––––––. *Lady Poverty,* trans. by Paul J. Oligny. Chicago: FHP, 1963.

Corstanje, Auspicius Van. *The Covenant with God's Poor: A Biblical Interpretation of the Testament of St. Fran-*

cis. Chicago: FHP, 1966.

Crosby, Jeremiah. *Bearing Witness: The Place of the Franciscan Family in the Church.* Chicago: FHP, 1966.

Dukker, Chrysostomus. *The Changing Heart: The Penance Concept of St. Francis of Assisi,* trans. by Bruce Malina. Chicago: FHP, 1963.

Engemann, Antonellus. *The New Song: Faith, Hope, and Charity in Franciscan Spirituality,* trans. by Isabel and Florence McHugh. Chicago: FHP, 1964.

Esser, Cajetan. *The Order of St. Francis: Its Spirit and Its Mission in the Kingdom of God,* trans. by Ignatius Brady. Chicago: FHP, 1959.

_____. *Origins of the Franciscan Order,* trans. by Aedan Daly and Irina Lynch. Chicago: FHP, 1970.

_____. *Repair My House,* ed. by Luc Mely, trans. by Michael D. Meilach. Chicago: FHP, 1963.

and Fngelbert Grau. *Love's Reply,* trans. by Ingnatius Brady. Chicago: FHP, 1963.

Eugene, Christian. *Our Lady: Devotion to Mary in Franciscan Tradition.* Chicago: FHP, 1954.

Felder, Hilarin. *The Ideals of St. Francis of Assisi,* trans. by Berchmans Bittle. New York: Benziger, 1925.

Glemelli, Agostino. *Franciscan Message to the World (Il francescanesimo).* London: Burns, Oates and Washbourne, 1934.

_____. *The Message of St. Francis,* trans. by Paul J. Oligny. Chicago: FHP, 1963.

Habig, Marion A. *The Franciscan Book of Saints.* Chicago: FHP, 1959.

_____. *New Catechism of the Third Order.* Revised edition. Chicago: FHP, 1967.

_____. *Franciscan Pictorial Book.* Chicago: FHP, 1963.

and Albert J. Nimeth. *Franciscan Pictorial Book Two.* Chicago: FHP, 1966.

Hallack, Cecily, and Peter F. Anson. *These Made Peace: Studies in the Lives of the Beatified and Canonized Members of the Third Order of St. Francis of Assisi,* ed.

by Marion A. Habig. London: Burns and Oates; Paterson, N.J.: St. Anthony Guild Press, 1957.

Hanson, Warren G. *St. Francis of Assisi: Patron of Environment.* Chicago: FHP, 1971.

Hegener, Mark, ed. *The Franciscan Vision of Life: The Address "Nel Darvi" of Pope Pius XII with Articles Explaining the Franciscan Way of Living.* Chicago: FHP, 1957.

———— and Marion A. Habig. *A Short History of the Third Order.* Chicago: FHP, 1963.

Hermann, Placid. *The Way of St. Francis.* Chicago: FHP, 1964.

Kann, Sr. Jean M. *I Found Francis in Assisi.* Chicago: FHP, 1960.

Leclerq, Eloi. *Wisdom of the Poverello,* trans. by Marie Louise Johnson. Chicago: FHP, 1961.

Lekeux, Martial. *Twentieth Century Litany to the Poverello.* Chicago: FHP, 1958.

Longpré, Efrem. *A Poor Man's Peace (the Spirit of St. Francis),* trans. by Paul Barrett. Chicago: FHP, 1968.

Masseron, Alexandre, and Marion A. Habig. *The Franciscans: St. Francis of Assisi and His Three Orders.* Chicago: FHP, 1960.

Meyer, James. *A Primer of Perfection for Everybody.* Chicago: FHP, 1946.

————. *Social Ideals of St. Francis: Eight Lessons in Applied Christianity.* Second revised edition. St. Louis and London: B. Herder, 1948.

Moorman, John. *A History of the Franciscan Order from Its Origins to the Year 1517.* Oxford: Clarendon, 1968.

Moreau, Abel. *On Leave from Heaven,* trans. by Flavian Frey. Chicago: FHP, 1960.

Motte, John Francis. *Face to the World: The Third Order in Modern Society,* trans. by Margaret Sullivan. Chicago: FHP, 1955.

O'Rourke, Daniel. *How to Live in a Layman's Order.* Chicago: FHP, 1964.

Piat, Stephane J. *How to Be an Instrument of Peace: The Message of Saint Francis to the World,* trans. by Paul J. Oligny and Barnabas Abel. Chicago: FHP, 1955.
_____. *Riches and the Spirit,* trans. by Paul J. Oligny. Chicago: FHP, 1958.

Pidoux de la Maduere, Sylvain. *Our Brother the Death of the Body,* trans. by James Meyer. Chicago: FHP, 1947.

Pope Leo XIII and Successors. *Rome Hath Spoken* (papal encyclicals on the Third Order of St. Francis), trans. by James Meyer. Chicago: FHP, 1943.

Schneider, Reinhold. *The Hour of Saint Francis of Assisi,* trans. by James Meyer. Chicago, FHP: 1953.

Wroblewski, Sergius. *Christian Perfection for the Layman.* Chicago: FHP, 1963.